The Ecology of the Barí

The Ecology of the Barí

Rainforest Horticulturalists of South America

STEPHEN BECKERMAN
AND ROBERTO LIZARRALDE

University of Texas Press ⬥ *Austin*

Requests for permission to reproduce material from this work should be sent to:
    Permissions
    University of Texas Press
    P.O. Box 7819
    Austin, TX 78713–7819
    http://utpress.utexas.edu/index.php/rp-form

♾ The paper used in this book meets the minimum requirements of ANSI/NISO
Z39.48–1992 (R1997) (Permanence of Paper).

Library of Congress Cataloging-in-Publication Data
Beckerman, Stephen.
    The ecology of the Barí : rainforest horticulturalists of South America /
by Stephen Beckerman and Roberto Lizarralde.
        pages   cm.
    Includes bibliographical references and index.
    ISBN 978-0-292-74819-4 (cl. : alk. paper)
    ISBN 978-1-4773-0207-1 (paperback)
1. Motilon Indians—Agriculture—Venezuela—Maracaibo Basin.   2. Motilon
Indians—Venezuela—Maracaibo Basin—Social conditions.   3. Indigenous
peoples—Ecology—Venezuela—Maracaibo Basin.   4. Rain forest ecology—
Venezuela—Maracaibo Basin.   5. Traditional ecological knowledge—Venezuela—
Maracaibo Basin.   6. Maracaibo Basin (Venezuela)—Environmental conditions.
7. Maracaibo Basin (Venezuela)—Social life and customs.   I. Lizarralde, Roberto.
II. Title.
    F2319.2.M6B43   2013
    305.898′2087—dc23   2013000152

doi:10:7560/748194

Contents

Kinship Abbreviations Used in Chapter Six

B = Brother
D = Daughter
F = Father
H = Husband
M = Mother
S = Son
W = Wife
Z = Sister

Preface

This is not the preface I originally wrote. The manuscript for this book was finished, except for the concluding chapter and a few final entries in the bibliography. The maps had been done and redone. The tables were at last formatted correctly. I began the preface by saying that Roberto Lizarralde and I hoped the current book on the ecology of the Barí would be followed by a volume on the social anthropology of the Barí. I intended to call Bob in a day or two to talk about how we might describe that second book, and who would be coauthor with the two old men who had just finished the ecology volume. Then I received an e-mail telling me to call Manuel Lizarralde, Bob's son. My friend and colleague of nearly forty years had just died.

Here is an early version of his obituary, very hastily written by Manuel and me and posted online:

> Roberto Lizarralde, dean and godfather of cultural anthropology in Venezuela, died in the late afternoon of February 25, 2011 at the age of 84. Most generous and gentlest of men, he had survived 10 years with cancer, spending his last decade, in the words of John Nichols, playing seven card stud with the angel of death, winning every hand. It was not the cancer that actually killed him. He used to walk every day and took a rest one morning (February 17th) on the railing of a small bridge on his property near Mérida; the railing gave way and he fell five feet onto his back. He died a few days later of pneumonia and other complications, as the result of the trauma and the effects of 10 years of chemotherapy.
>
> It is difficult to think of a single anthropologist who has worked in Venezuela over the last 58 years who does not owe a debt to Bob Lizarralde. With his beautiful smile and clear mind he welcomed any stranger

like a friend or family member. Bob was very considerate and unpretentious to others. Unfailingly generous with his time, advice, his own fieldwork data and vast knowledge of the geography and peoples of his country, he aided, advised and guided many generations of Venezuelan and foreign anthropologists. He made (at the risk of his life) the first modern peaceful contact with the Barí people of the Maracaibo Basin, and was constantly and energetically involved in efforts to secure their lands and promote their wellbeing from that moment on.

Since the time of his contact with the Barí, Bob had been carefully searching for the best way to help the Barí protect their territory. In 1989 he was able to receive funding from the European Union to start his dream project to help the Barí protect their territorial rights. Beginning in 1989 he started a series of field trips to help them in demarcating and securing their remaining lands. This demarcation became a requirement around the turn of the millennium, when it was decreed that all Indian lands in Venezuela were to be titled and henceforth protected from invasion and appropriation. It was Bob Lizarralde, already in his mid-70s, who for months covered nearly ten kilometers a day by foot in the Barí territory with a group of community leaders. He and his son Manuel cut many trails and established reference points for the demarcation of Barí land, working until 2006. Bob then produced the maps required for the titling process, drawing on his remarkable cartographic skills and his total control of the geography and settlement history of the region. Bob's Barí maps and detailed reports of the boundaries of Barí territory were the first to be delivered for any indigenous group in Venezuela and served as a model for subsequent land titling requests by other tribes. In the last years, while he was fighting cancer, the Venezuelan government approached him to participate in a workshop about indigenous people's land demarcations around the country, to help other indigenous nations. Bob was also actively involved with the Misión Guaicaipuro. When it became clear in the last few years that Barí lands would not be titled (national politics again overriding Indian rights), Bob responded with a characteristic lack of bitterness, although there was a sadness about him when the subject came up.

Roberto Lizarralde was born on September 13, 1926, in Nice, southern France, where his father, Enrique, was the cultural attaché *ad honorem* of the Uruguayan embassy until his death in 1940. Bob had an older brother, Manuel (now deceased), and a younger sister, Maïta (who lives in Olympic Valley, California). While living in occupied France during the Second World War, the Lizarralde family was involved in helping the 9th Air Force pilot ("Teddy," Theodore Roosevelt Stablein) of a downed twin-prop A-20 light bomber whom they found in the woods not far from their home on June 4th, 1944. They hid and fed him for several months, until the American forces took control of the region at the end of August of that year. Events such as these clearly piqued his lifelong sense of exploration and adventure.

Bob lived most of his first 18 years in France, mostly in Paris and Normandy (the latter in 1941–1944), spending one year in Uruguay (1929–1930), where his father had grown up. His complex ancestry explains why destiny brought him to Venezuela and his interest in anthropology. He was ethnically French and genetically Basque. His family spoke mostly French and Spanish at home, with some Basque (Bob's father was fluent), English and German (his mother was fluent in both). His mother, Isabel Seminario, was born in Paris and grew up in Hamburg, but her father, Victor Manuel Seminario, was from Piura (Peru, about which Bob used to say that "In Piura, there is only cactus, goats and Seminarios") and her mother, Bob's maternal grandmother, Julia Leseur, was from Caracas, Venezuela. Through her lineage, Bob was the great-great-grandson of the famous General Francisco Avendaño, one of the most important "Próceres" in the Venezuelan war of independence, as well as being another Basque. Therefore, his roots were deeply divided between France and Venezuela, and most of his ancestors were from the Basque region, in the province of Guipúzcoa.

Bob studied economics at the University of Lausanne in Switzerland; English and geography at Exeter University in the UK; and received his BS in geography at Northwestern University in the US in 1949. He earned an MA in geography from the University of Wisconsin in Madison in 1952. Although he completed the coursework for his PhD at the same institution, he did not turn in a dissertation, an omission that seemed to weigh on him.

Bob first came to Venezuela in September of 1952 to join a multidisciplinary team doing socioeconomic research in rural communities in the Venezuelan Andes. Over the next three years he participated in many additional research projects. While working in Venezuela, Bob met his wife, Elizabeth (Lilette) Coyne, in Caracas, at a party at the French consulate, and they were married in July of 1954. Together, they had three children, Ivan, born in 1955; Manuel, 1958; and Anne Isabel, 1959.

One project that took him to the Warao Indians at the mouth of the Orinoco in 1954 and another dealing with migration in the Andean piedmont were especially notable. He returned to the US in 1955 to resume his studies at Wisconsin, and later spent one academic year (1957–1958) teaching at Rutgers. By the summer of 1958 he was back in Venezuela, where he was appointed as the Chief of Fieldwork for the Venezuelan Indian Commission for three years. In this position, he carried out research and instituted programs among the Wayú (Guajiro), the Pumé (Yaruro), the Warao, and the Wóthuha (Piaroa).

It was also in this period and as part of his official responsibilities that he made peaceful contact with the Barí on July 19, 1960, jumping out of a helicopter into the ring of bare earth around an occupied longhouse. His portfolio as Chief of Fieldwork was to solve political problems and help develop education projects, as well as establish a durable peace between the Barí and their neighbors. However, within a few days of this contact, the Capuchins, a group of Spanish monks whose order had maintained missions to the Barí from 1772 until 1818, managed to get this portfolio, along with its budget, transferred to their order, and to have all employees of the Indian Commission prohibited from entering Barí lands. Bob immediately quit his job and continued to work with the Barí, but he had to do so unobtrusively for years.

By 1961, he had been hired to teach anthropology and cultural geography at the Universidad de Zulia, in Maracaibo. He was close to the Barí there and completed dozens of fieldwork sessions with them over the next seven years. In 1968, he moved to the School of Anthropology at UCV, the Central University of Venezuela, in Caracas, where he remained for the rest of his academic career, retiring in 1993 with the rank of Profesor Titular, equivalent to Distinguished Professor at an American university. From his post at UCV he carried out fieldwork with the Barí, the Yukpa, the Pumé, and the E'ñepá (Panare). In his long teaching career spanning four decades, many graduate students asked his advice on their research and academic works. One of his students, Alejandro J. Signi Sánchez, in his personal handwritten dedication in his book (2008) wrote eloquently: "Receive this work with all affection and care from one of your pupils, who implemented part of your teaching, and fundamentally, the perseverance and humility of the investigator, and respect to all our indigenous peoples."

It was while at UCV that he had a major role as coordinator and census taker in two national censuses. In 1982–1983 he helped design the first national Indian census in Venezuela, and administered all the questionnaires himself among the Barí, the Pumé, and the Hiwi (Guajibo). He also administered substantial numbers of forms among the E'ñepá and the Yanomami.

A decade later, he reprised his census role, again scouring the field for all Barí, Pumé, and Hiwi individuals living in Venezuela. He also coordinated the many census takers for the first Wayú partial census in 1958 and again for the Binational Wayú Census in 1992, when they numbered nearly 180,000. This census was very challenging and it was well known that it could not have been possible without the unstinting help and participation of Bob.

After his retirement from UCV, Bob, his wife, and their eldest son, Ivan, moved to a piece of land near the city of Mérida, in Manzano Alto, in the Venezuelan Andes. There, in sight of the Pico Bolívar (the tallest peak in Venezuela), they built a sort of Eden, with lush pasture and dairy cattle, roses and fruit trees, and a vegetable garden. His home has a red tiled roof, white walls (resembling his Basque ancestors' homes), and is filled with books, paintings and ethnographic artifacts. It is surrounded by cloud forest where howler monkeys can often be heard in the distance. Bob continued his research there, visiting Barí territory as often as his health and the perilous Barí political situation permitted. He completed 96 field trips to the Barí between 1960 and 2006. When he was at home, Barí often came to see him—seeking political advice, bringing news, and simply visiting with "Bobé" (his Barí name), a trusted friend. The Barí considered him a member of their nation and outsiders were recommended to talk to him for his evaluation. In one case, a filmmaker from Maracaibo, Emerita Fuenmayor, went to the Barí to make a film in the early 1990s and the Barí quickly recommended she talk to "Bobé." She thought they must be referring to a Barí headman. But when she asked where to find him, they sent her to Mérida, where she discovered that it was her beloved professor! His advice was taken quite seriously, like that of the *ñatubay* (headman) of the community.

Bob's generosity extended further by sharing a significant proportion of his small retirement salary with the Barí, subsidizing expeditions to clear demarcation paths, helping to pay for formal high school and university educations for a good number of Barí youth, and helping the first Barí doctor to finish medical school—in Cuba in 2010. Over the last 30 years of his career as fieldworker, he made sure to bring many antivenin kits for several of the larger Barí villages to help prevent the mortality of the regular bites of the deadly fer-de-lance snake. His legacy as a fieldworker among the Barí set an example that will be very hard for other anthropologists to match.

A man of extraordinary meticulousness, Bob had never published abundantly. He produced many manuscripts, but there was always one more datum to be added, one more draft to be completed. While writing, he would carefully select the perfect word for a sentence, sometimes thinking an entire afternoon and repeatedly consulting his dictionaries. Some of his manuscripts, such as the history of the contact with the Barí, took several years of finesse until he was satisfied. This goal of attempting perfection was a characteristic that is often one of the first traits that friends and colleagues mention when describing their friend.

A second characteristic that all agree on is that his memory was spectacular in every way. Friends swore he had never forgotten anything he had ever seen or heard, or the route to anyplace he had ever visited. He could recall events many decades ago by their specific dates, names of participants and characteristics of the surroundings. Recently, his son Manuel asked about Walter Dupouy's work and the indigenous commission affairs; Bob could recall not only all the details of Walter's background but also the budgets and names of the staff, even though it happened half a century ago. His geographical memory in particular was phenomenal. He knew the names of all the Barí territory creeks and rivers, not only in Spanish but also in Barí-aa. He was an important contributor to the National Cartography Office and supplied the names of geographical features in the southwestern part of the state of Zulia. While taking Manuel to the airport in El Vigía last month, Bob mentioned while crossing a little creek that it had a Barí name, *buubogyí*, "the creek of the hawks," which for him was evidence of its having been part of Barí territory in colonial times. He saw himself moving across the surface of the earth, as if observed from an anchored balloon, and retained everything he perceived. He was literally incapable of getting lost.

It is sad to realize that with the death of Roberto Lizarralde, we lost one of the greatest troves of knowledge about the ethnography and anthropology of Venezuela. His loss is like a whole library vanishing. Now that he has gone to the land of the *bashungchingbá* (the Barí world of the dead, where there is an abundance of happiness and food), the living are deprived. Anthropology has lost a knowledgeable and generous mind; the Barí have lost a wise and loyal friend; and his friends and family have lost a courtly, learned, gentle man who, although utterly without arrogance, was also entirely without fear.

Now that Bob is dead, this book becomes one of his memorials. Like the man, it is not a standard contribution to anthropology. In fact, it is as much a natural history of the Barí as it is an ethnography. (It remains to be seen if the second volume, on the social anthropology of the Barí, will be written.) The idea behind the book is straightforward: The Barí deserve an unusual sort of book because their anthropological situation is unusual.

The Barí are one of the very few peoples who were contacted by modern, quantitatively oriented social scientists while their aboriginal systems for obtaining food and organizing mating and marrying practices were intact and still largely cut off from the modern world system. They offered an opportunity to count, to measure, to record and examine aspects of tribal culture that are universally held to be foundational in the production and reproduction of society but that usually have to be reconstructed conjecturally, particularly in their quantitative parameters, after they have been substantially altered by conquest, trade, missionization, forced migration, compulsory education, and governmental oversight.

I do not mean to suggest here that the Barí of the 1960s and 1970s were some sort of pristine isolate. As discussed in chapter 3, they had a long history of hostile relations with surrounding peoples, and a large number of them underwent a two-generation-long period of coercive missionization around 1800. Nevertheless, when Bob made the first modern contact with them in summer 1960, they had had essentially no peaceful relations with other societies for over a century. Their subsistence practices were uninfluenced by market forces, their settlements situated without regard for the proximity of schools and stores, their reproductive behavior unsupervised by missionaries. That largely autochthonous situation is what Bob and I observed in our fieldwork—the ethnographic context in which we weighed and measured, timed and counted—and is what we record here.

Bob began work with the Venezuelan Barí in 1960. I started with the Colombian Barí in 1970. Over the decades, he made ninety-six field trips to the Barí. I made only eighteen (and that is counting as a separate trip every time I came and went from the field during my three years of dissertation fieldwork). After Colombian Barí territories became excessively exciting in the 1980s as a result of narcoguerrilla activity, I moved over to Venezuela, and Bob and I began doing fieldwork together.

During those decades, several institutions funded my work, both before and after Bob and I began working together. They include the Ford Foundation, the University of New Mexico, Southern Methodist University, the Pennsylvania State University, the National Geographic Society, the Wenner-Gren Foundation, the Vanguard Foundation, the National Science Foundation, the Instituto Venezolano de Investigaciones Científicas (which employed me as a visiting researcher for a year), and the Fulbright Foundation. The Instituto Colombiano de Antropología arranged legal permission for me to work with the Colombian Barí, and the Universidad de los Andes in Mérida took me on as a visiting professor for a year. As important, many people provided help and support of various nonfinancial kinds. Among non-Barí, I am especially indebted to the generosity and hospitality of Bruce Olson, who was key to my coming successfully to the Barí, and to Karl Schwerin, my learned and patient dissertation adviser. Others who helped my early fieldwork along in one way or another and from one place or another were Alfred Abboud, Ken Ames, Darrell Bartee, Rosenell Baud, Patrice Bidou, Horacio Calle, John Campbell, Robert Carneiro, Ramon Cubaque, Brigitte Fecht, Simone Fiorini, Sylvia Forman, Nina and Bob Friedemann, Patrick Gallagher, Yvon LeBot, Ed Lieuwen, Federico Medem, Noah and Kathy Neff, François Picon, Gerardo Reichel-Dolmatoff, Hernando Rueda, Nicolas and Estela Suescún, and Brian Weiss—and Hope Boylston, who later became my wife. The dissertation itself would not have been written without the help of Linda Kierstadt, Carolyn Reeves, Dennis and Jeanne Stanford, Dave and Cindy Stuart, and Pamela Erickson, with whom I continue to collaborate.

Ian Bennett and Tanya Marcuse later contributed data from their own fieldwork. My subsequent fieldwork was helped and encouraged by Alfredo Angulo, Carol Ballew, Jacqueline Clarac, Darrell Holman, the entire Lizarralde family, Manuel Martinez, Carlos Schubert and Erika Wagner, Paul and Anna Valentine, Renata Wulff, Maria Eugenia Zaldívar, and my wife and children. Compilation and analysis of data were aided by Jessie Bai, Darrell Holman, Dina Dajani, Sissel Schroeder, Jim Boster, Warren Morrill, and a host of undergraduate coauthors. My son Matías Martinez made the genealogical diagrams for this book.

Hundreds of Barí men, women, and children contributed generously to my work in the field, housing and feeding me, guiding me along trails, and putting up with long and sometimes tedious interviews. Among those who were exceptionally giving were Ashtacara and Abacachara, Aishigdora, Agdó and Atakbara, Asendoda, Obiara and Mamasugba, Acuchara, Lorenzo Aburuma and Jacinta Adankimbi, and Sara Oroksá. Nubia Koromoto Korombara was a source of great insight and conducted some of the most recent interviews herself.

Most of Roberto Lizarralde's Barí fieldwork was funded by the Venezuelan institutions that employed him over his long career: the Venezuelan Comisión Indigenista, the Universidad de Zulia (LUZ), the Universidad Central de Venezuela (UCV), and the Venezuelan Oficina Central de Estadística e Informática (OCEI); he also received funding from the European Union and the National Geographical Society. People who aided him in one way or another are legion. He was a well-loved man; he would have produced a very long catalog of non-Barí as well as Barí. He never had a chance to write the former list, but his son Manuel found among his papers an unpublished manuscript in which he expressed his thanks to the following Barí men and women: "Andrés y Jaime Achirabú, Akaeragdou, Undachí, Akairokbá, Asebo, Ashana, Ikrukrú, Adodongba, Adarobaeg, Aboksorón, Akatroriya, Ashibogdá, Ariká, Asabé, Wairidou, Akuéro, Akirihdá, Ashímbya, Achirirí, Ashrirokó, Abarú, Ashiboroko, Arakdou, Bakainshó, Abuyokba, Abarubí, Abokoré, Ataktabá, Ankobá, Ihtángda, Arukbá, Ushurí, Arokbarí, Atraktrá, Akurukbá, Gabriel Abea, Darío Abísosou, Mandabó, Ashkoró, Oroksá, Aidanshá, Abiraikiriré, Ashkerañá, Adoaira, Agyá, Addye, Akokoma, Arengda, Arochí, Aktrui-nagyá, Addakarabá, and in particular to David Aleobaddá, and many more Barí men and women and their descendants."

Bob's son Manuel Lizarralde produced the maps for this book; Bob and I shared a deep sense of satisfaction at seeing our sons participate in this common enterprise of their fathers.

The Ecology of the Barí

CHAPTER 1

Introduction

The Barí are a group of native South Americans who live in the rain forests of Colombia and Venezuela. They are known in Spanish as the Motilón Indians, or simply the Motilones, and their land is sometimes called Motilonia. This book is about them and what the study of their culture has contributed to anthropology.

Anthropology at base is about the variability of human nature, about the limits and possibilities of being human. The anthropological justification for studying the Barí, or any other culture, is ultimately to find out what it can tell us about human capacities—the abilities, tendencies, and limitations of our species. Obviously, no one culture is able to inform us about the full range of human possibilities; but anthropologists presume that every culture has some aspects that can enlighten us about some part of the human condition.

The kind of enlightenment we pursue depends on the theoretical perspective from which we ask questions. We write here from an ecological perspective. The sorts of questions raised—about the Barí in particular and about human nature in general—and the kinds of answers found come from ecological theory. The questions have to do with how people survive and reproduce in a given environment; and the answers have to do with people's interactions with that environment and with each other.

The core of this book, chapters 4 through 6, is arranged according to the three fundamental issues addressed by ecological anthropology: production, protection, and reproduction. Production concerns how people make a living—how they obtain, distribute, process, and consume food and other necessities. Protection concerns how people defend themselves against the dangers of life, from accidents and diseases and enemies. Reproduction concerns how people find mates, form and sustain families, and bear and raise their children.

Chapter 4 is devoted to production—the farming, fishing, hunting, and gathering by which the Barí fed themselves in the "ethnographic present," that time around first contact when their traditional culture was intact. (For purposes of this book, the ethnographic present runs from June 1960, the date of the first anthropological observations, to around 1975, when even the remotest Barí longhouses began to be overcome by Western culture.) Chapter 5, on protection, focuses on the various strategies the Barí traditionally used to defend themselves from the threats of malaria, Indian killers, and such dangers of rain forest life as drowning and poisonous snakes. Chapter 6, on reproduction, looks at the Barí way of courtship and marriage, family formation and child raising. We pay considerable attention in this chapter to the institution of partible paternity, in which all the men who have sex with a woman during a pregnancy are believed to share the fatherhood of her child.

With respect to the universal human challenges of providing for production, protection, and reproduction, we focus on current debates and issues in ecological anthropology and use them to organize our information. These organizing issues are set out at the beginning of each of the three central chapters.

As a study in ecological anthropology, this book must begin with a description of the two kinds of environment the Barí inhabit, the natural and the cultural. The Barí live in the southwestern lobe of the Lake of Maracaibo, a region bisected by the Colombia-Venezuela border. Their homeland is a pocket of lowland neotropical rain forest enclosed on all sides by different biomes. To the west and south, the lowland rain forest shades into submontane and montane forests, as one climbs the slopes of the eastern cordillera of the Andes, which divides, just south of Barí lands, into a giant Y whose arms enclose the Maracaibo Basin. To the north, rainfall diminishes and the rain forest gives way to lowland semideciduous and deciduous forest and eventually to savannah. Precipitation is also lower to the east, but there, instead of savannah and deciduous forest, most of the landscape is taken over by the swamps that fringe this section of Lake Maracaibo. Although the Barí certainly raided outside the area just described and may have had settlements there in some historical periods, there is some evidence that Barí territory often coincided with the limits of evergreen tropical rain forest.

Although their forest has been inhabited by human beings for centuries and although the human inhabitants have introduced a few agricultural domesticates, affecting the the abundance of some wild species, there is no evidence that the basic composition of the Barí forests is largely a result of human activity, as has been argued for some neotropical forests in Brazil, for instance (Balée 1994). As far as we know, the natural environment of the central Barí homeland was for the most part unchanged by human presence until the last half of the twentieth century. In order to survive and reproduce, the Barí needed to adapt to the plants and animals that made up the rain forest, their abundance, distributions, and activities.

Just as the natural environment of the Barí was made up of the populations and behaviors of the nonhuman animal and plant species of the rain forest, their cultural environment consisted of the populations and activities of their human neighbors. These neighbors included other native South American peoples, as well as European and African migrants to the region. With the exception of a four-decade period between the 1770s and 1810s and another that began in 1960, relations with those human neighbors have been hostile. In the same way that the Barí had to adapt to the abundance, distribution, and behaviors of the game animals they hunted, they had to adapt to the abundance, distributions, and behaviors of the human enemies who hunted them. Hence the chapter that follows our synopsis of the natural environment is a summing up of the social environment. Because the social environment changed dramatically over time, the only sensible way to explore it is historically, so this chapter is a history of the relations of the Barí with their neighbors from earliest historical times to the present.

In this historical chapter we introduce another important aspect of the environment to which the Barí had to adapt, one that comprised both the natural and social environments. Disease organisms, particularly the infectious microorganisms of Old World diseases such as malaria, hepatitis, and measles, found their vectors or reservoirs in the human populations surrounding the Barí. In the historical chapter we take a first look at these killers.

All these ecological conditions, the impositions of the two kinds of environment, were the basic forces that operated on the daily activities of individual Barí, as well as the size, growth rate, and movements of the whole Barí population and its local subdivisions. They enabled the population to grow and spread at some times and in some places, and they limited and reversed its growth and expansion at others.

Of course, no individual Barí thought of the situation in those terms. The Barí, like people everywhere, thought of a good meal, a hard day's work, a move to a new house, the birth of a daughter, the death of a father.

Nevertheless, the sum of those individual events of personal satisfaction and sadness produced a population, a demographic profile, and a human geography. The Barí as a whole became more or less numerous; the rates at which they reproduced, and at which they died, changed over time; they subsisted on one array of foods in the rainy season, on a somewhat different one in the dry season; they migrated into areas abandoned by non-Indians in the latter part of the nineteenth century and away from frontiers of non-Indian colonization in the first half of the twentieth century.

The importance of both kinds of environment in the vital processes of birth and death, and the ways that personal events translated themselves into demographic patterns, are illustrated in the life history of a single Barí woman, whom we call "Tótubi." Most of the Barí in the accounts that follow are given fictitious names, mainly the names of long dead people from other regions and occasionally the names of geographic features. Those Barí who were murdered during the wars of their neighbors against them are mentioned by their real names, because we do not want to conceal or diminish in any way the crimes committed against these people. Non-Barí are likewise called by their real names.

What follows is based on our original field notes from 1988, when we interviewed Tótubi at her home in a large mission village. She was able to take for granted that we were generally familiar with Barí life. Here we have expanded the original field notes with descriptions of particulars of Barí culture and environment where they are needed. Even with those additions, most of what we provide here is no more than a copy of what one or the other of us wrote in his notebook as Tótubi patiently answered our questions about the story of her life. We want to be clear that Tótubi is a real person, not a composite of several different informants or a fictionalized individual with typical life experiences. She really exists, and the events described here occurred in her life in the given order, as far as we know.

Tótubi was born in the early to mid-1930s, probably around 1934, the fourth child and third daughter of her parents. Her next older sibling was a brother, Abusanki, who was destined to play an important role in her life. A few years after Tótubi was born, her mother, Aseba, gave birth to her second boy, Akirikbá. This younger brother would also be an important figure in Tótubi's life.

Like all Barí in the precontact period, Tótubi's family lived in a section of a large, internally undivided longhouse built and occupied by a sizable group of people. This capacious communal dwelling held over fifty residents, with room for a similar number of visitors. It was shaped something like a keeled half watermelon sliced from end to end lying with the flat side down (Fig. 1.1).

Fig. I.I. Barí longhouse Baridoákaira in the middle of its house-surrounding field in May 1961.

All Barí longhouses were built in the middle of a garden whose main crop was manioc, a starchy root. Mature manioc, of the native Barí varieties, grew taller than a man's head. A bare ring of earth of variable width separated the longhouse from its surrounding garden (Fig. 1.2).

People slept in clusters of hammocks slung between the sloping wall of the longhouse and an internal ring of stout outward-leaning posts that supported the wall (Fig. 1.3). Enclosed by the ring of posts was a central area where people cooked (Fig. 1.4). Each clump of hammocks around the rim of the longhouse was near a cooking place in its central area. These hearths were made of a few large stones rolled around a slight depression where a fire was built. Often a roasting rack of green sticks was built over the fire.

The people whose food was cooked at one of these hearths and who slept in the cluster of hammocks slung near it made up a hearth group. Tótubi's hearth group when she was a little girl consisted of the following people: Tótubi's mother, Aseba, and father, Akoba; Tótubi herself and her brothers and sisters; Tótubi's oldest sister's husband, Asakadú; and Tótubi's oldest sister's husband's elderly father, Akokdaká (Fig. 1.5). About a dozen similar hearth groups lived in this longhouse.

It was usual practice among the Barí for a man to join his wife's family's hearth group when he married, just as Tótubi's oldest sister's husband had

Fig. I.2. Barí longhouse Karibaigdakaira in the middle of its house-surrounding field in June 1960.

Fig. I.3. The hammock ring of a Barí longhouse. This house was seasonally unoccupied, and most residents had taken their hammocks to another house, revealing the structure of the building. When occupied, a longhouse had so many hammocks in its external ring that it was difficult to see the architecture.

Fig. I.4. The central cooking area of an unoccupied longhouse. The vertical slats of wood surrounding the hearth area are drying firewood. The long roasting rack running the length of the hearth area is a temporary structure, used for smoking fish shortly before the residents left.

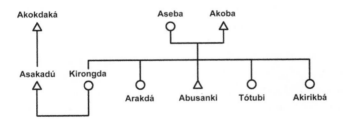

Fig. I.5. Tótubi's hearth group when she was a little girl.

done. It was less common for a father to follow his son when the young man married. But in this case the old man was a widower, and apparently frail, and may have had no other options.

Customarily each local group of Barí maintained several longhousess at the same time. These longhouses had as chiefs the men who had proposed and directed their construction. As is common in South American tropical forest societies, these chiefs had only the power of moral suasion; if they started acting too bossy, their people simply picked up and moved to another longhouse, built by someone else, or built a new house. But Barí life was largely free of abuses and resentments. In general, the people of a local group cycled amicably from one to the other of their longhouses, according to the season. During the dry season, when spear fishing was good, people tended to be at a longhouse near a sizable river. In the wet season, when the muddy rivers were too high and opaque for spear fishing, upland longhouses were occupied, and men spent their time hunting. People preferred to stay at each of their longhouses for a period sufficient to weed the gardens (in addition to a surrounding field, longhouses had satellite fields carved out of the nearby forest), after which they moved on to the next. This semisedentary settlement strategy was the rhythm of life Tótubi was born to.

As a baby, she spent the nights in her mother's hammock, sleeping on her mother's chest, nursing at will throughout the night, until she was close to fully weaned, at the age of two or three. Then she probably received her own hammock, although she might have graduated to sharing a hammock with her next older sister.

When she had grown to be a little girl, like all Barí children, Tótubi led a largely idyllic life. She helped her mother and older sisters cook—when she wanted to. She probably had a little knife of her own, and must have sat on a mat next to the hearth with the women of her hearth group, wielding her knife with her small hands as she helped her mother and sisters peel manioc roots. When the women went to fill water gourds at dawn, for boiling the morning manioc, she must have accompanied them—when she wanted to. When the entire longhouse group went off through the rain forest to spear fish at a river branch on one side of an island, she trotted along, riding on her mother's back when she grew tired—digging her little toes into the waist of her mother's skirt and holding on around her neck— or sitting on her father's shoulders when there was a river to be forded or swum. When her mother went to the manioc field to harvest roots for the next few days, she went with her and helped carry a root or two back to the longhouse—when she wanted to. When her mother needed a *Heliconia* leaf to serve the cooked manioc on, or when her father wanted some thread to bind an arrow he was repairing, she fetched things—when she wanted to. For the Barí did not compel anyone, even a small child, to do anything that he or she did not want to do. A parent might ask, or cajole, or try to make the chore sound like the most fun anyone could have in this world, but if in the last instance the child still refused, the parent got up and fetched her own leaf, his own thread. In this world of the longhouse she was indulged; she was protected; she was presumed to be a distinct, self-possessed person from the day of her birth.

The tolerant, safe world of the longhouse was continually menaced, however, by the hostile social environment of human enemies.

Tótubi's local group was at a longhouse named Jirikikairora when she experienced her first attack. She was about five years old at the time, dating the attack to the late 1930s. As discussed in more detail in chapter 3, this decade was a time when Venezuelan ranchers, aided by Colombian laborers, many of them laid-off oilfield workers, invaded Barí territory with increasing ferocity, attracted by the prospect of clearing the rain forest to acquire large cattle ranches and small homesteads, respectively. A few days before this attack, the occupants of Jirikikairora had made a raid on the invading Venezuelans. A reprisal was expected.

Several hours before dawn, Tótubi's oldest sister, Kirongda, woke Tótubi and the other children in her hearth group and led them out of their hammocks and into the dark, dew-wet manioc field surrounding the longhouse. They brought along mats with them, the kind that women sat on when they cooked and wove, plaited of the stiff central veins of palm leaves and strips of supple inner bark. At the edge of the field, close to the dark wall of the surrounding rain forest, they lay down on their mats and pulled more mats on top of them. Then they put manioc leaves on top of the mats. When the attack came Tótubi and her siblings were hidden, poised to flee to the rain forest. The children of all the other hearth groups were in the longhouse. These different responses to imminent danger reflect the autonomy of the hearth group and the lack of central authority within the longhouse. Each hearth group did as its head of household thought best.

In the dim light just before dawn, the killers assaulted the house. A man named Abikdaing (his real name) was warming himself by a fire. He was shot in the spine. Other men and women were also killed, as well as children. There were many attackers, evidently professional Indian killers. A child was captured and taken off, probably to be sold to a city family wanting a servant. Jirikikairora was burned to the ground. Its inhabitants fled to one of their other longhouses. Everyone in Tótubi's hearth group escaped unharmed. Other hearth groups were not so lucky, although Tótubi cannot remember the names of any of the victims except Abikdaing.

Deaths from other causes were inevitably added to those from human enemies. A few months after this massacre, Tótubi's oldest sister's father-in-law, Akokdaká, died at a lowland longhouse named Karikandiyakaira

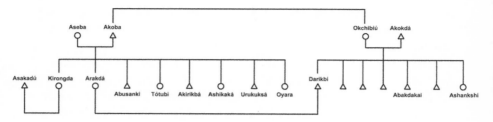

Fig. I.6. Tótubi's hearth group after it was joined by her father's sister's family.

that belonged to her local group. It was the dry season, and the group was residing at this longhouse specifically built for dry season fishing. It was convenient to a number of profitable fishing spots, locations where a river was parted by an island in the middle and one branch of the river could be cut off by building a pair of weirs stretching from the upstream and downstream ends of the island to the closest points on the adjacent shore.

In this house, occupied at the time of year when living was easiest, food most abundant and undemanding to obtain, travel most pleasant, and social visiting most frequent, the old man had a dream one night. He dreamed that a female *dlabikdu*, a spirit of death, came to his hammock during the night, and he had sex with her. When he woke in the morning, he knew he was going to die.

A few days later his body was carried from the longhouse in his hammock and buried in the forest, in a place corresponding to the location of his hammock on the circumference of the longhouse.

Some months after this death, Tótubi's local group migrated to another of their longhouses, Bandutchdu. One day, a group of relatives, Tótubi's father's sister, Okchibiú, and her husband, Akokdá, along with their sons, arrived at Bandutchdu. Their arrival was more than a temporary visit; it was a change of residence for the newcomers, again reflecting the autonomy of the hearth group. They had left the local group with which they had been living to join this one. Marriage was one motive for their migration, since Tótubi's parents had several daughters, and the new couple had many sons and only one daughter. The two families fused to form a very large hearth group of twenty people (Fig. 1.6).

Transfers of a hearth group from one local group to another were not rare, particularly when the local groups belonged to the same territorial group. In these traditional times, each Barí local group was associated with one to three other local groups in a territorial group, with a total population of up to three hundred. The territorial group possessed an expanse of land that might vary from 400 to 1,000 km². Its two to four component local groups placed their longhouses wherever they chose within this territory. They were usually scattered in such a way that it was impossible to say that a certain section of the territory belonged to a particular local group; rather each local group used the whole territory. There was no position of territorial chief corresponding to that of longhouse chief within the local group.

There were four territorial groups in the Venezuelan part of Barí lands around the mid-twentieth century. The exact number in Colombia is not known; there were at least four, but one of these may have been in the process of dividing into two (Map 1.1). Within four years of the peace-

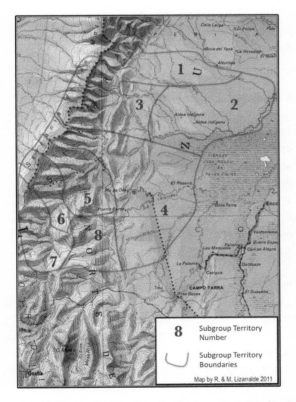

Map 1.1. The territories of the Barí in the years just before peaceful contact. The make-up and boundaries of the four Venezuelan territorial groups (Territories 1–4) are well established; those of the Colombian groups much less so.

ful contact of 1960, epidemics and slaughters reduced all four Venezuelan territorial groups to a single local group each, each one composed of the agglomerated survivors of the former local groups. The situation in Colombia was similar.

A month or so after the union of the two hearth groups, Tótubi's second oldest sister, Arakdá, married the oldest son of the newcomers, a man named Darikbí. In marrying her father's sister's son while her new husband married his mother's brother's daughter, Arakdá was making a marriage with a first cross cousin, a kind of match highly approved by the Barí as well as many other tribal peoples.

Within a year of Arakdá's marriage, while the hearth group was living in a dry season longhouse named Loksojikaira, Tótubi's eldest sister, Kirongda, gave birth to a baby girl. The birth began a series of tragedies. The baby died soon after birth and was buried in the surrounding forest. About ten days later, Kirongda died, too, apparently from complications surrounding the birth. Her husband, Asakadú, buried her in the forest, in a place corresponding to the position of her hammock in the longhouse, next to her baby.

About a year after the deaths of his wife and child, Asakadú also died. He had remained with his deceased wife's family, fishing and hunting for them, until his death. This sort of devotion of a man to his in-laws, and particularly the bond between a young man and his father-in-law, was characteristic of ideal Barí domestic relations. The bond between a son-in-law and a father-in-law was in principle one of the closest relations in Barí society, a model of loyalty.

All these deaths, except the baby's, were attributed to a dlabikdu, a death spirit. The baby was believed to have been killed by a *shungbaraba*, another kind of dangerous spirit, who lives in the earth and reaches up to seize young children.

A little later, another of Tótubi's brothers was born. The hearth group began to grow again.

A couple of years later, when Tótubi was eight or nine, she received her first *dukdura*, or woman's skirt. Her mother wove it herself and gave it to her in the longhouse, telling her that she must be clothed from now on so that boys could not see her genitals. Her mother also told her that she must learn to cook. And now she was to fetch water from the river every morning, in the tree gourds that the Barí used as canteens. Also, she needed to bathe in the river every morning, in order to grow. These instructions, in particular the admonition that Tótubi should now look on fetching water as a regular duty and not something she did when she felt like it, were an indication that she was growing up and should begin to take on some of the responsibilities of an adult.

The day after she received her first dukdura, Tótubi and her mother went alone to the river. They bathed together, Tótubi in her new dukdura, and when they returned to the longhouse she put on a dry dukdura, also new and also woven for her by her mother.

As the pace of invasion of Barí land increased in the 1940s and early 1950s, this sympathetic supervision of Tótubi's progress toward adulthood was again assaulted by the external social environment. The second attack on this local group of Barí occurred when Tótubi's mother was pregnant with her next child. The name of the longhouse where they were assaulted was Shisabai; this attack can be dated precisely, because it was reported in the regional newspapers. It took place in early January 1941. Again, Tótubi was concealed with her brothers and sisters in the field surrounding the house. Again, her hearth group was the only one in the longhouse to take this precaution. This attack began after dawn. The killers shot into the house, then burned it.

Tótubi's entire family escaped. They fled toward Karikandiyakaira, a hard day's walk. Tótubi cannot have been more than ten years old, perhaps as young as seven, but she carried her next younger brother, Akirikbá, all day. Her father and her pregnant mother took turns carrying the youngest boy and the household goods they had been able to escape with. Eventually, they reached Karikandiyakaira. The girl Tótubi's mother had been pregnant with during the attack was born shortly after.

Three or four years later Tótubi had her first period, a major event for a Barí girl. Her hearth group was again in Loksojikaira, the lowland fishing house where Kirongda and her daughter had died. Inside this longhouse her mother leaned two large mats against the wall, screening a little internal hut near the hearth group's hammocks. Tótubi had to remain inside the mat enclosure until her menstrual flow stopped. She was allowed outside only to relieve herself very early in the morning when everyone in the house was asleep or later in the day when everyone was away fishing.

(The Bari say they believe that in general a girl does not have her first period until she has intercourse. Tótubi probably had had sex before these events took place, but she did not mention her first lover when we interviewed her.)

If any men had seen her while she was in menstrual seclusion for her first period they would have lost their marksmanship with bow and arrow and fallen from trees when they climbed them to retrieve fruit and arboreal game. While Tótubi was in the little hut of mats, her mother and surviving older sister, Arakdá, brought her food (she could not eat salt or sugarcane or the tripe of howler monkey) and talked to her. They talked about menstruation, among other things. She was in the little hut for six days, sleeping on the ground on a mat. She was happy.

When her bleeding stopped, she left the little mat hut and bathed with her mother and older sister. When they returned to the house her father gave her a new name, in front of the whole hearth group. She was now a grown woman.

Now that Tótubi had completed her puberty ritual, she was allowed to take lovers and to sing. The major Barí ceremonial activity involved visiting, singing, and exchanging gifts. During the dry season people from one local group of Barí visited one of the longhouses of another local group. The guests and hosts sang together and exchanged gifts. Usually men sang with men and women sang with women. Sometimes men and women sang together. After a pair of men or a pair of women had finished singing, they exchanged gifts—bundles of arrows in the case of men, skirts in the case of women.

In Tótubi's case, on the first occasion she sang she was about sixteen, again residing in Loksojikaira and still unmarried. She sang with only one of the visitors, a married woman with two small children named Abakú. For the singing, Abakú lay on her back in a hammock that had been lowered so that it barely cleared the floor when she lay in it. Tótubi sat in the hammock with her back to Abakú. Each of them threw an arm over her head to protect her ears from extraneous, evil sounds.

Then they swung the hammock back and forth and took turns singing traditional words to each other in a simple, repetitive melody. The words said in effect, "I am going to give you a skirt, it will be yours, you will wear it"; and the response was, "Yes, I will wear your skirt." Their songs mixed with those of other pairs of women and men who were singing at the same time, no pair coordinated with any other.

The women sang softly and swayed their low-slung hammocks gently. The men, whose hammocks were suspended from the highest part of the longhouse roof, eight or ten meters above the ground, sang at the top of their voices and swung their hammocks so violently that there was a constant danger that one would tear loose and dump its occupants on the dirt floor below.

When Tótubi and Abakú finished singing (the song dialogue usually took the better part of an hour) the two women, who had never met before this visit, exchanged new skirts they had woven for the ceremony. A few days later Abakú and the other visitors from her local group returned to one of their own longhouses. The two women never saw each other again. But they had exchanged voices and garments they had made with their own hands, and each knew the other to be the sort of person with whom one might have such relations.

While Tótubi was growing to womanhood her father's sister's family, which had joined her family to form a single hearth group when she was a little girl, continued to share a hearth with Tótubi and her nuclear family. Tótubi's mother, Aseba, continued to bear children.

Tótubi's oldest sister, Kirongda, was now dead, along with her baby and her husband, Asakadú. Tótubi's second oldest sister, Arakdá, had married the oldest of her father's sister's sons, Darikbí, and a year or two thereafter gave birth to a baby. Within a few years this new birth was balanced by an unexpected death within the hearth group.

Urukuksá was Tótubi's youngest brother and her mother's next to last child. A perfectly healthy boy, he was bitten by a snake and died in his early teens, again at Loksojikaira. It was his cousin and brother-in-law, Arakdá's husband, Darikbí, who buried him.

Now Tótubi was attracted to the fifth of her father's sister's sons, a robust boy several years younger than she was who was a first-rate hunter and fisherman. He was very young when the two families merged, so he had known her essentially all his life.

His name was Abakdakai. Eventually they married. Tótubi was in her mid-twenties, unusually old for a first-time Barí bride.

A Barí marriage was a private event, without ceremony, usually accomplished when the bride's father, speaking for himself and his wife, said a discreet word to the groom indicating that they were willing to accept him as a son-in-law and explicitly "turning her over" to him. Almost always the young couple had been having sex for some time before marriage, and that was no one's business but theirs (unless they were of the wrong kinship categories and incest was involved.) The suitor had made his aspirations known to the girl's father, who then discussed the matter with her mother (it was usually the mother who had the final word on her daughter's marriage) and usually with the girl herself and in due course responded to the boy. Usually, after the father had turned over his daughter, the groom joined his father-in-law's hearth group, and his hammock was hung directly above his new bride's hammock. The new position of his hammock counted as a public announcement of the marriage. (A common way in which a man assented to turn over his daughter was to say to the suitor, while the local group was on a migration from one of its longhouses to another, that in the new house he would be welcome to hang his hammock above hers.) In Tótubi's case, her husband was already a member of her father's hearth group, so his hammock moved only a few feet.

At the time of Tótubi's marriage, her father spit tobacco juice on her and rubbed it into her skin, so that she would not get *kokshibadyi*, a skin disease. (In our culture, spitting on someone is the height of insult. Among the Barí—and the custom is not uncommon throughout the world—spitting on a person, particularly spitting the juice of a magical plant, was a means of curing or blessing, parallel in symbolism to holy unction.)

Marriage did not change Tótubi's daily routine greatly. She continued to live with her parents and to participate in the economic life of the hearth group, planting, weeding, harvesting, and replanting manioc and other crops; cooking and cleaning; and taking part in communal fishing expeditions and in the occasional construction of new longhouses. The major difference in her life was the man with whom these activities were directly associated.

For example, each longhouse in which she lived was surrounded by an oval field whose major crop was manioc. Most of these fields were circled by a ring of bananas and plantains, with rings of minor crops near their centers, just beyond the area of cleared earth that surrounded the longhouse. Conceptually, these fields were divided into wedges, like pie slices, with each wedge belonging to the adult male who had planted the crops there and to whose hammock location within the house the tip of the wedge pointed. Since the wedges cut across the concentric rings, each man owned the full complement of crops. Previously Tótubi had helped her mother weed, harvest, and replant her father's section of the field. Now she worked in her husband's section.

Because she and her new husband were already in the same hearth group, there was no major change in Tótubi's cooking activities. She continued to take her turn cooking for the whole group.

But now when the entire local group engaged in communal spear fishing, there was a subtle change in her activities. The most common kind of spear-fishing expedition involved cutting off one arm of a river where it parted around an island by piling up stones in a pair of weirs. The upstream weir was built by the men of the local group and the downstream one by the women. Tótubi continued to participate in building the women's weir, but now when the men speared the trapped fish and tossed them to the shore it was her husband's fish that she scaled and gutted, rather than her father's, and his catch that she packed home in a basket while he raced ahead with the other men.

Tótubi had a good womb, as she told us, and she was pregnant less than six months after she was officially married. In addition to her new husband, during this pregnancy she also had sex with his younger brother (a custom known among many lowland South American tribes). About a quarter of all pregnancies among the Barí involved a lover as well as a husband. Their belief was that the fetus needed repeated anointing with semen to make it grow fast and strong. All the men who had intercourse with a woman during a pregnancy were thus believed to contribute to the development of the fetus, and all of them in principle had fatherly obligations to the child.

When the time came to give birth, Tótubi's people were back at Loksojikaira. When her labor pains came strong and fast, she walked through the field that surrounded the longhouse to a place she had chosen just at the edge of the forest, corresponding to the location of her hammock in the longhouse. Her mother and elder sister, Arakdá, came with her. Accompanying them were two women who stood in an affinal relationship to Tótubi.

In her chosen spot she put down a mat that her mother had woven. The women covered it with *Heliconia* leaves, the same giant leaves that the Barí used to eat from and to wrap food in. Tótubi squatted over the leaves, holding herself upright by grasping a low overhead branch. She was also supported by the accompanying women, one of whom knelt behind her, ready to squeeze her belly if the child had difficulty emerging. Her mother caught the baby. One of the affinal women cut the umbilical cord with a knife, because the baby was a girl. If the baby had been a boy the cord would have been cut with the beak of an anhinga (a neotropical bird that uses its long, sharp beak to spear fish) so that he would grow up to be a good spear fisherman.

Tótubi's mother bathed the baby and wrapped the placenta in *Heliconia* leaves and buried it at the foot of a tree. While Tótubi nursed her newborn child, one of the affinal women returned to the longhouse and said to Abakdakai and his brother, "You have a daughter."

Soon after the birth Tótubi's husband spit tobacco juice on her stomach to stop the postpartum bleeding. For three months after the birth Tótubi could not have sex, cook, eat salt, or go to the garden. Her husband went to the garden to harvest manioc; her sister cooked for her.

Tótubi and her husband and their new daughter continued to live with her natal hearth group. He fished and hunted for the common pot and cleared land for gardens; she weeded and harvested and took her turn cooking for the hearth group, rotating with her mother, her older sisters, and her father's sister. It was the usual rule among the Barí that only one married woman, usually aided by her young daughters, cooked at any one time. If there were two or more married woman in a hearth group they took turns of a few days each.

When her daughter was about three years old, the girl's grandmother, Tótubi's husband's mother, who was also Tótubi's father's sister, dreamed that a dlabikdu had had sexual intercourse with her during the night. After this vision she gave her granddaughter some food she had been eating, a reckless thing to do. As anticipated by her vision, the old woman died. About a week later, after days of diarrhea and vomiting, the little girl died, too.

Tótubi's husband was evidently too grief-stricken to manage the task of laying his daughter to rest. Tótubi's father buried his granddaughter, close by in the forest, in a place corresponding to the position of her mother's hammock in the longhouse. It happened that the people were again at Loksojikaira. The little girl was buried in the forest not far from where she had been born.

With his sister dead, Tótubi's father soon married the old woman's last child, Ashankshí, her only unmarried daughter. Uncle-niece marriages are widely recorded in lowland South America and were not uncommon among the Barí. The timing of this marriage suggests that Tótubi's father and his former brother-in-law, the new bride's father and now also Tótubi's father's father-in-law, were deliberately forging a new kinship link to hold the two large nuclear families together in a single hearth group (Fig. 1.7). One child, a girl, was born from this marriage.

Tótubi continued to sing ceremonially from time to time and to establish the relationships that came from exchanging songs and gifts. Twice she went off with a group of three other women to visit another longhouse. On the first of these trips, traveling with only their hammocks and the skirts they were wearing, the women had to turn back when the longhouse house they reached, Burubungdakaira, turned out to be unoccupied, its inhabitants having migrated to another of their longhouses, Bakshikokdori. On the second try they went straight to Bakshikokdori and found their hosts. Tótubi sang with two people, a man and a woman. Both of them were her relatives, in the Barí way of reckoning, because Tótubi's father's brother had had sexual relations with their mothers. Thus they were "like siblings." The man gave her a necklace of toucan breast feathers; the woman gave her two skirts.

While the singing and visiting was going on, Tótubi and the other visiting women from her longhouse ate and slept close to each other in a part of the longhouse that their hosts had given over to them. It worked

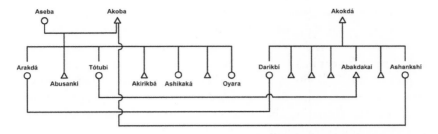

Fig. I.7. Tótubi's hearth group after her daughter and her father's sister died and her father married his sister's daughter.

that way when women came alone to sing. When whole families or hearth groups visited, each family was parceled out to a host hearth group and ate and slept in the host hearth group's part of the longhouse.

A few months later, after her visit to Bakshikokdori, the man who had given Tótubi the toucan feather necklace came alone to the longhouse where her people were residing. He sang only with her. Then she gave him a *tarikbá*, a man's loincloth she had woven, freeing herself from obligation and repaying her debt to him.

Soon Tótubi was pregnant again. In the longhouse Bariduá she gave birth to a boy, again attended by her mother and elder sister. While this boy was still nursing, Tótubi's hearth group made a visit to Burubungda-kaira, a longhouse belonging to the local group she had previously visited with the group of women. Both her surviving brothers were still unmarried at this time, and the visit was largely a search for wives for them.

There was a great deal of singing, and a young unmarried man of Burubungdakaira named Bakdererei sang with both of Tótubi's brothers and with her husband. Tótubi herself sang with a woman named Akchirú and received a skirt from her, when it became clear that her younger brother Akirikbá intended to marry Akchirú.

When Tótubi's little boy was two years old her local group was again in Bariduá when one night she took him with her when she left the house to urinate. She heard him cry out when a dlabikdu grabbed him by the wrist. Very soon, he was seized by a fever, his small heart pounding rapidly. Six days later he was dead.

The obligations of social life continued after the latest domestic tragedy. Akchirú had given Tótubi a skirt she had woven; this debt had not yet been paid. When Akchirú visited Bariduá Tótubi sang with her and presented her with a skirt she had made. Tótubi was now pregnant with her third child.

The social environment of the Barí changed dramatically toward the end of this pregnancy, while Tótubi was residing in Bariduá. Roberto Lizarralde, working for the Venezuelan Bureau of Indian Affairs, established peaceful contact with the Barí, descending from a hovering helicopter on July 19, 1960. For a few hours it looked as if Lizarralde would be in charge of helping the Barí make their place in the modern nation of Venezuela. However, when news of his successful connection became public Lizarralde was relieved of his duties, and his charge, along with the budget to carry it out, was transferred to Capuchin missionaries. The Capuchin order had had a mission to the Barí for a few decades around the turn of the nineteenth century, achieving the partial pacification of the tribe. (See chapter 3 below; and Lizarralde and Beckerman 1982.)

The twentieth-century Capuchins began enthusiastically visiting Barí longhouses and planning missions, often accompanied by employees from their already existing missions to the Yukpa, a nearby tribe who were traditional enemies of the Barí. The central Capuchin mission compound, still in existence, is named Tukuko.

A few months after Lizarralde's peaceful contact, at a longhouse named Ohbadyá, Tótubi gave birth to another child, a daughter. Her mother attended the birth as usual, but her older sister was asleep in the house. Oyara, Tótubi's youngest sister, took her place. A few weeks later the local group returned to Bariduá.

At Bariduá a Capuchin priest, Father Adolfo, encouraged the people to build a new longhouse, Arikbakantung, at the foot of the mountains, more convenient to his mission base at Tukuko. It was there, in August 1960, that the first of the contact epidemics found the Barí. Arikbakantung was newly occupied, and Father Adolfo and the two Yukpas with him had been there for about a week. The major disease was measles, deadly in a population with no epidemiological experience of it and thus no immunity within any age group. Hepatitis and influenza may have been involved, too.

Tótubi's recollection is that as people got sick, Father Adolfo gave them pills. Then, after mass, one of the Yukpa helpers, a man named Paulino, gave injections to the sick ones. People began dying after that.

Father Adolfo left but soon returned and told the sick people to follow him to the mission at Tukuko. Tótubi stayed in Arikbakantung to care for her family. She was one of only two people there who did not get sick. Other people were feverish, initially with pains in their chests, diarrhea, and respiratory problems; then measles spots appeared. Most of them, typically for traditional Barí, saw their sickness as a shameful thing, lost hope, and abandoned themselves to death. Tótubi's mother died in this longhouse.

After the death of her mother Tótubi's family fled back to Bariduá. She and the baby and one other adult were apparently the only ones in this group of refugees who were not already sick. In Bariduá she was able to care for her sister and for a man named Baraká. But her husband, Abakdakai, took to his hammock and said, "I am too sick. I have to die." Her father, too, was very ill and seems to have abandoned hope.

Her sister and Baraká, who allowed her to bring them water and food, survived. Many others, including her husband and her father, did not. Tótubi covered them with blankets and waited. She remembers the names of fifteen men and seven women who died. She does not remember the names of all the children. When the end came she and the only other person in the longhouse who was not sick could only drag the dead outside and leave them. Crying, she had to drag her own father outside.

Months later, after her sister recovered, they went to the longhouse Ohbadyá. A couple of days after they arrived, another Capuchin, Padre Romualdo, found them there; he and Paulino, the Yukpa mission employee, took them to the Tukuko mission, where many other Barí had also been gathered. The Barí were fed by the nuns at Tukuko, since they had no gardens there and many of them were too sick and confused to be able to care for themselves.

As these devastating and confused events suggest, Barí society was falling apart. By the middle of 1966, only five years after peaceful contact, between one-fourth and one-half of all the Barí had died—from epidemic disease, from the deliberate poisoning described in chapter 3, and perhaps from despair itself. Some of them, including Tótubi, managed to survive and carry on with their lives.

At the mission compound where she had been brought, Tótubi lived with her surviving sisters and brothers and their spouses. After Tótubi's father's death her older brother, Abusanki, had married his father's widow, Ashankshi, who was also his father's sister's daughter. Again, this marriage may have been an attempt to keep the two nuclear families together as a single hearth group. But although the marriage was unimpeachable in terms of the kin relations between husband and wife, Abusanki's new wife did not care for him.

One day at Tukuko (it was May or June 1961) a nine-year-old girl was holding Tótubi's daughter, her only surviving child, who was then about nine months old. The little girl dropped the baby, and *shungbaraba*, earth spirits, grabbed the baby girl. She died four days later.

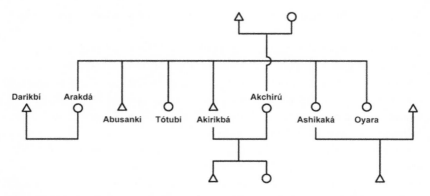

Fig. I.8. Tótubi's hearth group after the epidemic deaths and the flight from the mission at Tukuko.

With her mother, father, husband, and all her children dead, Tótubi's only remaining ties were to her brothers and sisters. She slept next to her younger sisters.

The family stayed at Tukuko for over a year. Eventually Abusanki's wife left him for another man, and he led the remaining family away from Tukuko. The departing group included Abusanki, his brother Akirikbá and his wife and two children; his sisters, Arakdá, Ashikaká, Oyara, and Tótubi and the husbands of the first two sisters, along with the only child of the second. When they left, in addition to his siblings and their spouses and children, Abusanki was accompanied by the parents of Akchirú, the wife of his younger brother Akirikbá (Fig. 1.8).

He took everyone first to Dakuma, a hamlet built by Father Adolfo with Colombian and Yukpa workers. They stayed there for two nights, during which time a man named Achirokdó and his two young daughters (about eight and ten) began to eat with them. Achirokdó's relationship to Tótubi and her brothers and sisters illustrates Barí ideas of relatedness.

Achirokdó's father had slept with Tótubi's mother when she was pregnant with Tótubi. Thus, according to Barí beliefs about conception and fetal growth, he had contributed to forming Tótubi while she was in the womb. He was a secondary father to Tótubi, not as crucial as her primary father but undeniably involved in creating her. So Achirokdó was Tótubi's half brother through their shared father and a legitimate member of her group of siblings.

The full group of siblings, Achirokdó and his daughters now included, left Dakuma after two nights and went to the traditional longhouse of Birokdoteintein. There they stayed for several months. Eventually, though, the married couples and their children, more than half the group, returned to Tukuko. The unmarried adults—Tótubi; her older brother, Abusanki; her half brother, Achirokdó; and her youngest sister, Oyara—went on to Okbadyá, a traditional longhouse belonging to Tótubi's local group, and the house at which Tótubi's second daughter had been born. Achirokdó sent his daughters back to the nuns at Tukuko with Tótubi's married brother and sisters.

Abusanki, Achirokdó, Tótubi, and Oyara were alone in Okbadyá for about three months. The men fished and hunted, and the women gardened and cooked. The pronounced sexual division of labor among the Barí made it impossible for an individual of either sex to live alone. Virtually all activities required the participation of members of both sexes. Men hunted alone or in all-male groups, but it was women who cooked the game. Women did all the spinning and weaving, but it was men who set up their looms. Single adults were rare and married as soon as they could. While single they lived with their parents, with adult siblings of the opposite sex, as was the case with Tótubi's sibling set, or, if they were elderly, with their adult children.

When Tótubi's sibling set was alone at Okbadyá the men and the women ate together but slept in separate parts of the house. The Barí had a horror of anything that hinted at even the possibility of sexual relations between consanguinal relatives. Brothers and sisters were not permitted to see each other's genitals or mention sexual matters in each other's presence, even jokingly. In the longhouse people classified by kinship terminology as consanguinal relatives always slept apart, either physically distant or separated by an affinal relative sleeping between them.

One night (it must have been late 1961 or early 1962) there arrived in Okbadyá three Barí men, half brothers by the same father, from a longhouse named Buribungdakaira. They said they were on their way to Tukuko. One of them was Bakdererei, the young man who had sung with Tótubi's husband and brothers when they had visited Buribungdakaira years before. The others were his half brothers, Abagyí and Bachkiri. The visitors spent the night at Okbadyá. The next morning when Abusanki and Achirokdó awoke they discovered Bakdererei in Tótubi's hammock, and Abagyí in a hammock with her sister Oyara.

Abusanki said to the men, "If you are going to marry my sisters, then stay here" (i.e., instead of going to Tukuko). And they answered, "We are going to be your *okdyibara* [brothers-in-law]."

Then Abagyí said to Abusanki, "I have married your sister; I will bring you my sister to marry."

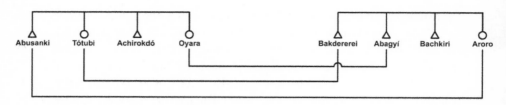

Fig. I.9. Tótubi's hearth group after she, her sister, and her brother remarried.

Abagyí returned to Buribungdakaira and brought his sister Aroro to Okbadyá. She asked, "Why did you bring me?"

Abagyí answered, "I have married the sister of Abusanki. For that I brought you."

And Aroro replied, "Yes, I will marry Abusanki."

So it happened that five days after his sisters found new husbands, Abusanki found a new wife. The great French anthropologist Claude Lévi-Strauss argued that sister exchange is the oldest and most fundamental form of marriage: two men contract that each will hand over his sister to the other as a wife. The case of Abusanki's marriage is as clear an example as one could imagine (Fig. 1.9).

Soon the newly married couples went to another traditional longhouse, Barandanku, and a month later to yet another, Birokdoteintein. After three months there they were again taken to the mission at Tukuko, this time in a Toyota Land Cruiser. Roads were now cutting through the rain forest.

After a short time they left the Tukuko mission, returned to Birokdoteintein, and then went to the new mission settlement of Dakuma, where Tótubi became pregnant. At Dakuma, Tótubi and her new husband, Bakdererei, shared a hearth with her brother Abusanki and his new wife. This two-couple hearth group again left the hamlet of Dakuma, moving from longhouse to longhouse in the traditional semisedentary pattern. At Akokburung, a temporary shelter on the way to Birokdoteintein, Tótubi gave birth to a son, Aboksó, in December 1962.

As they moved back and forth from mission to longhouse in this transitional period in their lives, Tótubi and Bakdererei and Abusanki and Aroro not only changed location but also their basic form of residential life. In the missions they lived in small, peasant-style houses designed as single-family dwellings. In the longhouses they lived in large communal dwellings with no walls between one family and the next. The surviving Barí were trying to find their feet in the new circumstances, going from one cultural adaptation to another, trying to build new lives and finding that new lives would require a new culture as well.

When Tótubi had her next son, Atdyeraká, the hearth group was back at the Tukuko mission. Abusanki soon said that with the new child it was a burden for the two families to share a hearth. He established a separate household for his nuclear family.

Tótubi's next five children, three boys and two girls, were born at the mission settlement of Dakuma. Of the seven children Tótubi had with Bakdererai, three had secondary fathers. One of these men was her sister's husband, another was her husband's brother, and the third had no close kin connection.

After the last child was born the family moved to a village that had grown up as the main mission to the Barí. It is now the largest Barí settlement. There the children were able to go to the mission school.

Pregnant at this settlement, Tótubi tripped over a vine one day while wearing heavy boots and fell on her stomach. The miscarried fetus was a boy. Since then she has not been able to get pregnant, although she has wanted to.

These days Tótubi and her husband still have a house at this mission village and another on a piece of land she and her husband farm. In the settlement she lives in a peasant-style house with her husband and four of her surviving six children. Her oldest son is married and has his own house, as does her third son. Her second son is also married, and he and his wife live in the same house as their parents. Her two daughters and her youngest son have not yet married.

Just a few steps away from Tótubi's house is the house belonging to Akirikbá, the younger brother whose life she saved when they were children. When we interviewed him he kept returning to that episode.

"She carried me all day. She was very strong."

The descriptions in the chapters that follow explore the aggregate patterns that emerge in the lives of the Barí. Although those patterns are central to this book, we believe it is important to keep in mind that they emerge from individual activity and experience. Thus, in Tótubi's biography we emphasized her activities in the fields of production, protection, and reproduction, the central concerns of the book. She made no attempt to dramatize the events she recounted; nor did we in our retelling. Nevertheless we hope that the unvarnished account she provided allows readers to infer the lived experience of this woman and imagine the perceptions and emotions that accompanied her as she moved through her life.

For instance, we described ordinary Barí subsistence activities from the perspective of a participant. When in chapter 4 we present measurements of kilograms/man-hour rates of return from fishing and the labor demands and productivity of manioc horticulture we want it to be clear that those quotients arise from totals calculated from the subsistence activities of individual people such as Tótubi and her father, as narrated above. There was more than tabulation and calculation involved. When fishing, there was also sweat and the heat of the sun on the shoulders, the chill of cold water on the legs, the shrill buzz of insects, the banter of the fishermen, and the smiles of the women as they bathed their children and cleaned the fish their husbands tossed to them. When clearing a field, there were blisters on the hands and the constant worry that the fall of a giant tree might crush someone. When planting a field, there was the smell of the recently burned slash, the heat of the afternoon, and the practiced coordination of men and women working together.

We reported the deaths of Tótubi's parents and sisters and brothers and husband and children as she remembered them, with a slow voice and a heavy face, because when we discuss the impact of disease and violence in chapters 3 and 5 we want it known that pain and tears were entailed as well as changes in actuarial parameters. We reported the raids in which members of her longhouse were murdered as she recalled them, not as predator-prey relations, but as moments of terror and horror and flight.

We recounted the history and individual circumstances of Tótubi's marriages because when we deal with reproduction in chapter 6 we want to underline that here as everywhere affection and courtship and all the rest of the intricate dance of human mating and marriage have a great deal to do with birth rates and that the survivorship of one's children is bound up with domestic arrangements and social relations. The intent is not to "put a human face" on foraging practices or population dynamics but rather to insist that the latter emerge from multitudes of individual human faces and minds and bodies. These last are the places any ethnography must begin.

CHAPTER 2

Physical Environment

Many of the particulars of the Barí natural environment derive from two general characteristics of its location: a northern tropical latitude and a landscape marked by mountain ranges on the south and west. From these features descends a string of consequences displaying two patterns, one temporal and one spatial. Temporally, this environment is marked by bimodal oscillations: two rainfall peaks per year, two river rises per year, and so forth. Spatially, it is arranged as a series of concentric rings (ring segments, strictly speaking) whose geometric center is near the mouth of the río Catatumbo. The annular order is manifested in landforms, soil types, vegetation zones, and other geographic features. The interplay of the two patterns is the basis for the organization of this chapter.

Landscape and Climate

The Maracaibo Basin is a structural depression, approximately bisected by the line of 10° N latitude, bounded by the arms of an enormous, tilted Y formed by the Eastern Cordillera of the Andes. The north-south arm of the Y, the Sierra de Perijá, forms the western border of the basin. On the south and east the basin is enclosed by the northeast-southwest arm of the cordillera, known as the Venezuelan Cordillera of the Andes or the Mérida Cordillera. The center of the basin holds Lake Maracaibo, a large body of slightly saline water (equivalent to about 3% seawater [Redfield et al. 1955: iii] since the dredging of its mouth in the early 1950s) open on the north to the Caribbean Sea, with which it communicates through a strait (el Estrecho de Maracaibo), a bay (el Tablazo), and a shallow gulf (el Golfo de Venezuela) (Map 2.1).

Map 2.1. The Maracaibo Basin and the location of the Barí within it.

The area of the whole Maracaibo system, including the continental shelf in the Gulf of Venezuela and the Coro and Guajiro Peninsulas that enclose this shallow marine area on the east and west, respectively, is close to 125,000 km² in extent. The hydrographic basin defined by the mildly brackish lake properly speaking and the rivers draining directly into it have an area of about 78,000 km², with roughly 62,000 km² in Venezuela and 16,000 km² in Colombia (MARNR 1979: 170–171; Parra Pardi et al. 1979: 4; Acevedo Latorre 1969: ix). Lake Maracaibo itself has an area of 13,000 km² and a maximum depth of only 34 m; it is about 150 km long from north to south and 120 km wide at its maximum east-west dimension (Ginés 1982: 25; Rodrígues 1973: 21).

A geologically well-studied section (Servicio Geológico Nacional e Inventario Minero Nacional 1967) of one Colombian section of Motilonia, around the oil town of Tibú, can serve as a snapshot of the underlying geology of the region—at least on its western edge. The basement formation is made up of igneous and metamorphic rocks—schists, gneisses, and intrusive granites, largely Devonian and all pre-Mesozoic. Overlaying the basement rocks are middle and upper Cretaceous sediments up to 2 km thick, laid down in six formations of sandstones, limestones, and shales. Many of the limestones are fossiliferous, and five of the six formations have yielded oil. Of special interest here is the fact that a 45 to 86 m thick limestone formation named La Luna, from the early upper Cretaceous, is capped by phosphate deposits of sufficient richness to be commercially exploitable. One outcropping of this stratum occurs about 20 km west of Tibú, along the banks of the río Orú, a tributary of the Catatumbo; another is found about 15 km south of the town of Petrólea, not far from the río Sardinata, another tributary of the Catabumbo; a third one occurs along the course of the Catatumbo itself, near the town of La Gabarra. The significance of the phosphate stratum and its restricted outcroppings is discussed below. It is also of consequence that the topmost upper Cretaceous formation, the Catatumbo, contains coal.

Overlying the Cretaceous sediments are seven Tertiary formations, primarily of sandstones and shales from the Paleocene, Eocene, and Oligocene and of sands and clays from the Miocene and Pliocene. These strata are up to 4 km thick in some places. The Barco formation, from the Lower Paleocene, is the major oil producer for the whole section. It is overlain by the Los Cuervos formation, from the Upper Paleocene, which has eight to ten coal strata in its lower part. These strata, of both lignite and bituminous coal, vary in thickness from 0.1 to 2.5 m and constitute a considerable coal deposit. There is also coal in the later Carbonera formation, which straddles the Eocene-Oligocene boundary.

The Quaternary is represented by the Necesidad formation of clays interbedded with sandstones, bridging the Pliocene-Pleistocene boundary, and by Recent alluvial and colluvial deposits. All the strata below the Carbonera, and a good part of the Carbonera itself, were laid down before Lake Maracaibo existed.

In the early Eocene all northwestern South America was probably a relatively flat area without major relief between the regions that are now the separate basins of the Magdalena River on the west, Lake Maracaibo in the middle, and the upper río Orinoco tributaries in the east (Perez Lozano 1990). The Maracaibo Basin was brought into existence by the orogenesis of the northern Andes, in a process that began in the late Eocene and was nearly completed by the Pliocene (Rodrígues 1973: 24–26). The Central Cordillera of the Andes was the first of the current three cordilleras to appear. It is thought that the Eastern Cordillera, separating the drainage of the Orinoco Basin from those of the Maracaibo and Magdalena Basins, began to arise in the late Miocene. The orogenesis of the northern extension of the Eastern Cordillera, the Sierra de Perijá, at the end of the Pliocene, separated the Maracaibo drainage from that of the Magdalena. The timing of these events is reflected in the greater similarity of the ichthyfauna of the río Catatumbo (the largest river in the Maracaibo Basin) to that of the río Magdalena than to that of the río Orinoco (Galvis et al. 1997).

As the enclosing mountain ranges rose and the basin sank, the level of the sea changed, in response to global climatic fluctuations. The size and shape of the Lake Maracaibo depression were stable throughout the Pleistocene and Holocene, but the advances and retreats of the Caribbean changed it from a freshwater lake with interior drainage (during glacial maxima with lowered sea level) to a coastal lagoon (during glacial minima with raised sea level) several times (Graf 1969). The strait of Maracaibo is believed to be the drowned valley of a river that drained the freshwater lake into the sea around the end of the last glacial period. The opening of the strait has been variously estimated at dates between 4000 and 8000 BP (Rodrígues 1973: 28).

On the western edge of the Maracaibo Basin, the Sierra de Perijá runs almost due north from the bifurcation point of the Eastern Cordillera of the Andes, south of the Colombian city of Cúcuta, for over 350 km, finally subsiding north of the city of Maracaibo. Its crest is above 1,500 m altitude throughout that distance, and in some lengthy stretches it rises above 2,000 m. In its central portion it reaches above 3,000 m and shows evidence of having been glaciated in the past (Schubert 1975).

The other arm of the Y, the Venezuelan Cordillera of the Andes, extends northeast from the same location south of Cúcuta for about 700 km before turning due east near the Venezuelan city of Barquisimeto. In their northeasterly run, the Venezuelan Andes' crest never dips below 1,000 m. With the important exception of a pass just south of Cúcuta, where one upper branch of the río Zulia (the río Táchira) nearly touches the headwaters of the río Quinimari (an Orinoco affluent), the crest stays above 1,500 m. Indeed, the Venezuelan Andes are substantial mountains: with a crest of over 2,000 m for 400 km of their length and peaks of up to 5,000 m, they are a considerable barrier, even to high altitude winds. Thus the southern pass through the Venezuelan Andes, where the cordillera dips to barely 1,000 m, is crucially important for the wind and weather of the Maracaibo Basin.

The region of the Maracaibo Basin of interest in connection with the Barí is its southwestern lobe, here called historical Motilonia, a zone made up primarily of the basins of the ríos Santa Ana, Catatumbo, and Escalante. A few smaller rivers also drain parts of the sector, and a sizable swampy area communicates directly with the lake as well. Assimilating the minor rivers to the basins of the three major rivers provides a rough but convenient comparison of the watersheds. The basins of the Santa Ana and Escalante are entirely within Venezuela and encompass about 6,700 km² and 4,800 km², respectively. The Catatumbo Basin covers over 10,400 km² in Venezuela and an additional 16,400 km² upriver in Colombia, for a total of 26,800 km². The swampy area (sometimes differentiated by water color as two swamps, la Cienega de Juan Manuel de Aguas Claras and la Cienega de Juan Manuel de Aguas Negras) covers about 1,500 km² (ICLAM 1991: 40). The drainage basins within which historical Motilonia is located, then, total nearly 40,000 km², or about half the area of the hydrographic basin of the lake.

This realm is the rainy quarter of the basin, where prevailing winds, a land-water transition, and significant relief combine to produce heavy precipitation. In ways specified below, the tropical latitude of historical Motilonia combines with its landforms to produce consequences that extend to the region's climate, geomorphology, soils, flora, and fauna. The effective environment to which the Barí must accommodate themselves is generated by a complex causal history. This history begins with the latitude, the climate, and the biannual fluctuation of the local weather.

The general circulatory pattern of the earth's atmosphere is driven by the input of solar energy. The solar equator (the parallel of latitude at which the sun is directly overhead at noon) moves from 21° N of the geographical equator on June 21 (the summer solstice) to 21° S of the geographic equator on December 21 (the winter solstice). The parallel at which the sun is directly overhead receives more solar energy per unit area than other latitudes, where the slanting sunlight spreads more thinly. Because much of the energy of the sun's rays is transferred to the atmosphere as heat, the air around the solar equator becomes warmer and less dense than adjacent air masses, rising to produce a planet-ringing low pressure zone known as the equatorial trough. This low pressure zone, over 1,000 km in width, has its center at a mean annual position of around 5° N latitude (the so-called meteorological equator) and migrates north and south with the orientation of the earth's axis to the sun—northward in our summer, southward in winter. This migration lags behind the zenithal position of the sun, however, and is confined to a narrower band of latitude—about 20° total range over land and fewer than 10° over ocean (Snow 1976: 296). The movements of the equatorial trough vary somewhat from year to year; it is usually farthest south in February and March and farthest north in September and October.

In the region with which we are concerned, the trade winds blow across the Caribbean from the northeast, as denser temperate air flows toward the low pressure trough to the south. From December through April, when the equatorial trough is well to the south, the trades blow vigorously, enter the Maracaibo Basin, and are forced south when they strike the Sierra de Perijá (Snow 1976: 296–298; Rodrígues 1973: 39–40; Goldbrunner 1963: 105–107).

From May through November, the equatorial trough is farther north, and the trade winds blow too weakly to enter the Maracaibo Basin in force (Snow 1976: 296–298; Rodrígues 1973: 39–40). Local winds then predominate.

Year round the Maracaibo Basin experiences local winds caused by the unequal heating and cooling of the land and water. During the day the land heats more rapidly than the lake and transfers heat to the adjacent air, which begins to rise. The air over the lake remains cooler and denser and flows toward the land, producing an onshore breeze. This local wind begins in mid-morning and dies down at dusk; after dark the land cools more quickly than the water, and the inverse process produces an offshore breeze (Rodrígues 1973: 39–40). The force of these winds varies with the amount of temperature difference between land and water, which in turn is determined by the strength of local solar radiation (Goldbrunner 1963:

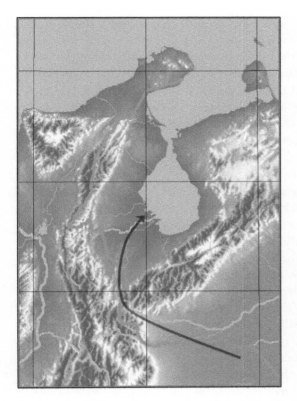

Map 2.2. The southerly winds that enter the Maracaibo Basin through the pass south of Cúcuta. Base map from Sandalmelik 2007. Source: http://wikipedia.org /wiki/Archivo:Colombia_Topography.png (accessed Feb. 5, 2011).

106, 108). The region receives two local maxima of solar radiation, in May and in August.

The result of this mixture of trade and local winds within the basin is a nearly permanent low pressure area, oscillating north and south across the mouth of the río Catatumbo over the course of the year (Goldbrunner 1963: 105–109; Rodrígues 1973: 41, 49–50). At most times of the year but especially when this local low pressure center is in the far south, moist continental winds enter the basin from the south and southeast, spilling over the Andes from the great humid rain forests of central South America through the mountain pass in the Venezuelan Andes just south of Cúcuta (Map 2.2; Goldbrunner 1963: 108). These southerly winds meet the northerly trade winds in a zone of local convergence that runs diagonally southwest-northeast across the lake from around the río Catatumbo on the western shore to somewhat south of the town of Cabimas in the east (MARNR 1979: 188).

The combination of the local convergence of the trades and the continental winds, and the daily wind reversal caused by the land-water transition, produces abundant rain (Rodrígues 1973: 50). Indeed, the thunderstorms of the region are famous, producing the legendary "relámpago del Catatumbo" (lightning of the Catatumbo) evident as far away as the city of Maracaibo, 150 km north. It is a conspicuous feature of the weather that rain mainly falls at night, usually beginning shortly before midnight and winding down slowly to a misty dawn.

Like other coastal areas of northern South America, the region has an essentially marine climate with two rainfall maxima (Snow 1976: 295, 332), the larger one here in October-November and the smaller in May (Fig. 2.1, Map 2.3), nearly coinciding with the two yearly maxima of solar radiation. The precipitation maxima are separated by two somewhat drier seasons. Of these two periods of reduced precipitation, the major (drier) one is also the more stable, centering reliably on February in virtually all of historical Motilonia. The minor (wetter) dry season is less predictable. Although it occurs mainly in July, there are locations in which its midpoint comes in June and one or two where it falls in August.

In general, annual rainfall in historical Motilonia increases as one moves south and west—that is, away from the lake (Map 2.3). In most of the area, only the three months centering on February ever experience so little rainfall as to raise the question of a water deficit; and for most of the region where the Barí of the ethnographic present live, even February normally sees rainfall sufficient to prevent water stress in most vegetation. In the Koeppen classification, historical Motilonia has both Af and Am climates, supporting tall, moist forest.

The bimodal rainfall regime is reflected in the discharge rates of the region's rivers (Sutton and Arnett 1973: G1), whose changing flows reflect a twice yearly oscillation in the amount of water carried and also in the nutrient and sediment load, clarity, and (probably) pH of the water. The relative dryness of the northern rim of historical Motilonia, the Santa Ana Basin, is manifested in the abrupt flow rate changes of the río Santa Ana with the alternation of the wet and dry seasons. These oscillations can be compared with the less marked fluctuations of the río Catatumbo, which drains a larger and wetter basin. The Catatumbo contributes 69% of the fresh water that annually enters Lake Maracaibo, while the Santa Ana carries only about 8%. The smaller río Escalante, draining a basin under

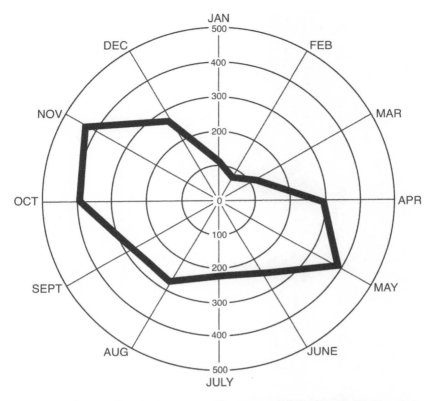

Fig. 2.1. Rainfall rose showing the two annual precipitation peaks (mm/mo.) in historical Motilonia. Figures are averages from four weather stations with 15 to 20 years of records each.

a somewhat different rainfall regime, also shows low variability in river flow—and a shift in the timing of the minor rainy season. Less than 5% of the fresh water in the lake enters by way of the Escalante (Parra Pardi et al. 1979: 45, 180).

The mean annual temperature for the lowlands of this region is around 27°C, with a difference of under 2° between the mean for the hottest month (August) and the coldest (January) (Beckerman 1975: 248–252). There is no biannual cycle in the temperature regime; rather, as is characteristic of marine climates, the temperature manifests a single yearly peak. Daily temperature change is greater than annual or altitudinal variation, typically moving from an early morning low near 23°C just before sunrise to a high close to 34°C around three o'clock in the afternoon (Beckerman

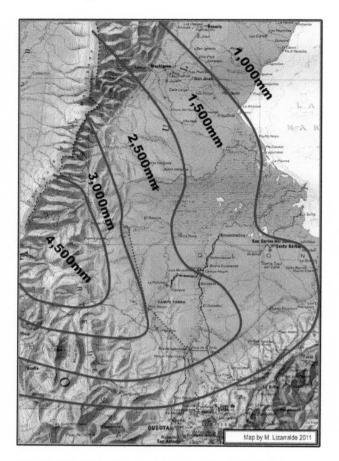

Map 2.3. Rainfall distribution in historical Motilonia. Redrawn from MOP 1973.

1975: 248–252). In this zone, annual mean temperature declines about 0.6°C with each 100 m gain in altitude (Snow 1976: 338), a trend reflected in the flora and fauna of the region.

The Terrestrial System

As regards the spatial patterning of historical Motilonia, both the geomorphology and the pedology of the region show the effects of abundant rainfall and high year-round temperatures on the geological features of the Maracaibo Basin.

The geomorphology is heavily influenced by the flow of warm water derived from the heavy rainfall. On the western rim of historical Motilonia, where the Sierra de Perijá confines the region, there is a rather regular succession of geomorphological features as one moves east toward the lake (COPLANARH 1975: 8). The highest parts of the Sierra de Perijá are composed largely of hard sandstones and conglomerates, but the lower slopes are of softer, interbedded shales and sandstones. Still lower is a depositional valley floor through which flow the upper courses of the Catatumbo and Santa Ana and many of their affluents. For the most part, these rivers begin at higher altitudes as eastward-flowing streams, then turn north or south and run through the long, north-south valley (la Valle de los Motilones) between the main cordillera of the Sierra de Perijá and the cordillera's eastern foothills (la Serranía de Abousanqui,) until they cut through passes in the latter and resume their eastward course (see Maps 1.1 and 2.1). The floor of the valley is covered with colluvial (and some alluvial) deposits from the bordering uplands. It has for the past half century or more been regarded by the Barí as the most favorable environment remaining in their Venezuelan territory, with good fishing and hunting as well as substantial deposits of agriculturally desirable soil. Most of it lies within Territory 3, as shown on Map 1.1. The Serranía de Abousanqui, the foothills bordering the Valle de los Motilones on the east, which the rivers eventually slice through, is a set of broken hills with sharp crests that soon give way farther east to low hilly country with slopes of only 3 to 5%, then to a long topographic plain, slightly inclined and little cut. This plain is composed of fine-grained colluvial material washed down from the hills, with some alluvial additions.

Still farther east, one reaches the alluvial systems of the Catatumbo and Santa Ana, a low tropical plain with a slope of under .05%. While the upper and middle stretches of the rivers have well-conformed channels that flood regularly in the rainy season, these lower reaches have less stable riverbeds, due to the increased water volume and decreased slope in the plain. Fluvial dynamics are unstable here, with numerous abandoned meanders and filled channels.

Between the Catatumbo and the Santa Ana, in the most easterly, lowest reaches of these rivers' courses, is a permanently inundated tectonic depression—a great swamp. Two portions of it are distinguished on the basis of water color—la Cienega de Juan Manuel de Aguas Negras has darker water than la Cienega de Juan Manuel de Aguas Claras, but these sections are not hydrographically separated. The swamp communicates directly with the lake (COPLANARH 1975: 8–9) and is vitally important in the life history of many of the fish in the Catatumbo Basin, in particular the bocachico, the most important fish in the Barí diet.

On the southern edge of historical Motilonia, the situation is similar to that found on the west, except that the Andes have no outlying range of foothills here, and thus there is no large intermontane valley (CO-PLANARH 1975: 9–10). The generally northward-flowing rivers have deposited numerous debris cones in the piedmont band. Deeply cut alluvial terraces are also common at these altitudes. Lower down and farther north, a patchy band of alluvial fans, deposited by the frequent flooding of the poorly conformed rivers, separates the piedmont from the alluvial plain properly speaking.

This plain is made up here of the sedimentation zones of the ríos Zulia and Escalante. The Zulia is the major southern tributary of the Catatumbo, and the Escalante flows parallel to the Zulia and enters Lake Maracaibo south of the Catatumbo. The Zulia-Escalante plain was formed by the continuous filling of the lowest areas of their basins by these heavily laden rivers. The process deposited large quantities of sediment and promoted considerable instability of the river courses, producing frequent lateral shifts in river channels and numerous forkings as well. The result is considerable heterogeneity in soils, vertically as well as horizontally. Sheet sediments from generalized overflow are the major feature, except around the somewhat swampy deltaic region between the mouth of the Escalante and the Zulia-Catatumbo confluence, where filled, abandoned meanders are common (COPLANARH 1975: 10).

A critical distinction in this sloping basin terrain is that between erosional and depositional aspects of the landscape. Where the ground is high and steep, erosional processes predominate, and the land is subject to ablation by water, wind, and gravity. On lower, flatter ground, the products of these ongoing erosional forces accumulate as deposits, sometimes of considerable depth. The distinction is important for such crucial matters as soil development, depth, and texture.

To illustrate the connection between altitude and the erosional-depositional distinction, consider the Venezualan portion of western Motilonia, where both gemorphological and topological maps are available. An idea of the relationship can be gained by examining geomorphological types along the 200, 400, and 600 m contour lines. In the region between the ríos Catatumbo and Tukuko, about one-third of the land cut by the 200 m line is a depositional environment, most of it made up of colluvial deposits in the intermontane valley mentioned above. At 400 m only about an eighth of the intercepted land is depositional; and at 600 m the depositional fraction of the landscape is too small to show up on the maps. The significance of this pattern to the Barí results from pockets of depositional, especially alluvial, soils that are important for their agriculture.

In sum, the geomorphological map of historical Motilonia reveals a broadly similar succession of features as one moves from the mountains toward the lake, whether one starts on the western or the southern rim of the basin. This general picture of concentric rings of features, centering on the swamps around the mouth of the Catatumbo, is a repeated pattern, manifested by other geographic features of the region, including the soils.

There is no good, detailed soil map of historical Motilonia, particularly in its Colombian reaches. Available information (COPLANARH 1975: 11–16) is consistent with local climate and geography. Heavy rainfall and steep slopes drive an ongoing geomorphological reworking of the landscape. Most of the low altitude soils are Entisols and Inceptisols, the soil orders composed of the newest, least developed classes of soils — attributes due here largely to the recent deposition of the soil forming material by alluvial and colluvial transport and the constant washing of these materials by abundant warm water.

For the lower reaches of the region — under about 300 m — where most soil work has been done, it is possible to speak of a spotty but discernible overall pattern, even though that pattern is locally obscured at many points. The general picture is one of concentric bands of different soil suborders, radially cut by spokes of one of those suborders, the spokes bordering the rivers that converge on this section of the lake (Map 2.4).

The center of the region is made up of the swampy soil orders, Aquents and Histosols, deposited in the great swamp bordering the lake around and between the mouths of the Santa Ana, Catatumbo, and Escalante and in a few swampy areas back from the lake. The Aquents are very young, continuously wet mineral soils. As Entisols, they show little or no development of horizontal zonation through soil forming processes. The Histosols are the order made up of similarly wet and immature organic soils; most of their bulk is plant remains. Aquents and Histosols are characteristic of swamps and bogs. They are generally of little agricultural use and as far as anyone knows were never cultivated by the Barí.

Roughly ringing the swamp soils is a band of Tropaquepts. These are Inceptisols, young but somewhat evolved mineral soils with slight to moderate horizon development. (In terms of soil evolution, the Inceptisols stand between the undeveloped Entisols and the more developed soils such as Ultisols and Alfisols.) Tropaquepts are wet Inceptisols under a

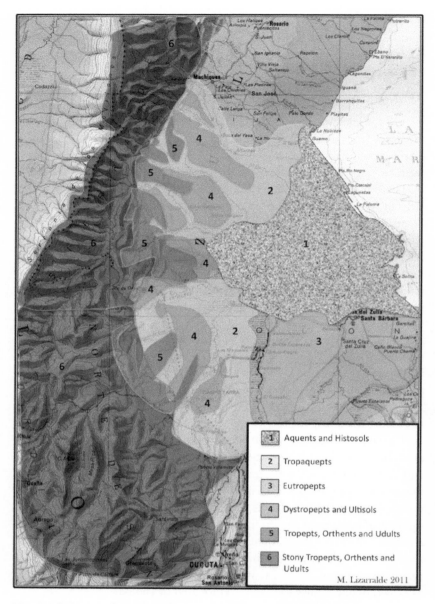

Map 2.4. Soil types of historical Motilonia. Redrawn from COPLANARH 1975.

constantly warm temperature regime. The Tropaquepts of historical Motilonia occur in depostional environments, mainly formed of the alluvium laid down along the courses of the major rivers and in the alluvial plains of the Santa Ana, Catatumbo, Zulia, and Escalante. These plains are nearly contiguous around the edge of the tectonic depression where the rivers disgorge, and thus the swamp is effectively surrounded by a band of Tropaquepts. These Tropaquepts also flank the major rivers up- and downsteam from the alluvial plain, as a result of flood bank sediment deposition, so that the Tropaquept ring is joined by spokes of the same soil passing through it along the courses of the rivers. As tropical soils go, Tropaquepts are not necessarily unsatisfactory for agricultural purposes, if cultivation concentrates on crops tolerant of a high water table.

The next ring out is composed, in the southern part of the region, largely of river deposits of Eutropepts, Inceptisols formed under a constant temperature regime but under conditions of less constant moisture than that producing Tropaquepts. These Eutropepts have high base saturation and are generally considered desirable soils for the sort of slash-and-burn agriculture practiced by the Barí. They are prevalent between the Zulia and the Escalante, an area from which the Barí were permanently removed by the construction of the La Fría-Encontrados railway line around the turn of the nineteenth century. To the northwest of this area, in the Catatumbo and Santa Ana Basins, the depositional Eutropepts are replaced by a largely erosional complex of Dystropepts—Inceptisols formed under similar moisture and temperature regimes but of low base status and much reduced agricultural desirability—and by Ultisols, with the Ultisols approximately twice as abundant as the Dystropepts.

These chiefly erosional Ultisols are evolved soils with a distinct clay horizon and a low base status. The Ultisol suborder Udults contains the classic infertile tropical soils. The Udults prominent in this ring are Paleudults and Plinthudults, the latter being the kind of tropical soil often called laterite, which hardens into an ironstone hardpan on removal of the protecting vegetation.

Slightly higher in elevation is another erosional ring, found on steeper, more broken ground, composed largely of Tropaquepts and other Inceptisols in the south; and Tropepts, Orthents (shallow, often rocky Entisols, undergoing active erosion), and Udults in the west. This band terminates below 300 m in the west and even lower in the south.

Above that level, little pedological work has been done, although it is clear that prominent among the higher elevation soils must be similar but thinner erosional Tropepts, Orthents, and Udults, with small (but agriculturally important) pockets of deeper Tropaquepts on the deposit banks of rivers and in old, filled-in meanders.

Although significant for agriculture, soil type is not as important for natural vegetation cover in the wet tropics as in some other regions, the looser association being due to a well-known attribute of tropical rain forests: in these complex communities, most of the nutrients are cycled within the living and dead vegetation itself, and the soil serves more as a means of structural support than as a nutrient bank. Nitrogen and phosphorus are generally the only nutrients found primarily in the soil (Salati and Vose 1984: 131). Although obviously limited by the gross physical properties of the soil—amount of moisture, depth of the soil layer to which roots can penetrate, and so on—the overall character of rain forest vegetation is to some extent unresponsive to chemical variation in the ground in which it roots. This statement must not be interpreted to mean that no individual species of rain forest trees are sensitive to soil type and soil chemistry, or that these qualities are not important to agriculture. Rather the broad-brush typological attributes of the tropical rain forest, its mean canopy height, tree density, trunk diameter distribution, and the like, are not necessarily directly reflective of soil type.

Indeed, another major attribute of the tropical forest, the proportion of trees that lose their leaves during the driest months, may not map well either (in at least some parts of this region) to the physical boundaries most commonly taken as governing deciduousness. Mean annual rainfall and number of physiologically dry months, closely correlated with each other, may not be good predictors of the limits of evergreen and semideciduous tropical forest in much of historical Motilonia.

This issue is important for the ecology of the Barí because modern clearing has removed most of the forest on the northern and virtually all the forest on the southern borders of historical Motilonia. To investigate the influence of various vegetational associations (otherwise called life zones, ecozones, vegetation formations, forest types, phytogeographical units, etc.) on the distribution and activities of the pre- and pericontact Barí, it is of course necessary to know the extent of those associations at the relevant times, so present purposes require a historical as well as a modern review of the phytogeography of the region.

The classification and mapping of the vegetation types in historical Motilonia and adjacent regions began in the 1910s with the fieldwork of the Swiss botanist Henri Pittier. His 1920 ecological map of Venezuela (reproduced in MARNR 1985: 3) shows an area of "selvas pluviales" (rain forests) covering almost all of historical Motilonia. Swamp vegetation is not differentiated from the forest in this area. The rain forest is terminated in the mountains on the south and west by "selvas templadas" (temperate forests) beginning at an altitude of under 100 m; and on the north by "selvas veraneras" (monsoon forests, by which Pittier means raingreen, or tropical deciduous, forests) whose line of contact with the rain forests is a SW-NE diagonal running from near the río de Oro confluence with the Catatumbo up to the mouth of the río Apón (see Map 2.5).

Pittier was apparently the only author of a vegetation map of Venezuela or Colombia who did fieldwork well within historical Motilonia. It is of interest for the history of the Barí that his map shows agricultural removal of the forests only in three reduced areas: around the town of Encontrados at the Catatumbo-Zulia confluence; near the towns of Santa Cruz and San Carlos-Santa Barbara on the Escalante; and in a small patch between the Escalante and the Zulia near the present-day village of Los Conucos.

Later vegetation maps prepared by Karl Hueck (published in MAC 1960: 12), Jean-Pierre Veillon (in MARNR 1985: 33), and Otto Huber and Clara Alarcón (1988), refine Pittier's work in some aspects (e.g., distinguishing swamp vegetation from forest and recognizing altitudinal zones within the forest) and contradict it in others (e.g., where they locate the northern transition zone between evergreen and semideciduous forest).

M. Lizarralde, who conducted extensive ethnobotanical research with the Barí in this area, is the most recent and reliable authority on the vegetation of historical Motilonia. According to him, "The vegetation is basically evergreen medium-tall rain forest (up to 50 m), much wetter and seasonally flooded in the south around the Catatumbo and the río de Oro region in the rainy season" (M. Lizarralde 1997: 19). He goes on to note that "the northernmost Barí territory has a few deciduous trees. Between the Aricuasá River and the río de Oro, the land is totally covered by evergreen forest" (20). His sketch map shows remnants of semideciduous forest only in the upper río Santa Ana drainage and farther north (20).

Modern research seems to converge on the conclusion that the natural transition zone between lowland evergreen and lowland semideciduous forest is the line running northwest to southeast in the vicinity of the río Negro-río Santa Ana watercourse. The most recent mapping of the phytogeography also indicates that the lowland swamp forest around the great swamp, even its eastern edge, is evergreen, despite the relatively low rainfall there (Huber and Alarcón 1988). In the flat eastern area of the region, the water table is very high (as evidenced by the presence of the swamp), and during months of low rainfall even trees outside the swamp apparently obtain, from the groundwater, moisture that has fallen at higher, rainier elevations to the west.

The undisturbed natural vegetation of precontact Motilonia, to sum up, repeated the concentric pattern noted for soils and landforms: a low-lying swamp covered mostly with grassy plants was largely surrounded by a narrow band of swamp forest, which was in turn backed by a broad ring of evergreen forest limited by higher-elevation forest in the south and west and drier forest in the north. The higher-elevation forest (piedmont and basimontane, in Huber and Alarcón's terms) shaded from semideciduous in the north to evergreen in the south.

Merging these field observations with the combined data of the various phytogeographical maps, an aerial photograph–based map of forest cover remaining around midcentury (MAC 1961), and the Barí territory maps in Lizarralde and Beckerman (1982) provides a rough picture of Barí habitat in the generation preceding contact in 1960 (Map 2.5). It is important to remember that the Barí had been expelled from much of this habitat (see chapter 3) before the trees were felled. Described below are the limits of the remaining contiguous evergreen and semideciduous forests; these forests were larger than the Barí range within them.

Around 1950 the northern border of Motilonia was already partly set by human activity, in that agricultural clearing had removed much of the forest just south of the río Negro, in the region west of its confluence with the Yasa. At one point, ranchers and farmers had reached south of the río Tukuko as far as the río Santa Rosa. To the east of the Negro-Yasa confluence, some forest remained south of a line running roughly from that confluence east to the mouth of the río Riecito. Thus in the northeastern reaches of historical Motilonia a phytogeographical boundary still crossed the forest, since the woods north of the Negro–Santa Ana watercourse were almost certainly semideciduous.

South of the Santa Ana system, Barí territory was crossed on the west by phytogeographical boundaries consequent on increasing altitude, as lowland forest gave way to piedmont, basimontane, and eventually submontane forests, where the Sierra de Perijá mounted above the lake basin. Little or no forest had been felled on this western border before contact.

The forest ended at the great swamp (las Cienegas de Juan Manuel de Aguas Clara y Juan Manuel de Aguas Negras) on the northern half of its eastern boundary as late as the early 1950s; and at the cleared corridor in Colombia surrounding the Petrólea-Orú-Tibú-río de Oro oil camps in the southern part of the eastern edge. That is to say, even by midcentury

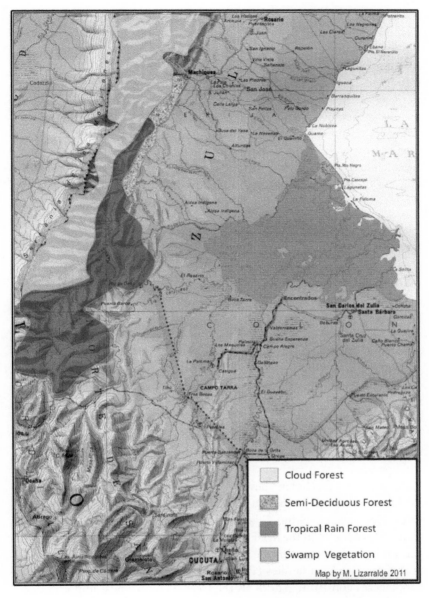

Map 2.5. Current vegetation of historical Motilonia. Redrawn from Huber and Alarcón 1988 and M. Lizarralde 1997.

much of the lowland forest had been felled between the río Zulia and the Colombian portion of the río Catatumbo.

On the southern end, the forest was cut by a road and an oil pipeline running from Tibú and Orú through Convención and El Cármen on the western slope of the Sierra de Perijá and west of it. (A small group of Barí were cut off, south of this road, when it was built in the 1930s [Lizarralde and Beckerman 1982: 21].) The pipeline traversed high ground in its western reaches, and thus the southern limits of Barí habitat, like those in the west, were crossed by altitudinally determined phytogeographical boundaries. Here in the south the higher forests of the piedmont and basimontane region were evergreen, in contrast to those of the north, which were semideciduous.

Even today forest remains in large areas of Barí territory (Map 2.6). These areas are impressive in the size and diversity of their vegetation; they share the typical features of neotropical evergreen forest: the canopy is over 30 m high, and emergent trees may reach a height of 60 m. As is typical of neotropical rain forests, most trunks are relatively slender and do not branch below the canopy. Abundant vines bind the trees to each other. With the exception of the palms and a few understory species, most leaves are of about the same size and shape—smaller than a woman's hand and shaped like a laurel leaf. Flowers are generally inconspicuous from the ground and may appear on virtually any part of a tree. Despite the apparent repetition of form, there is a great variety of species. The old tropical naturalists' saying that one can walk for a mile in the jungle without passing the same species of tree twice is seldom strictly true anywhere in the tropics, and is conspicuously inappropriate for historical Motilonia, but it gives an idea of the richness of the tropical rain forest in comparison to a temperate forest.

A number of scholars have characterized the flora of Motilonia. M. Lizarralde (1997) conducted an ethnobotanical study of thirty-three forest plots located within 10 km of the largest contemporary Barí settlement, Samaidodyi, in the drier northern part of the current area of occupation. In these forest plots he identified 2,325 individual trees. He found that "four botanical familes (Palmae, Leguminosae, Euphorbiaceae and Sapotaceae) constitute half of all the trees. . . . The most important botanical family is Palmae. One in every five trees is a palm" (M. Lizarralde 1997: 23).

The most common palms were *Oenocarpus bataua* (= *Jessenia bataua*, *J. polycarpa*, etc.), *O. mapora*, and *Bactris major*, all of which provided edible fruits used by the Barí. Another important comestible palm was

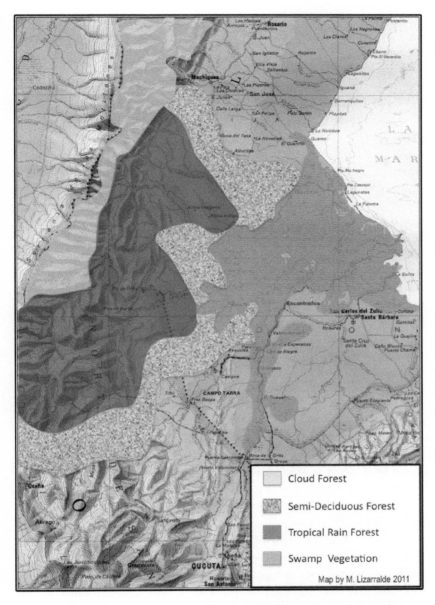

Map 2.6. Vegetation of historical Motilonia around 1950. Redrawn from Huber and Alarcón 1988 and M. Lizarralde 1997.

Attalea butyraceae, which M. Lizarralde (pers. com.) now believes is found only around old habitation sites and thus was probably a cultivar in the recent past.

A number of other species have been identified as characteristic of the forests of Motilonia. Pittier (1971: 46); Huber and Alarcón (1988); Behrens, Baksh, and Mothes (1994: 299); and M. Lizarralde (1997: 22) concur that *Cariniana pyriformis* and *Ceiba pentandra* are especially prominent.

In comparison to other lowland areas of tropical forest in South America, the woods of northern historical Motilonia are toward the low end of tree species diversity. M. Lizarralde (1997: 25–26) found 223 tree species in his plots, but only 38 of these constituted 74% of all the individual trees he identified. The average number of tree species per hectare was around 100. These figures suggest that the forests of Motilonia have perceptibly fewer species overall, and more species that are rather common, than one might expect to find in the lowland rain forests of the Amazon, to use the obvious comparison. "The diversity for the Amazonian forest in Brazil, Ecuador and Peru is between 100 and 400 species [per hectare]" (M. Lizarralde 1997: 26). A similar conclusion about the relative lack of floristic diversity was reached by Dueñas-C., Betancur, and Galindo-T. (2007) in their study of the forest near the Colombian Barí settlement of Bridicayra. This later study is problematic for current purposes because the study plot was at 700 m altitude, higher than the traditional Colombian Barí lived, and because the study plot had been selectively logged.

No biomass and productivity measurements have been made in Motilonia, but there is no reason to think the region's forests are markedly different from other South American forests of similar edaphic and climatic regimes. Consequently, it is probably safe to estimate the aboveground living biomass of the evergreen forest as 350–450 tons per hectare (t/ha), dry weight; with a belowground living biomass of 15–50 t/ha, dry weight; and a total dead biomass of 100–150 t/ha, dry weight (Klinge and Rodrigues 1974: 343; Pires 1978: 615; Beckerman 1987: 64–65; Jordan 1989: 23). Net primary production is probably around the neotropical wet forest mean of 10 t/ha/yr, dry weight (Pires 1978: 615; Leigh and Windsor 1982: 117). The higher-elevation, piedmont and basimontane forests are somewhat smaller than the lowland evergreen forest, particularly in their northern reaches where they are semideciduous, but they may have a production not markedly different from that of the lowland forest.

The distribution of standing biomass in a tropical forest is not strikingly different from that of a temperate forest, but the trees allocate their net primary production differently. In a temperate forest, most fresh growth goes into wood; in tropical forests, the majority of new biomass is leaves (Jordan and Murphy 1978). One result is a relative abundance of arboreal foliavores in the fauna of the forests, browsing tender new leaves in the canopy. This elevated situation of potential game species is a circumstance to which the forest's human inhabitants adapt in various ways.

Leaves are more or less uniformly distributed in space throughout the forest canopy, and their abundance and quality change only moderately over time, particularly in the wetter areas of Motilonia. Fruits have a more disjointed distribution in space, time, and desirability. There are no relevant studies for the forests of historical Motilonia, but for a semi-deciduous tropical forest in Panama that is geographically close to historical Motilonia and shares quite a few tree species, Leigh and Windsor (1982: 118) estimate an average annual fruit production of over 1 t/ha, dry weight. It must be emphasized that this figure is an average, summed over local abundances and deficits, both temporal and spatial. The greater the degree of deciduousness, the patchier becomes both the temporal and spatial distributions of fruit.

The great majority of fruit—upwards of 80%—is not consumed by herbivores on the tree but falls to the ground (Leigh and Windsor 1982: 118). Despite the heavy presence of arboreal folivores, most leaf production—again over 80 or 85%—also ends on the forest floor (Leigh and Windsor 1982: 113-117; Coley 1982: 130). The dry weight of leaf and twig litter falling to the ground in tropical rain forests is typically around ten times that of the fruit fall (Leigh and Windsor 1982: 117). This combined litter fall is the source of the nutrients that the shallow and surficial roots of the tropical forest trees recycle without allowing them to sink into the soil and of the allochthonous production that enriches the rivers and streams of the forest.

Litter fall increases during the drier months, as the more water-sensitive trees shed more of their leaves. Many—although by no means all—tree species also show some synchronization of their flowering and fruiting schedules with rainfall. For instance, *O. bataua*, the palm of greatest importance to the Barí, appears to present the greatest abundance of fruit toward the ends of the two dry seasons and to have little or no ripe fruit at the peaks of the two wet seasons (Beckerman 1977). Other plants, including nontree species, are more regular. The giant grass *Gynerium*

Table 2.I. Most important mammals in the Barí diet (abridged from Beckerman 1975)

Family	Species and Genus	Common Name	Extrapolated Total Weight Eaten per Person per Year (kg)
Tayassuidae	*Tayassu pecari*	white-lipped peccary	6.0
	Pecari tajacu	collared peccary	3.7
Dasyproctidae	*Dasyprocta punctata*	agouti	5.9
Cuniculidae	*Cuniculus paca*	lapa or paca	0.8 (est.)
Atelidae	*Ateles hybridus*	spider monkey	3.6
	Alouatta seniculus	howler monkey	2.5
Cebidae	*Cebus albifrons*	capuchin monkey	1.8
Aotidae	*Aotus griseimembra*	owl monkey	1.0
Myrmecophagidae	*Tamandua tetradactyla*	lesser anteater	1.5
Procyonidae	*Potos flavus*	kinkajou	1.2
Sciuridae	*Sciurus granatensis*	red-tailed squirrel	0.8

sagittatum, called "arrow cane," flowers synchronously each May through July, putting out long, thin peduncles used as arrow shafts. The flowering and fruiting cycles of the vegetation clearly affect the behavior of the animals that consume these parts, although data on this subject are few.

The terrestrial fauna (at least the vertebrate component) of historical Motilonia is parallel to the flora in that it is similar to but somewhat less diverse than that of Amazonia. Currently, 118 mammal species and subspecies have been identified in the literature, of which 8 are endemic to the region. Also reported are 624 species and subspecies of birds (46 endemics) and 89 species and subspecies of reptiles (5 endemics) (Viloria and Calchi La C. 1993).

Within this terrestrial fauna, only eight mammals are really important to the Barí, in terms of the frequency with which they are taken and the amount of food they supply (Table 2.1). They are two large rodents, the agouti (*Dasyprocta punctata*) of the family Dasyproctidae and the paca (*Cuniculus paca*) of the family Cuniculidae, and two species of peccaries, the collared peccary (*Pecari tajacu*) and the white-lipped peccary (*Tayassu pecari*), both of the family Tayassuidae; and four species of monkeys, the spider monkey (*Ateles hybridus*) and the red howler monkey (*Alouatta seniculus*) of the family Atelidae, the white-fronted capuchin monkey

(*Cebus albifrons*) of the family Cebidae, and the owl (or night) monkey (*Aotus griseimembra*) of the family Aotidae.

Various guans (South American relatives of the turkey) of the family Cracidae also make a significant contribution to Barí meat intake (Beckerman 1980a: 92). Prominent are several species of the genera Crax and Penelope.

Less important mammals in the diet are the red-tailed squirrel (*Sciurus granatensis*), in the family Sciuridae, which is taken fairly often but is so small that it makes little nutritional contribution; the kinkajou (*Potos flavus*) and the coatimundi (*Nasua nasua*), both in the family Procyonidae; the prehensile tailed porcupine *Coendu prehensilis*, family Erethizontidae; and the nine-banded armadillo (*Dasypus novemcinctus*), family Dasipodidae; the tamandua or lesser anteater (*Tamandua tetradactyla*), family Myrmecophagidae; the red brocket deer (*Mazama americana*), family Cervidae; and the tapir (*Tapirus terrestris*), family Tapiridae. This last, the largest wild mammal in South America, is by far the most desired game animal, but it is so rare — perhaps by now extinct in the Maracaibo Basin — that it makes only a minor contribution to the Barí diet.

Aside from the guans mentioned above, other sizable birds are taken often enough to contribute appreciable amounts of meat when considered together. These birds include parrots and macaws, doves, toucans, and tinamous.

The Barí do not eat birds of prey — or snakes or felids. They do eat the spectacled bear (*Tremarctos ornatus*), family Ursidae, but in a manner so filled with ceremonial prohibitions and injunctions that are uncharacteristic of the Barí as to make it clear that the consumption is ritual, not alimentary.

The Barí do eat turtles on occasion. Viloria and Calchi La C. (1993) list six species known from the Barí region. One of them, *Rhinoclemmys diademata* (Emydidae) is the most common, in our experience; it is not large (15–20 cm long by 10–12 cm wide).

Another reptile, this one of considerable importance, although not as food, is the highly poisonous snake, *Bothrops asper*, the fer-de-lance (family Viviperidae). Sometimes called "the ultimate pit viper," this large, fast, and excitable serpent, said to be the leading cause of snakebite death wherever it is found, is a nontrivial cause of death among the Barí and grounds for constant watchfulness while on the trail.

There are a few invertebrates that present themselves to the Barí either as food or as danger. In the first category is the land snail, *Strophocheilus oblongus*, family Strophocheilidae. It is about the size of a child's fist and can occur in densities of up to one snail every 2 or 3 m², especially in riverside stands of *Heliconia*. Considerably less abundant is the large riverine snail *Pomacea exima*, Ampullariidae. These mollusks, about the size of a man's fist, are solitary.

The larvae of the palm weevil (*Rhynchophorus palmarum*), Curculionidae, extracted from the trunks of fallen palm trees, are an important fallback source of fat and protein. These grubs are about the size of the last two joints of a man's little finger.

In the danger category, the most important invertebrates are the *Anopheles* mosquito, the carrier of malaria; and the sandfly *Phlebotomus*, which carries Leishmaniasis, an ulcerating infection of the skin. The ways in which the Barí traditionally dealt with these threats are described in Chapter 5.

All the terrestrial animals eaten by the Barí fall to secondary importance in comparison to fish. To know the fish, one must understand the waters in which they live.

The Riverine System

The clear-water rivers and creeks where the Barí fish with their long, graceful spears are the peripheral veins of a vast, complicated circulatory system whose heart is Lake Maracaibo. The perimeter rivers—Caño Martillo, the ríos de Oro, Suroeste, and Barankay; the upper reaches of the Santa Ana, the Aricuaisá, the Lora, and the Socuavo—are clear except on days following a rainstorm. Farther downriver we have never seen the Catatumbo clear below its confluence with the río de Oro. In the terms usually employed for Amazonia, it is a "whitewater" river. The Escalante is similarly turbid year round. The Santa Ana is only seasonally turbid and has darker waters than the other rivers. According to Sutton (pers. com.), the Santa Ana "comes to Lake Maracaibo as a dark amber most of the year." In this trait, it resembles the "blackwater" rivers of the Guiana Shield, although the water of the Santa Ana is neither as dark nor as impoverished in nutrients, vegetation, and fish as the water of a typical blackwater river. (The río Negro, a northern tributary of the Santa Ana, is more representative of a blackwater river.)

Where the Santa Ana, Catatumbo, and Escalante flow vaguely over the almost imperceptible slope of their lower alluvial plain and spill into the final large tectonic depression of the southwestern basin, these streams communicate directly, when in flood, with the great swamp that merges into the lake—although their main courses continue to channel most of their flow directly into the lake. The deposition of suspended sediment, especially heavy during flood months, has produced sizable deltas where the mouths of the three rivers enter the lake.

Despite a considerable knowledge of Lake Maracaibo itself (acquired as a result of the oil deposits beneath it), surprisingly little is known about the southwestern rivers that discharge over 80% of the fresh water into the lake. Most data concerning river chemistry (Parra Pardi et al. 1979; ICLAM 1983) refer to recent years when pollution from agricultural runoff had already become an issue.

Although these data incline toward ratifying the visual evaluations of the rivers as clear-water (the río de Oro and other upstream Catatumbo tributaries), whitewater (the Catatumbo itself, the Zulia, and the Escalante), and "tending toward blackwater" (the Santa Ana), they are hardly conclusive on this point. Information with respect to their chemistry shows the limits of this initial classification.

These rivers have several salient chemical properties: the clear-water rivers of the Catatumbo Basin (especially in the northwest) have a near neutral pH of around 6.7, in contrast to the acid waters of Amazonian clear-water rivers (Galvis, Mojica, and Camargo 1997: 15). They are extraordinarily rich in phosphorus (P) (mean P concentration, 1.62 mg/lt, range 0.43–2.62 mg/lt). They are also high in nitrogen (N) (although not to the remarkable extent of their phosphorus content: mean N concentration 1.53 mg/lt); and the relation of the two elements, the N/P ratio, is in the range of 1.4 to 2.2—a notably low figure (Parra Pardi et al. 1979: 57–59).

The seasonal variation in the chemistry of the ríos Catatumbo and Santa Ana shows a positive correlation of P concentration with flow rate, although there are some strong deviations in P concentration associated with relatively minor changes in flow (Parra Pardi et al. 1979: 41–43). These findings are consistent with a regime in which local rainfall on the localized outcrops of the phosphate-rich Cretaceous stratum in the underlying rock is a major source of phosphorus.

A similar positive correlation obtains between N concentration and amount of flow for the Catatumbo but not for the Santa Ana. No significant correlation has been found between flow and either N or P concentration in the Escalante (Parra Pardi et al. 1979: 41–43).

The remarkably low N/P ratio has an interesting biological implication. Under this chemical regime, it is likely that the limiting nutrient for algal growth in these river waters is nitrogen (Parra Pardi et al. 1979:

57). This conclusion was borne out for the lake waters (although not the rivers) by bioassay experiments in which the addition of nitrogen generally stimulated algal growth while the addition of phosphorus alone had little or no effect (Parra Pardi et al. 1979: 57). It is to be noted, however, that nitrogen is limiting in the river water only by comparison with the superabundance of phosphorus; overall, by temperate standards at least, these are nutrient-rich waters. The significance of these findings for the food chain topped by the Barí is twofold: on the one hand, the rivers carry nutrients capable of supporting a rich algal flora as the base of a trophic pyramid; on the other, those nutrients are generally present in highest concentrations in the rainiest months, when the sunlight necessary for algal growth is least able to penetrate the cloudy river water.

Redfield, Ketchum, and Bumpus (1955: 7) assessed the transparency of the Catatumbo at a point about 11 km above its mouth in May 1955 (the beginning of the minor dry season) and found that a Secchi disc was visible only to a depth of 15 cm. (Barí would not even consider spear fishing in such opaque waters.) Gessner (1953, 1956) collected water from the mouth of the Catatumbo in October 1952 (onset of the major rainy season); in a measurement made at that time he found that only 37% of incident sunlight reached a depth of 10 cm.

A river's clarity is related to the load of suspended solids carried by its water. Figures for suspended solids in water samples taken in the Santa Ana, Catatumbo, and Escalante Rivers by Sutton and Arnett (1973: 82) in September 1972 and March 1973, along with figures from ICLAM (1983) for samples from the Catatumbo, the río de Oro, the Socuavo, the Tarra, and the Zulia collected in May 1982 confirm the opacity of even generally clear-water rivers during the minor rainy season and suggest strongly that light, rather than nutrients, may establish the limit on algal growth in these river waters for most of the year.

As suggested below, light-limited algal growth at the base of the trophic pyramid is consistent with fish migration patterns. Another influence on algal growth, and one of the changes fish encounter in their migrations, is that of water temperature.

Beckerman took the temperature of the Shubacbarina, a small, clear, briskly flowing tributary of the río de Oro, which in turn flows into the Catatumbo, at the end of March 1972 and recorded a temperature of 24.5°C. Both Redfield et al. (1955: 7) and Gessner (1956) reported water temperatures all within a half degree of 29°C for measurements made in October 1952 and May 1953 at various depths and locations within a few kilometers of the mouth of the Catatumbo. The downstream temperature rise reflects the solar warming taking place in the last lazy miles of the Catatumbo's descent to the lake.

It is where the rivers reach the great swamp that the richness of their nutrient load is fully expressed. The bimodal rainfall regime of this basin ensures that twice a year the rivers swell (peaks in May and November) with rain that has washed the relatively new rocks and soils of the Andean Cordilleras, filling them with turbid, fertile water. Floating vegetation, particularly *Eichhornia* spp. and *Pistia* spp., flourishes in the swamp into which they flow. An abundant growth of algae and other organisms adheres to the underwater stems and roots of the surface vegetation, which form a rich bottom detritus when they decompose (Galvis, Mojica, and Camargo 1997: 17).

When the rains diminish and the rivers fall, the turbid water of the swamp decants. Submerged vegetation (in particular Charales, freshwater branched algae), and free-floating plankton, now prosper in the swamp (Galvis, Mojica, and Camargo 1997: 17). In addition, in the clear-water rivers above the swamp, sunlight can now penetrate the water, and various algae form a coating on the bottom rocks and other submerged substrates (e.g., sunken logs). The major fish in the Barí diet feed on algae and detritus.

From the heart to the outermost veins, lake, swamp, rivers, and tributary streams all play a part in the biology of the fish on which the Barí depend for three quarters of the meat in their diet.

The freshwater ichthyfauna of the Maracaibo Basin is similar to but less diverse than the ichthyfauna of the Magdalena River Valley to its west. As noted above, the two basins were one until the orogenesis of the Andes, beginning in the late Eocene and lasting through the Pliocene, divided them. It is likely that some fish species were trapped on the western side of the Sierra de Perijá when the Andes rose, that others died out due to the transgressions of seawater into the Maracaibo Basin during the Miocene, and that a later, partial recolonization of the Maracaibo Basin from the Magdalena Valley took place during or after the Pliocene (Perez Lozano 1990).

There are 107 species of native freshwater fish known in the entire Maracaibo Basin (Pérez Lozano 1990: 24). In the Catatumbo Basin, 84 of these species occur, of which 26 are endemics (Galvis, Mojica, and Camargo 1997). Of these 84, about a dozen are of particular importance to the Barí, and one—the bocachico (*Prochilodus reticulatus*, family Curimatidae)—by itself makes up half of the animal flesh eaten by the Barí (Beckerman 1980a).

Despite its commercial importance (it ranks third or fourth in the catch of the Lake Maracaibo fishing fleet, and 8 million individuals per year were taken in the late 1960s [Nemoto 1971: 7; de Espinosa and Gimenez B. 1974: 7]), little work has been done on the natural history of the bocachico in this region. The following description relies on early work with the same species in the Sinú Basin of Colombia (Dahl 1963, 1971; Ramos Henao 1963) and on captive breeding experiments in that country (Patiño R. 1973; Solano M. 1974), as well as on information provided by Novoa (1982) and Taphorn (pers. com.) for a closely related species in the Venezuelan llanos. The resulting description of Maracaibo Basin bocachico natural history needs onsite confirmation.

The bocachico is a fast-swimming, scaly fish of the order Characiformes; it reaches an adult length of 25 cm or more and an average (fresh, uncleaned) weight of 350 to 400 g in Motilonia. It achieves large populations. The Lake Maracaibo commercial fisheries recorded in the period 1967–1971 a yearly average catch of over 2,800 metric tons of bocachico disembarked in the ports serving the area of the lake into which the Santa Ana, Catatumbo, and Escalante discharge (de Espinosa and Gimenez B. 1974: 20). This fresh weight translates to an annual harvest of somewhere around 8 million individuals. It is the trophic position of the bocachico that allows it to attain such numbers.

> It is an iliophagous fish, that is to say, it feeds on the algae and organic detritus present in the mud or muck of lakes, swamps, and oxbows, as well as the periphyton adhering to the rocks and branches in the rivers. The shape of its bucal apparatus allows it to suck up these materials, which are accumulated and compressed in a double stomach (cardiac and pyloric) with thick, muscular walls. After a process of trituration similar to the grinding [that takes place in] granivorous birds, the thick cellular wall of the diatoms and other algae common in the absorbed mud becomes weakened or broken, thereby facilitating its attack by digestive enzymes throughout the length of the strongly folded intestinal tube. It is, thus, a short chain consumer. (Patiño R. 1973: 79–80; our translation)

A great deal of Barí behavior is influenced by the fact that the bocachico is migratory, moving from the great swamp at the eastern edge of Lake Maracaibo up tributary rivers and streams and back each year. A similar migration was described for the same species in the Magdalena River.

When it reaches gonadal maturation, it leaves lentic waters and begins an upstream migration . . . that will culminate in the expulsion
of its gametes . . . and the formation of millions of transparent larvae
which, carried by the current during the rainy season, enter the swamps
or oxbows where they will begin a new cycle. (Patiño 1973: 80; our
translation)

The migratory cycle is poorly known in Motilonia, but some conclusions can be tentatively drawn from scattered regional data here and more
thorough studies elsewhere. Most adult bocachico are apparently in and
around the swamps near the mouths of the ríos Santa Ana, Catatumbo,
and Escalante in October and November, when the rainy season is at its
height and the rivers are at their fullest. Many feed in the lake itself, and
some enter in the lower courses of the rivers, but the still, shallow waters
of the swamps probably provide the richest habitat at this time, when the
swollen, muddy rivers deprive algae of transmitted sunlight. As the rains
diminish, the river level drops and the temperature of the swamp water increases while its oxygen content decreases; pH may also increase, making
the swamps uncomfortably alkaline as well as hot and oxygen-poor.

In December and January, at the beginning of the dry season, many
mature bocachico begin a migration, heading for the upstream rivers
where lack of rain has cleared the water and the algal bottom flora is
blooming under strong sunlight. It is likely that some of them also migrate downstream at this time and enter the lake. It is also likely, based on
observations in the Uré River in Colombia and on studies of the commercial catch in Lake Maracaibo (de Espinosa and Gimenez B. 1974), that the
females begin this migration, and their return, before the males.

The December–January exodus from the swamps produces one of the
two yearly peaks in the commercial catch and contributes to a seasonal
upturn in Barí fishing success. The adult fish move upstream in schools,
grazing on the diatom- and algae-encrusted bottom. In the Cauca valley
of Colombia, they have been reported to move with some speed: "at least
10–15 kilometers every 24 hours," although it has also been observed that
"at times they halt for a day or two in the large pools" (Dahl 1963: 96; our
translation).

By February, the driest month, the bocachico are amply distributed
throughout Motilonia and have ascended as far as the small waterways
at the outermost reaches of the system. There they can be seen in abundance, grazing on the algae that encrust bottom cobbles in clear, sunny

streams. Most of the time they appear to favor rather shallow water with a cobble bottom, probably because of luxuriant algal growth there under conditions of abundant sunlight. These conditions are of course also optimal for spear fishing.

Fish taken upstream at this time are notably fat. As the rains of the minor rainy season come on in March and April, fat is converted to reproductive tissue (Ramos Henao 1963: 72–75), particularly in females, for whom eggs may come to make up 20% of total body weight (Ramos Henao 1963: 75–78).

The clouding of the rivers by the rains of the minor rainy season, beginning in March, apparently induces many bocachico, particularly females with mature eggs, to begin a descent of the rivers. Once the downstream migrating fish reach cloudy waters (either of whitewater rivers such as the Catatumbo or of seasonally opaque clear-water rivers), where drifting eggs and larvae will be hidden from potential predators, they spawn in late April and May, and the fertilized eggs begin their rapid development. The drifting larvae shortly fetch up in the great swamps around the mouths of the rivers, where they feed and develop rapidly into fish. The young fish apparently remain in the swamps for a year and a half, before leaving with the coming of the second major dry season after their arrival as tiny larvae. Indeed, some of them may not leave the swamps until the third major dry season after their arrival (Dahl 1963: 98; de Espinosa and Gimenez B. 1974: 11, 28–29).

After the eggs are laid in late April and in May, by June no females with mature eggs are to be found in the lake or the rivers, as far as we are aware (de Espinosa and Gimenez B. 1974: 10, 23; Beckerman, field notes 1971–1972).

Development of the newly laid and fertilized egg is rapid. From an initial size between 1.5 and 2.0 mm, it undergoes four blastomeric divisions and doubles in diameter in only forty-five minutes. The embryo appears in about seven hours, and eclosion (the escape of the larva from the egg sack) occurs between thirteen and sixteen hours after fertilization. The transparent, 4.0 to 4.5 mm-long larvae are immediately capable of some movement, a helical trajectory toward the water surface; they develop characteristic fins, mouth parts, and so on, over the next forty-eight hours. By the end of this period, about two and a half days from fertilization, the larvae are able to swim horizontally and have a digestive system that allows them to feed with ease on zooplankton, the food of the larval bocachico. Two to three weeks later, the larvae look like small bocachico, 10–15 mm in length (Solano M. 1974: 14–17). It is reported that in

a closely related Brazilian species the larvae next pass through a phyto-
phagous stage, before becoming definitively iliophagous (Ramos Henao
1963: 83–84). One study (Dahl 1963: 98) suggests that young bocachico
do not leave the swamps to which they have drifted until they have reached
a skeletal length of over 12 cm, corresponding to an age of about eighteen
months (see de Espinosa and Gimenez B. 1974: 17, 29).

Our reconstruction of the postspawning pattern of migration in Motilonia (based on Barí statements and our field observations but uncon-
firmed, we hasten to add, by professional ichthyological fieldwork) is
tentative. The movements of the adults after spawning are known only
well enough to make it clear that they do not all move in the same direction. The respectable hourly catch rates the Barí obtain in their upriver region in July and August make it clear that in Motilonia the entire
bocachico population does not simply abandon the tributary rivers for
downstream waters after spawning, as it apparently does in some other
areas. Rather, Barí upriver fishing data suggest that after spawning in May
some bocachico move back upriver and spend June, July, and August in
the clear-water streams of Motilonia and then swim down to the swamps
and the lake in August and September, whereas others return directly to
the downstream waters in May and June. It may be that in each of these
downstream migrations, corresponding to the onset of the major and the
minor rainy seasons, respectively, the females begin to move before the
males and that some males do not migrate at all in some years.

This discussion concentrates on general migratory trends, and it must
be stressed that these are only statistical tendencies. There are no months
in which the commercial catch from the lake and adjacent waters falls to
under 5% of the yearly total; and there are no months (with the possible
exception of May) when bocachico are entirely absent from locations as
far upstream as the río de Oro–río Intermedio confluence. Although dramatic changes in bocachico abundance are of enormous importance to
Barí ecology, it is clear that these fish do not move like a regiment on
parade. There are always stragglers and wanderers, and at times these
individuals may make up significant local populations.

There are many fish in addition to the bocachico in the rivers of Motilonia. Common but very seldom taken by aboriginal spearing methods—
apparently because it avoids the clear, shallow water where spear fishing
takes place—is the manamana, *Potamorhyna laticeps* (= *Anodus laticeps*),
another fish in the family Curimatidae. It is of roughly similar size and
shape to the bocachico but has much smaller, silvery scales.

Next in importance to the bocachico as food come various species of the family Loricaridae. These fish are prehistoric-looking armored cat-fish. (Small ones are used as cleaner fish in hobbyist aquariums.) Mostly solitary bottom feeders, they tend to prefer silty riverbeds with crevasses in which to hide. There are at least twenty-one species known from Moti-lonia (Cassler et al. 1990; Viloria and Calchi La C. 1993; Galvis, Mojica, and Camargo 1997). Some species attain a respectable size (> 20 cm adult total length), but much more abundant are smaller Loricarids (10 cm in length); they can often be taken in quantity during periods of high water or when larger fish and game resources are otherwise unavailable.

The Pimelodidae, or true catfish, are another family of food fishes; fourteen species are recorded from Motilonia (Galvis, Mojica, and Ca-margo 1997). The largest fish taken in the Catatumbo Basin are all catfishes.

A small fish, at times taken in some quantity, is *Piabucina pleurotae-nia* (Lebiasinidae) (Schultz 1947: 292–293; Galvis, Mojica, and Camargo 1997: 32). Those caught by the Barí can be up to 20 cm long but are usually under 10 cm. These fish, like the small Loricarids, can be taken from small streams at times of high and muddy water. The two kinds of small fry seem to inhabit different kinds of streams, however, for they are seldom taken on the same expedition.

Three additional food fish are the predatory *Hoplias malabiricus* (Ery-thrinidae), which attains lengths of up to 35 cm; the peculiarly elongated *Sternopygus macrurus* (Sternopygidae), which grows up to a meter long in these waters; and the only dangerous fishes in Motilonia, two rays, *Pota-motrygon magdalenae* and *P. yesezi* (Potamotrygonidae). A *P. yesezi* adult reaches a length of 40 cm or more. Basically a disk with a tail, it lies flat in the mud. If it can be spotted and speared from a distance, it is good eat-ing. When stepped on, however, it whips its tail up and over, producing a wound on the leg or, more commonly, the top of the foot. Such wounds, initially very painful, invariably become infected. They may take months to heal.

Thus the riverine fauna, like the terrestrial fauna, presents the Barí with both foodstuffs and dangers. They have learned to deal cleverly with each.

CHAPTER 3

Social Environment and Ethnohistory

All human groups relate to a natural environment of land and climate, flora and fauna, and to a social environment of other peoples. As described in chapter 2, the natural environment of the Barí seems to have been fairly constant over the last millennium or so. It has always presented daily fluctuations and seasonal changes, but over time the rain forest has remained reasonably constant, with a landscape, climate, flora, and fauna similar from one century to the next, until extensive forest clearing began in the 1920s.

The social environment is another story. It has manifested dramatic changes throughout the five hundred years for which we have written records. Thus this description of the social environment of the Barí is essentially an account of their history; and, vice versa, the study of their history is an indispensable part of a study of the ecology of these people. The main conclusion of an investigation of Barí history is that despite the profound transformations that the social environment has undergone, there have been two major forces originating in the social environment throughout most—but not all—of known Barí history. The first is that these people have been prey to stronger neighbors for most of the past half millennium, neighbors who enslaved and murdered them when they could find them. (There is reason to believe that this subjugation has deep pre-Columbian roots.) The second is that they have also been subjected to two documented—and several more possible—disastrous epidemics of Old World diseases, as well as the continuing threat of other, no less deadly endemic Old World diseases. Both the predations of neighboring humans and disease produced heavy death tolls. In one of those cynical ironies of history, the times of less intense human predation on the Barí have been those of the worst disease mortality. The dispersed Barí settle-

Table 3.I. Periodization of Barí history

1499–1591	From discovery of Lake Maracaibo to first use of tribal label "Motilón"	Period I 92 years
1592–1771	From first mention of "Motilones" to the first pacification	Period II 180 years
1772–1818	"Reduction to missions" of the first pacification	Period III 46 years
1819–1911	From abandonment of the missions to beginning of the oil invasions	Period IV 93 years
1912–1959	Oil and land invasions and intensification of warfare	Period V 47 years
1960–	Second pacification	Period VI 52 years

ment pattern and their semisedentary migration pattern played an important—probably decisive—role in saving the Barí from extinction in the face of these threats.

Barí history can be conveniently divided into six periods on the basis of the availability and quality of the historical data, as well as by the seminal events in that chronicle (Table 3.1).

The first period encompasses nearly a century, from the discovery of Lake Maracaibo in 1499 to the first use in a historical document of the word *Motilón*, usually in its plural form, *Motilones*—the name given to the Barí in all subsequent documents, until the name they used for themselves was learned half a century ago. (The Spanish word *Motilón*, from the verb *motilar*, means roughly "those who cut their hair short.") The label seems always to have included the Barí, and it is clear that it was applied to them alone from the seventeenth to the early nineteenth century. In this period we know a fair amount about the Lake Maracaibo region in general but little that is specific to the Barí.

According to known records, the label "Motilón" was first applied to an Indian tribe of the Maracaibo Basin in 1592. This appearance marks the beginning of the second period, which lasted until 1771. Like the first period of Barí history, this one was a time of considerable hostility and depopulation. Data specific to the Barí, although tantalizingly few, are available from this period.

In 1772 peaceful contact with the Barí was established, and over the course of the next few decades many of them were "reduced to missions," as the Spanish phrase of the time had it. The missionaries, Capuchin monks, were expelled from the Bolivarian countries in 1821 for their royalist sympathies; political infighting had already forced them from their missions to the Barí by 1818. In the course of this half century, 1772–1818, classified here as the third period, considerable ethnographic information was recorded.

The fourth period, remarkably obscure, began with the departure of the Capuchins and ended about ninety years later, with the invasion of Barí territory by international oil companies in the early years of the twentieth century. The events were complex, and the documentation is poor. At the beginning of the fourth period, armed hostility between Barí and *criollos* (Creoles) seems to have been diminished if not absent; by its end relations were belligerent again.

The fifth period—lasting about half a century—was distinguished from the fourth by a sudden increase in the frequency and ferocity of attacks on the Barí, as well as by better records of these activities.

The sixth, current period began in July 1960 when Roberto Lizarralde made peaceful contact with the surviving Barí. Documentation is, of course, best for these most recent five decades.

We follow the scheme laid out in Table 3.1 in examining the changing social environment and its effects on the Barí. Although our periodization is convenient, it is to some extent arbitrary, for there was considerable change within each period as well as from one period to the next.

First Period, 1499–1591

There is considerable evidence that when Alonso de Ojeda and Amerigo Vespucci first saw it in 1499, the Maracaibo Basin was inhabited by a complicated mosaic of distinct societies (Argüelles and Párraga 1579, cited in Arellano Moreno 1964: 205; Martín 1534, cited in Gabaldón Márques 1962, II:272; Perez de Tolosa 1564, cited in Arellano Moreno 1964: 6–7; Sánchez Sotomayor 157[?], cited in Breton 1921: 9–12; Simón 1627, cited in Simón 1963). The major distinction was between two contrasting subsistence strategies, one lacustrine and one terrestrial, each employed by a number of different language groups. The lacustrine peoples, who lived in pile houses in Lake Maracaibo, farmed a bit on adjacent shores but apparently concentrated much of their efforts on fishing and collecting salt from pans near the mouth of the lake. The various terrestrial peoples fished the rivers that drain into the lake but derived more food from farming (some of them grew maize as well as manioc) and did a good deal of hunting. The lake peoples and the inland peoples exchanged their major foodstuffs, terrestrial farmers trading manioc and balls of cooked maize for fish. There was also exchange with the peoples to the west, in which salt and fish (probably salted) from the lacustrine peoples and cotton cloths from the terrestrial peoples were traded out of the basin for gold from the Andes. Despite these clearly institutionalized trade networks, indigenous warfare was evidently endemic.

The Barí probably lived then, as now, in the southwestern corner of the Maracaibo Basin, in and around the nonswampy parts of the río Catatumbo drainage and adjacent areas in the drainages of the ríos Santa Ana to the north and Escalante to the south. They were of course one of the terrestrial peoples. The lacustrine people with whom they were most closely associated, a group known as the Quiriquiri (who spoke an Arawakan language), appear to have taken them as slaves (Martín de Horia 1638 in AGN, Encomiendas, T. 42, Fol. 106–107, cited in Dávila 1949: 87–89), although it is not clear at what times and how regularly this practice was followed. Nevertheless, it is clear that the Barí had experience with slaving neighbors even before the raids of the Europeans and Africans. The Quiriquiri built their pile houses on the southwestern shore of Lake Maracaibo, especially around the mouth of the Catatumbo, and in the swamps and lakes associated with the river mouth.

On their arrival, the conquistadors began taking their own slaves and setting up towns and *encomiendas*, agricultural estates based on Indian labor. Very soon there was frantic if initially uncoordinated general resistance on the part of the Maracaibo Basin Indians. Their defiance, however, bore little fruit. Most tribes were conquered or reduced to impotence in less than half a century. But the Barí remained free.

The first Spanish slaving and punitive expedition clearly targeting the Barí took place in 1583, although earlier expeditions—1531–1533, 1548–1549, and 1566 (Martín 1534, cited in Gabaldón Márques 1962, II:270]; Aguado 157[?], cited in Aguado 1987: 303–306]; Simón 1627, cited in Simón 1963, II:195, 600–601)—probably struck at them as well. The accounts of some of these early Spanish expeditions asserted that people who were probably Barí were continually at war with other Indians of the region. The evidence is discussed by Beckerman (1978).

To the European versions of warfare and slavery introduced in the first period were added the diseases of the Old World. In the greater Maracaibo Basin, bleeding dysentery, measles, cataria, and two smallpox epidemics had struck before 1580 (Ponce de León et al. 1578 and Pacheco 1579, cited in Arellano Moreno 1964: 148, 151–152, 164–165). Many Indian peoples disappeared or were reduced to such small populations during this period that they became extinct before the end of the next. The ancestors of the Barí survived, almost certainly due to their remoteness and the small size and geographical dispersion of their settlements. Diseases struck the more densely populated and compactly settled tribes with greater efficiency.

Although evidence is sketchy, the first period was clearly a century in which massive epidemic death, as well as new forms of warfare and servitude, entered a set of societies manifesting the well-known New World pattern of habitual trade relations combined with chronic war. The Barí were certainly affected by the increased violence, but they seem, thanks to their remote location and dispersed settlement pattern, to have escaped the worst ravages of the diseases. In this earliest period, we may also infer that the Barí remained peaceful, on the evidence of a 1579 document that describes the Lake Maracaibo region and reports that navigation on the "río Pamplona" (as the Catatumbo and Zulia were then called) was "pleasant, peaceful and without risk" (Argüelles and Párraga 1579, cited in Arellano Moreno 1964: 2006).

Second Period, 1592–1771

The second period opened with the first use of the tribal label "Motilón" in a known document. This document was the 1592 Real Cedula addressed to the "President and Judges of the New Kingdom Court." It refers to the "Province of Motilones."

In 1600 some Quiriquiri rebelled against their *encomenderos* (Spanish landowners who kept them in conditions of forced labor) and sacked and burned the town of Gibraltar at the southern tip of Lake Maracaibo; they escaped to the region around the mouth of the Catatumbo. For the next two generations, they defied the Spanish from this refuge, taking part in 1606 in a general uprising of Indians in the western Maracaibo Basin. It is likely, although hard evidence is minimal, that during this time the Quiriquiri held the swamps and adjacent areas near the mouth of the Catatumbo while the Barí controlled the higher reaches of the river and its tributaries.

Another document from these years, the 1622 investiture of the first governor of the province of La Grita, Juan Pacheco Maldonado, suggests that the Barí may have been a problem for the Spanish in their own right. The province of La Grita, according to this document, was created specifically to deal with "the nation of Indians who are called Motilones, fierce and cruel people, who, for twenty years, committing murders and robberies, are impeding the navigation of the río Zulia" (Nectario María 1977: 404). (Río Zulia is the old name for the middle and lower reaches of the río Catatumbo; the name now designates the major southern tributary of the Catatumbo.)

However, when the Barí agreed to make peace with the Spaniards, Governor Pacheco Maldonado gathered four hundred of them and took them across the Andes in a forced march with only twenty-two survivors, the rest succumbing to cold and exhaustion. Not surprisingly, this treatment provoked an uprising among the remaining Barí. The date of the rebellion is not recorded, but the "juicio de residencia" that evaluated Pacheco Maldonado's term in office specifies that it took place during his administration, 1622–1634 (AGI, Escribanía, L. 1188, 1637).

The Quiriquiri had been seriously hurt by Spanish campaigns in 1599, 1608, and 1617 and were essentially destroyed by a major military expedition in 1638 (Nectario María 1977: 406–407). It was a document relating to this conquest that recorded the possession of Motilón slaves by the Quiriquiri (Martín de Horia 1638, in AGN, Encomiendas, T. 42, Fol. 106–107, cited in Dávila 1949: 87–89). After the leveling of the Quiriquiri the Barí were probably too few and too remote from Spanish settlements to pose much of a military problem. Also, beginning around the mid-seventeenth century, towns around Lake Maracaibo were repeatedly sacked by French and English pirates as the entire Spanish imperial economy entered a decline. Shortly thereafter, colonial transport regulations prohibited the transshipment from this region of goods whose receipt and dispatch had previously enriched the local economy. In the midst of these European military and financial woes, the Spanish colonists paid little attention to the Barí, or indeed to the other Indian peoples inhabiting the southern basin, many of whom were never again mentioned in colonial documents. It can be inferred from the disappearance of their names from the Spanish records during this period that many of the tribes of the region simply passed out of existence from the early sixteenth to the late eighteenth century. Their extinction apparently provided the Barí with unoccupied territory south of the lake into which to expand.

Expansion also brought the Barí back into frequent contact with the Spanish. From 1713 the Motilones were known often to raid Spanish towns and haciendas on the periphery of their territory (Anon. 1787, cited in Arellano Moreno 1964: 415). Missions specifically intended to pacify and "reduce" the Yukpa Indians, the Barí's neighbors to the north, were founded in the 1730s. The Motilones raided the missions as well.

Spanish retaliation, despite the depressed economy of the region, was inevitable. In 1728 a Spanish troop of over a hundred men mounted a short campaign that captured two and killed eight Motilones—a woman and seven children (Cesáreo de Armellada 1962: 296–299). Three additional Spanish military expeditions against the Motilones took place between 1730 and 1735; there were other officially organized and financed armed expeditions in 1745, 1765, and 1767. These recorded campaigns alone took at least 113 captives in the years 1733–1767 (Beckerman and Lizarralde 1995); we have found no numerical record of the deaths resulting from the official incursions.

Of semiofficial standing were the repeated armed forays made by slaves and servants of hacendados under governmental license; these attacks were described as routine in a viceregal letter dated 1753 (Febres Cordero 1975: 32). A travel journal written in 1761 (de Oviedo 1970: 370–374) spoke repeatedly of the need to traverse Motilón territory only with an escort of four or five men regularly firing shotguns to frighten the Motilones away. On the other side, Motilón raids on the Spanish were reported to be numerous; prominent attacks took place in 1713, 1736, 1742, 1744, 1761 (in the course of which many tools and weapons were stolen), 1766 (when two men were killed in the city of Maracaibo itself), 1767, 1770, and 1771. It was reported that one mission was attacked at least once a year from 1753 to 1760 (Alcácer 1962: 72–143).

In sum, the second period opened in 1592 with ongoing hostilities directed primarily at the Quiriquiri, a lacustrine people with whom the Barí were somehow affiliated, probably as a subject population. After the elimination of the Quiriquiri in 1638, there were six or seven decades of decreased hostility, during which the Barí expanded their territory into land made available by the elimination of most other tribes in the region and by the declining Spanish colonial economy. A decade or so into the eighteenth century, there began six decades of guerrilla warfare in which both sides suffered serious losses.

The Barí were clearly using captured iron tools and weapons in the eighteenth century, and had begun to do so, to judge by the date of renewal of raiding and thefts of iron tools, at least as early as the mid-seventeenth century. Indeed, it is plausible, although only archaeological evidence can confirm this possibility, that the Barí began using iron tools as early as the sixteenth century, obtaining them through the old indigenous trade connections, and that they began raiding the Spanish only when this source of iron was eliminated by the extinction of the other aboriginal peoples.

Two Spanish documents from the end of the second period are significant for understanding the influence of the social environment on patterns of Barí culture. In the first document, the difficulty of fighting the Barí was specifically attributed, by an experienced Spanish military officer, to their dispersed multiple houses and their consequent ability to abandon an area rapidly and stay away for a long time (Collado 1755, cited in Beckerman 1980a: 540–541). In the second, the Barí motive for raiding the Spanish was explicitly given.

The punitive expedition of 1767 took among its captives a young woman—apparently from the Yukpa—who as a small girl had been carried off by the Barí years before after one of their raids on the Capuchin mission to the north of their territory. She was now married to a Barí man (also captured by the expedition) and had added the Barí language to the Spanish she remembered from her mission girlhood. This woman's Barí husband asserted through her that one reason for raiding Spanish settlements was to obtain iron tools; the other was revenge for the capture and deaths of Barí at the hands of the Spanish (del Río y Castro 1772, cited in Buenaventura de Carrocera 1973: 198; Guillén 1773, AHNC, Caciques e Indios, T. 62, Fol. 290–291).

Third Period, 1772–1818

The third period opened on April 5, 1772, when Alberto Gutiérrez, a Spanish officer, accompanied by about fifty soldiers and guided by the now Spanish-speaking captive husband of the Yukpa woman (now dead), established peaceful contact with the residents of a longhouse near the upper Santa Ana, the next river north of the Catatumbo (Gutiérrez 1772, cited in Buenaventura de Carrocera 1973: 212–224). A follow-up expedition headed by Sebastián Guillén, the Spanish official in whose house the bilingual Barí man was living and who was the original planner of the Gutiérrez expedition, ratified and expanded this peaceful contact in August of the same year. The account of this expedition (Guillén 1772, AHNC Milicias y Marina, T. 121, Fol. 130–150, cited in Alcácer 1962: 259–277) is the most comprehensive ethnohistoric document of the third period.

Over the next decades, thirteen Spanish missions were founded around the perimeter of Motilón territory. All but one were in its southern portion, on the banks of the ríos Escalante, Santa Rosa, Zulia, and Catatumbo. They were populated by Barí brought out of the forest by Capuchin monks, sometimes using persuasion alone, sometimes using the menace of the Spanish soldiers who often accompanied the monks. The first mission was founded in 1774 and the last in 1799. During this last period, Barí also began to be removed from their territory by newly arrived hacendados, who used them as laborers on their haciendas.

Total mission population hovered between a thousand and twelve hundred at the dates of various Capuchin censuses (Table 3.2), which presumably counted only Barí residents of their missions. Over two hundred additional Barí were recorded to have been settled on adjacent haciendas (Alcácer 1962: 173, 216–218). However—and this fact is crucial to understanding the survival of the Barí up until modern times—at the abandonment of the last missions by the Capuchins in 1818, there was still a substantial number of Barí living a traditional life in the upper Catatumbo region (Cesáreo de Armellada 1964b: 42).

Nine missions were included in the last Capuchin census of the Barí, in 1810. Shortly thereafter, the Capuchins' missionization came to an end, as Simón Bolívar led northern South America to independence from the Spanish crown. The Capuchins were royalists, and three of these mission settlements along the río Zulia were sacked by Bolívar's forces in early 1813, causing at least some of their residents to flee to the forest (Alcácer 1962: 226–230). A "Motilón brigade" was formed by a royalist colonel but quickly disintegrated.

In September 1813 the king of Spain issued a decree ordering his missionaries to cease administering their remaining Indian reductions, to put the Indians in charge of the settlements, and to distribute the land privately to the individual inhabitants under a law vaguely similar to the U.S. Homestead Act. This order made Indian land legally available for transfer to members of the Spanish population (Cunill Grau 1987, I:240), although the Capuchins remained at five missions to the Barí for several more years and apparently did what they could to slow this takeover. In 1818 these missions were abandoned by their monks after several months of ecclesiastical infighting (undoubtedly based in the turbulent civil politics of the time) between the head of the missions and the bishop of Mérida (Alcácer 1962: 229–234). The Capuchin order was forced to leave Venezuela in 1821.

The ethnographic evidence recorded in the third period, particularly by Guillén (1772, cited in Alcácer 1962: 259–277]), is remarkably informative with respect to diet, settlement, and other matters the Spanish could observe directly. The people visited by Guillén were Barí beyond any doubt, described with numerous decisive details immediately recognizable to an observer with Barí field experience.

The few discrepancies between the historical and the contemporary ethnography were discussed by Beckerman (1978). The most interesting difference between the Barí of 1772 and those of circa 1960 was the possible existence at the earlier date of multiple longhouse settlements (Gutiérrez 1772, cited in Buenaventura de Carrocera 1973: 191–224; Guillén 1772, cited in Alcácer 1962: 259–277). This pattern has not been recorded in Barí territory for the past century. However, a Barí informant spoke in 1988 of memories of side-by-side longhouse (Beckerman field notes 1988), and Lizarralde observed three relatively close longhouses built in the late 1960s, so even this divergence had some ethnographic support.

Guillén (1772, cited in Alcácer 1962: 262–263) left no doubt that local groups of Barí in the eighteenth century maintained contemporaneous longhouses in separate locations and migrated seasonally among them. Another intriguing reference in Guillén raised the possibility that maize may have been present as a minor crop among the eighteenth-century Barí, a suggestion echoed (see below) early in the present century.

The total territory controlled and hunted over by the Barí in 1772 was probably between 30,000 and 35,000 km². Of this whole, about 15,000 km² were under 600 m altitude, the upper limit of Barí settlement (cf. Beckerman 1978; as a result of subsequent research, the present figures differ from those given in this earlier reference). Thus the residential territory, the land in which the Motilones were able to establish most of their houses, was only around half of the land they defended to the exclusion of others (the territory designated "historical Motilonia").

There were probably not more than 2,500 to 3,000 Barí at the beginning of the third period, and the measles epidemic known to have struck some of the missions around the mid-1780s (Alcácer 1962: 188, 191), as well as unrecorded diseases, almost certainly reduced this population by several hundred by the end of the period (Beckerman 1978). The recorded mission population diminished by 17% between the censuses of 1799 and 1810 (Table 3.2), and this decrease took place while Barí were still being brought in to the missions from their longhouses.

The uncolonized regions still inhabited by traditional Barí, to which refugees from the missions must have returned in the early nineteenth century, had also shrunk considerably, probably to under 10,000 km² for the total territory.

Table 3.2. Barí mission population at known census dates

Year	Population	Source(s)
1786	887	Estevan de los Arcos 1786 (in Peña Vargas 1995: 318–320)
1797	998	Baltasar de Lodares 1930: 409–412
1799	1,233	Baltasar de Lodares 1930: 409–412
1805	1,131	Cesáreo de Armellada 1964a: 10–12
1810	1,025	Jahn 1927: 70

It is appropriate to close this section with an evaluation of the Barí made during this brief period of peaceful relations. The governor of the province of Maracaibo left a document in which he offered the opinion that "the Motilones' character is different and much superior to the other Indians I have seen in this province, in Guayana, Barinas, and this [Maracaibo], since among other properties they do not know drunkenness, theft, lying, and though ferocious before their conquest, today they are obedient" (Miyares 1799, cited in Archivo General de Venezuela 1876).

Fourth Period, 1819–1911

The opportunity to obtain mission land was heavily exploited by the criollo population of the Barí area after independence, especially on the lands bordering the ríos Zulia, Catatumbo, and Escalante, where the missions were established. Of the nine missions in existence in 1813, when the king's edict removed mission land from religious control, at least eight still remained as Barí mission villages (*pueblos de misión*) in the early 1820s. However, with the independence of Maracaibo in 1821, all missionaries were forced to leave Venezuela. Only five of those settlements retained significant numbers of Indian inhabitants by 1836, the Barí at the other missions having "disappeared" after "selling" their land (Cunill Grau 1987, II:1266, 1272)—largely to smallholders whose farming probably did not differ much from that practiced by the mission-raised Barí.

A law promulgated in 1836 in the province of Maracaibo ordered the distribution of the remaining Barí mission lands. This decree seems to have been the final legal step in the disappearance of missionized Barí as a separate entity.

The northernmost of the surviving Barí settlements (on the río Apón) lost its ethnic identity in the 1840s, when ranchers and farmers coming from the north occupied its lands and founded the contemporary city of Machiques. In general, cattle ranching continued to be the major economic activity on the northern border of Barí territory in the 1800s (Cunill Grau 1987, II: 1266), as it had been since the seventeenth century. It is likely that criollo smallholder farmers were displaced by ranching and that their displacement was one of the motives for attempts in the mid- and late 1800s to invade remaining Barí land, both that associated with the missions in the north and south and that remaining in the uncolonized area in which the "wild Motilones" still lived.

If the takeover of the mission land was successful, most invasion of the uncolonized territory was not. Apparently, the forest-dwelling Barí (and their traditional and ongoing enemies, the Carib-speaking Yukpa) constituted a recognized obstacle to colonization of the forested land remaining to them, the area south of the Apón and extending to the Catatumbo and the Zulia. Colonization was restricted to narrow corridors along the main rivers—the Catatumbo, Zulia, and Escalante. This limitation on invasion was recognized in land titles by the 1840s (Cunill Grau 1987, II:1266) and grew stronger with Barí raids on criollo targets throughout the last half of the nineteenth century (Cunill Grau 1987, II:1263; Alcácer 1965: 79). The only former mission to the Barí that had been near the middle course of the Catatumbo, El Pilar, by 1880 had become a completely criollo village. It was successively attacked in 1882, 1883, and 1894 and finally abandoned after the killing of many settlers (Jahn 1927: 82). There was a bloody encounter between Barí and Venezuelans in the vicinity of the río Tarra in 1911 (Jahn 1927: 78) and probably many others around that time. One such was reported by an American geologist in 1912 in the same region (Arnold, MacReady, and Barrington 1960: 289). It is likely that the Barí actually regained in these decades some of the land previously controlled by missions and ranchers, such as that around El Pilar. These gains came at the cost of reprisals, however.

In 1894 the U.S. Consul in Maracaibo made a recommendation: "A well organized raid upon these [Barí], giving no quarter, without regard to age or sex, is, in the opinion of those most competent to advise, the only method to pursue. Burning all houses and settlements and uprooting all plantations would naturally follow . . . the Motilones tribe can only be treated as beasts of prey" (Plumacher 1894).

An 1885 punitive expedition of landowners near the Zulia returned with the head of a Motilón man who had begged in broken Spanish not to be killed (Ernst 1887: 298–301). In a series of events indicating the contingent nature of Barí attacks (cf. M. Lizarralde 2008), an east-west cattle trail from Cúcuta to the Magdalena Valley was cut through Barí territory in 1895 and used peacefully until the drovers began stealing crops from Barí fields; the subsequent attacks forced the abandonment of the trail around 1907 (Holder 1947: 420; Reichel-Dolmatoff 1946: 385).

Another brake on the invasion of remaining Barí land (and on the retention of former Barí land) was disease. A malaria epidemic struck the criollo population of the southwestern Maracaibo Basin in 1844, others followed, and the region continued to be perceived as unhealthy through the 1870s (Cunill Grau 1987, II:1275), and indeed well into the twentieth century (Solano Benítez 1970–1971, IV:815).

None of these obstacles was sufficient to prevent the construction of a railway line along the río Zulia, connecting the towns of Encontrados and La Fría, in 1894. By forcing the Barí to retreat west, this railway line established an unbreachable eastern border on the southern part of their territory.

In sum, the fourth period began with peaceful relations and free access to iron tools—directly for the mission Barí and indirectly through them for the "wild Motilones" who remained unreduced. As mission Barí were driven off their land or assimilated, eliminating these lines of supply, new invasions of remaining Barí territory were attempted by criollos, both large ranchers and small farmers. It was this combination of loss of access to iron tools and new territorial invasions by Spanish-speaking people that was behind the renewed hostilities of the latter part of the fourth period. These hostilities, combined with disease, were responsible for small gains in territory by the end of the fourth period. From the control of probably under 10,000 km² total territory around 1818, the "wild Motilones" evidently increased their total territory to about 16,000 km² (with a residential territory of 13,000 km²) a little less than a century later (Lizarralde and Beckerman 1982). There were, of course, no population figures for this latter date.

Fifth Period, 1912–1959

The year 1912 marked the beginning of modern geologic exploration of the Barí region (Mendez 1975: 22; Notestein, Hubman, and Bowler 1944: 1170). It was also the year of the Capuchins' return to Venezuela—although, after establishing their first missions in the eastern part of the country, they had to wait until 1944 to obtain government permission to establish a mission in the Lake Maracaibo region.

In Colombia, however, the Capuchins established peaceful contact with the Yukpa (known as the Yuko on the Colombian side of the border), northern enemies of the Barí, in fall 1914 (Alcácer 1965: 111–142), and missionization of the Yukpa proceeded regularly from then on. Oil, however, was the driving force of the events of the fifth period.

Petroleum seeps had been discovered in the southern part of Barí territory during the second half of the nineteenth century. By 1905 a small plant for distilling oil had been established in the vicinity of the modern town of Petrólea by a Colombian military officer, Virgilio Barco. International oil companies took over exploration and drilling in 1914 on the Venezuelan side of the border, near the ríos de Oro and Tarra, but not until the early 1930s on the Colombian side. Many geologic scouting and prospecting expeditions entered the area between 1912 and 1931, after which oil exploration became more systematic (Notestein, Hubman, and Bowler 1944: 1167). A joint Colombian-Venezuelan border commission was appointed in the 1930s to survey and delimit this little-known section of the border between Colombia and Venezuela after the subsoil wealth became known, as part of a major border surveying project from the Caribbean coast to Amazonia. It was active in Barí territory in the early 1930s, each national commission accompanied by one hundred well-armed soldiers (M. Loboguerrero, pers. com., to R. Lizarralde, April 26, 1975). This little army, with its frequent shooting to scare away the Barí, apparently achieved its objective. After some initial, bloody attacks, the Barí allowed the commission to pursue its activities undisturbed most of the time (C. Ruiz, pers. com., to R. Lizarralde, January 21, 1958).

As a result of oil exploitation, the history of the fifth period is largely an account of the amputation of larger and larger sections of Barí territory, with ranchers and homesteaders following the roads and other infrastructure provided by the oil companies. The invasions were accompanied by extraordinary brutality and provoked bloody reprisals from the Barí, in addition to their habitual raids aimed at obtaining iron tools. The characteristics of the invasions and responses changed as the decades passed.

The Teens

By 1914 two oil camps had penetrated Barí territory from the south, within Venezuela. Two more were established in 1921, on the Colombian side of the border. These invasions cost the Barí about 12% of the total territory they held in 1912; as a result, by the early 1920s the Barí retained a total territory of only about 14,000 km² and a residential territory of roughly 11,000 km². At a rough estimate, based mainly on territory size, there were about two thousand Barí around 1920 (Lizarralde and Beckerman 1982: 16, 49).

In these early days of the fifth period, the head of the Colón Development Company (a subsidiary of Royal Dutch-Shell), the international oil company developing the Venezuelan side of the oil fields, wrote the president of that country about his company's efforts to contact the Motilones. The oilman was interested in the pacification of the Barí and noted that while Motilón attacks were terrible, it was also true that "the criollos are relentless with them; they hunt them like dreadful animals wherever they find them" (Murray [1915] 1988: 145; our translation). He also gave a description of a longhouse, its contents and associated fields, obtained from his field geologist, A. Faison Dixon, which clearly indicated that the location visited (in 1914) belonged to a group of Barí (who had evidently fled when the exploring party approached). An intriguing note was the observation by the company geologist that the longhouse contained some baskets of maize and that maize was also to be found in the fields, although manioc "appear[ed] to be the principal food of these Indians" (Murray [1915] 1988: 147). Maize was never recorded afterward in Barí fields, but in light of Goldman's (1963: 30) observation that the Cubeo gave up secondary maize cultivation in the first third of the twentieth century, the possibility of a similar change among the twentieth-century Barí must be seriously considered.

Although Murray clearly desired peaceful contact with the Barí, not all oilmen were intent on harmony. In January 1920 the same A. Faison Dixon took bows and arrows from an empty Barí house he encountered during a survey expedition along the río Lora. The result was a running battle between the geological party and the inhabitants of the longhouse in the course of which ten or twelve Barí were killed (Arnold, MacReady, and Barrington 1960: 301–302; Holder n.d.: 81).

Another set of events may have affected the Barí. The worldwide influenza epidemic associated with World War I reached the Colombian city of Cúcuta and its neighbors in 1918. Epidemic dysentery, often fatal, followed and persisted for two years. Finally, a notable malaria epidemic struck lower-altitude criollo regions of the Zulia drainage in 1921 (Solano Benítez 1970–71, I: 732–733). (It is significant that the town of La Fria, terminus of the rail line along the río Zulia, earned its name from its reputation as a focus of malarial fevers and chills.) There is no record that these diseases reached the Barí, but their presence upriver of the Barí in the same river basin, and the transmission of the latter two diseases by water and mosquitoes, respectively, leaves open that possibility.

The Twenties and Thirties

The combination of increased oil drilling in the twenties and thirties and the construction of a pipeline in Colombia across the southern part of Motilonia during the late thirties cost the Barí another 27% of what their landholdings had been in 1912, leaving them in 1940 with a total territory of about 9,700 km² and a residential territory of 7,400 km² (Lizarralde and Beckerman 1982: 21). The pressure of attack and land loss probably diminished their population as well.

A small island of territory had been cut off to the south of the pipeline; it was inhabited by one or two Barí families who were now isolated from the rest of their nation. It was also during the 1930s that the border commission was most active in the region, heavily guarded by Colombian and Venezuelan troops (Solano Benítez 1970–1971, III:51) and perhaps launching a new form of anti-Barí warfare.

When Beckerman first worked with the Barí in the early 1970s several American employees of Colpet, the oil company then working the wells in the Colombian fields, told him that "the company used to fly over Indian houses and drop gasoline drums on them." They all said these incidents happened "before my time" and left the impression that the culprits were former military pilots who had joined the company after World War II. When he mentioned these stories to the American anthropologist Preston Holder, who had attempted, along with the Colombian anthropologist Gerardo Reichel-Dolmatoff, to contact the Barí in 1946 at the request of the Colombian Petroleum Company, Holder commented that he had heard these stories told then not about oil company pilots but about pilots associated with the border commission of the previous decade. Lizarralde heard similar stories in the 1950s in Venezuela concerning the bombing of Barí longhouses by oil company airplanes. Both authors also heard stories of electrified fences surrounding oil company installations such as Campo Rosario.

It was also during the 1930s that there took place the small beginnings of the colonization of Barí land by individuals not associated with the oil companies. These first invasions were from the south. During the 1930s there were also at least two occasions on which unarmed Barí men showed themselves to oil company workers (Holder n.d.: 27–29).

The creation as early as 1922 of a charitable fund for an ongoing anti-malarial campaign among workers in the Catatumbo Basin oil fields (Solano Benítez 1970–1971, IV:815) illustrates the generally malarial nature of the region in these decades. An unidentified epidemic of an often-fatal fever in the Catatumbo and Santa Ana region in 1928 and an outbreak of typhus in Cúcuta in 1929 (Solano Benítez 1970–1971, I:479) may or may not have reached the Barí.

In 1939 the town police of Ocaña massacred about forty Barí men, women, and children in retaliation for Barí attacks near the town of Mercedes. The bodies were seen by a former Colombian Petroleum company worker, who described the incident to Lizarralde on August 17, 1960.

The Forties

During the 1940s the composition of the major invaders of Motilonia changed. While the oil companies made relatively slight incursions in this decade, colonization became the major threat. The new invaders were primarily large hacendados (in this case, mostly wealthy dairy ranchers) from around the city of Machiques at the northern end of Motilonia in Venezuela and *campesinos* (peasant homesteaders) at the southeastern end in Colombia. When the oil pipeline was completed in September 1939, about three thousand laborers were let go by the Colombian Petroleum Company (Solano Benítez 1970–1971, III:460); many of these men went to work on the ranches invading Motilonia from the north; some of them undoubtedly turned up among the homesteaders pushing in from the southeast. A description of a 1941 attack on a Barí longhouse, narrated by eyewitnesses, is recorded in R. Lizarralde (2004).

Gerardo Reichel-Dolmatoff, the Colombian anthropologist who with Preston Holder formed the unsuccessful contact team engaged by the Colombian Petroleum Company, recorded that in the early 1940s "the homesteaders considered the Indians as beasts of the forest, and they killed them wherever they found them. In the region of Mercedes attacks were organized with the goal of stealing women, and at the same time that the oil company workers were fighting with the Indians, the homesteaders declared war on them" (1946: 386; our translation).

(Holder and Reichel-Dolmatoff did manage to hand some gifts to the Barí family cut off south of the pipeline at their small longhouse. But these people, clearly terrified, refused further contact.)

Still worse, in 1947 *la violencia* reached the Colombian borders of Motilonia. "The violence" was a generation-long civil war that swept over

Colombia. In this region it lasted only until 1950. However, it left behind armed men known as *pájaros*, birds, who were like the jayhawkers, pro-slavery guerrilla bands during and after the U.S. Civil War, or the para-military gangs roaming the former Yugoslavia. Irregular troops who re-fused to lay down their guns, they looked for employment in their trade.

Invaders on both the Colombian and Venezuelan sides of the terri-tory were aided by the antimalarial campaign undertaken in the region in 1940–1950, which made the area considerably healthier for people with the closely packed settlement and housing habits of the criollos of the region (Lizarralde and Beckerman 1982: 24). Despite the largely suc-cessful control of malaria in this decade, yellow fever struck Colombian Petroleum Company camps in 1945 (Solano Benítez 1970–1971, IV:247). Again, it is not known whether this mosquito-borne disease made its way to the Barí.

Another significant event in this decade was the beginning of a cam-paign by the Capuchin missionary monks to establish contact with the Barí by means of what they called *bombas de paz* (peace bombs). These were packages of machetes, axes, knives, aluminum cooking pots, cloth, and so on, that were air-dropped, beginning in the second half of 1947, near occupied longhouses.

The quantity of these goods was sufficient enough that when the Barí were peacefully contacted by Roberto Lizarralde in July 1960, they no longer made pottery. It also is likely that the axes and machetes acquired from this source increased the amount of land the Barí could clear in a unit of time. (Even in the 1970s the bottleneck in felling trees in a large field was the number of axes available at a longhouse.) Thus the "peace bombs" may have helped the Barí colonize new locations, as they fled the Indian killers described below.

The Fifties

By 1950 Barí total territory had been reduced to 7,400 km², with 5,600 km² under 600 m.[1] About four thousand illegal homesteaders were re-ported to be on the Colombian-Venezuelan border in the Catatumbo re-gion, making a living by smuggling and stealing from oil camps as well as by farming (Solano Benítez 1970–1971, V:268–269). Some reputed Moti-lón raids may actually have been carried out by these people.

Authentic Barí raids against criollos did increase sharply in this period. In 1953 alone there were three reported raids on oil towns and two on missions to the Yukpa, in Colombia alone. A Colombian historian wrote, "It was said that the cause of so many Motilón attacks this year is due to the fact that on the Venezuelan side the Indians are being harried by the whites" (Solano Benítez 1970–1971, V:270).

Harried they were. According to local oral history, it was common in the 1950s (and perhaps a little earlier) for groups of Colombian pájaros to present themselves at ranchers' homes and stores in the Venezuelan cattle town of Machiques to strike a deal with the local people. "For such-and-such a quantity of money, food, and ammunition," they would say, "we will erase the Indians from the land you want—and fence it, if you provide the barbed wire."

These professional Indian killers were certainly responsible for most— but not all—of the killings reported to Lizarralde in the 1960s and recorded systematically by Beckerman and Lizarralde (1995) in interviews with survivors living in the northern part of the Venezuelan reserve. Most of these recollections could not be dated with certainty; they are all considered here in the section on the 1950s, although some fraction of them took place in the 1940s.

In those decades, solely among the half (roughly) of the Venezuelan Barí population represented by interviewees, twenty-seven incidents took place in which one or more Barí lives were lost. Over seventy-two people were killed outright, and an additional five or so children were kidnapped, presumably to be taken for rearing as domestic servants. In the attacks that resulted in these losses, the habitual strategy was to set fire to a longhouse just before dawn, when people were all inside asleep, and then shoot the residents as they tried to flee. Eyewitnesses reported the disemboweling of children and the mutilation of corpses.

These tactics were of course effective in forcing the Barí to attempt to escape. By the beginning of 1960, the territory size figures were 5,100 km² total and 2,500 km² residential (Lizarralde and Beckerman 1982: 24–31). The population may have been no more than 1,100 people (Lizarralde and Beckerman 1982: 49).

In sum, the fifth period began with a sharp increase in invasion, loss of territory, and the brutality accompanying these injuries, and by the end of the period the situation had become much worse. The Motilones had their backs to the wall by the middle of the twentieth century.

Sixth Period, 1960–Present

Roberto Lizarralde, in his role as an official of the Venezuela Indian Commission, made peaceful contact with the embattled Venezuelan Barí on July 19, 1960. Almost immediately thereafter the government removed him from the region and transferred his budget to the Capuchin order, which resumed its former missionary role among the Venezuelan Barí. A Protestant missionary, Bruce Olson, made another contact on the Colombian side of the border in 1961 and became the major missionary presence in that country, although nuns from the Order of the Mother Laura also opened a Colombian mission to the Barí in the early 1960s.

Postcontact history, with the profound acculturation it records, is treated extensively in R. Lizarralde's *Una breve historia de los contactos con los Barí de la Sierra de Perijá, Venezuela y Colombia* (under review). The major focus of the current volume is traditional culture as revealed by the pericontact Barí. However, a few postcontact events must be mentioned here, to illustrate the circumstances under which most of the data on the traditional culture were collected.

Within a few days of Lizarralde's contact in Venezuela, three heavily armed men in a helicopter landed at the largest Barí longhouse, Karibaigdakaira, and treated the Barí, jubilant at the promise of peace, to a sweet drink later described as "like red milk" (it may have been Kool-Aid). An hour or two after the men left, people began dying. The helicopter also visited Okbadyá and poisoned people in that longhouse with the same trick. Between fifty and one hundred Barí were killed this way in the first week of peaceful contact.

Disease mortality was far worse (Lizarralde and Beckerman n.d.). Measles struck two local groups of Venezuelan Barí in March 1962, infecting all their hundred-odd people and killing sixteen. Local health authorities treated eighty-six cases and certainly prevented many more deaths.

By 1964 missionization, which moved from north to south in Venezuela, had reached all the Venezuelan Barí, leaving them in regular communication with priests and nuns and their employees. The last uncontacted Barí group in Colombia received a brief visit in 1963 from a Colombian priest who had a well-known television show, but there were still several Colombian local groups living essentially traditional lives through the early 1970s.

In September-October 1964 there was a congregation of four Barí local groups near a Colombian oil camp, Campo Río de Oro, located on the river of the same name. People from Bakyubi, Aitrabá, and Ikikaig lived together in a new *bohío* (longhouse) named Sabituá on the Venezuelan side of the river, while people from Orobiá had a temporary shelter just to the side of the oil camp's airstrip on the Colombian side. These settlements were also struck by measles. Between 175 and 200 people were in these groups, and at least 63 of them died by November of that year. Again, without cosmopolitan medicine the toll would have been much higher.

Thirteen Barí were reported to have died at an isolated house in mid-1965. The cause was not determined.

The worst epidemic began in the first days of May 1966. It affected most of the southern half of Barí territory and reached groups totaling at least 250 people. Most of these people were in Colombia, where the Barí were no longer newsworthy. Medical intervention and evacuation came late. When the epidemic ended in late June, at least 164 people had died.

The population never again reached as low a level as it did in 1966, when there were probably no more than 850 Barí, dangerously close to the "magic number," ±500, below which a human population usually cannot replace itself.

Barí territory suffered parallel reductions. By 1970 it was reduced to a largely mountainous area of 3,300 km² total, 1,900 residential (Lizarralde and Beckerman 1982: 28–31). A reservation of 1,492 km² within this terrain, intended for the Barí and an adjacent group of their traditional enemies, the Yukpa, was created in Venezuela in 1961; in 1974 a reservation of 840 km² was created for the Barí in Colombia. In the 1960s fourteen small groups of Barí returned to the lowlands, to their former longhouse sites in Venezuela, now in the midst of ranchland from which they had been driven in previous decades. There they were generally tolerated, although only as squatters without true land rights. This toleration was not immediate, however.

As their history makes clear, for most of the past half millennium (and quite possibly for much longer) the Barí have been prey to more powerful populations around them. The threat—and the actual fact—of murder and slavery at the hands of their neighbors has been an influence on their culture as powerful as hunger and the dangers of the rain forest, and must be reckoned with in any discussion of the ecology of these people.

Note

1. This 600 m limit refers to Colombia in the twentieth century, a time for which oil company aerial photographs are available. In the same period in Venezuela, where low altitude land was more scarce, there were a few longhouses at altitudes as high as 800 m.

CHAPTER 4

Production

The natural environment is always a place of variable food availability. A major issue for subsistence economy human populations is stabilizing the supply of food.

The field of human ecology has been criticized for its excessive emphasis on how populations achieve and/or maintain homeostasis, and the point is in general well taken. Human beings do not as a rule maintain stationary populations, or seek to; history is full of examples of burgeoning populations linked to expanding territories and ravaged resources—and of displaced and conquered neighbors who suffer the consequences of these disequilibria. Contrariwise, one does not have to look far in history books to find examples of populations—sometimes those of whole continents—shrinking with catastrophic speed.

And with regard to the means of supporting human populations, history is full of instances of the adoption of new subsistence techniques that are more (or occasionally less) productive than those they replace: new tools, new ways of using them, new crops—and the abandonment of old ones—not to mention the extinction of numerous wild local species and the introduction of foreign species to new habitats. Clearly, such changes may disequilibrate the populations whose food they provide.

Nevertheless, it will not do to throw the dietary baby out with the ecological bathwater. All people want their daily bread or its local equivalent. The avoidance of a subsistence shortfall *is* a universal concern. And it is usually only after the introduction of substantial long-distance commerce that the production of a food surplus, that is, beyond what can be consumed locally, becomes a goal. In an egalitarian subsistence economy, in particular one with a high degree of family and local group autonomy, most people happily turn from the food quest to alternative activities as soon as they have assured themselves enough to eat and a comfortable margin against misfortune.

The Barí are no exception. Their subsistence problem is assuring a regular supply of food in the face of an irregular environment. They have no use for a food surplus above a reasonable excess for the possibility of adversity and the demands of hospitality. They are few enough (for reasons discussed in subsequent chapters) that in traditional times their nutritional demands constituted no threat to the natural environment. The issue for the Barí, then, is a constant need for food in an inconstant environment.

Inconstancy in this context has two faces. On the spatial scale, as one ascends the slopes of western and southern Motilonia, the rivers are smaller than in their lower courses, and run straighter and faster. Pockets of alluvium, furnishing agriculturally desirable soils such as Tropaquepts and Eutropepts, become fewer and smaller with increasing altitude. Horticulture is more laborious. Also, fish are smaller and less abundant (although sometimes more visible). Game, however, may be more abundant at higher elevations and hunting more productive, as there is less intense hunting pressure here compared to the lowlands. Many gathered food items appear to be spatially restricted by such factors as soil type, proximity to rivers, and other less sweeping patterns, as well as by altitude.

On the temporal scale, a field that is slashed just at the end of the major wet season and left to lie in the sun throughout much of the dry season will burn well. Because thoroughness of burn has agricultural implications, horticultural productivity may be related to the timing of field preparation. Fishing returns are strongly related to rainfall, as rain generates fish migrations and controls water clarity and depth. In contrast to the strong seasonality of fishing productivity, we have discovered no significant effect of seasonality per se on the abundance of terrestrial or arboreal game. Many gathered foods, however, are fruits with a seasonal peak of abundance.

Despite the spatiotemporal inconstancy of their natural environment, the Barí manage to provide themselves with a continuously adequate supply of food. We can expect that the Barí, like the great majority of peoples—like the great majority of organisms, in fact—are rate maximizers in their subsistence activities. That is, while engaged in subsistence activities, they try to obtain their food at the greatest rate achievable, to maximize the quotient of food obtained per time spent obtaining it. There is considerable evidence, summarized below, that this expectation is generally met. However, there are additional questions that arise in the context of maximization. This chapter is informed by five questions about Barí subsistence, three of them general concerns about the context and strategy of producing food and two of them more specific issues dealing with maximization:

1. Are the Barí hungry? That is, in the overall scheme of things, is their environment bountiful or niggardly, and do their subsistence practices generate scarcity or abundance?
2. How do the Barí deal with spatial variability in subsistence resource distribution and abundance?
3. How do the Barí deal with temporal variability in subsistence resource distribution and abundance?
4. Are the Barí bufferers in any of their subsistence activities? That is, do they attempt to minimize the likelihood of a shortfall in the production of any of their subsistence activities at the expense of rate maximization?
5. Given the evidence that the Barí are generally rate maximizers in their subsistence activities, is it because they are food maximizers or because they are time minimizers? That is, do they attempt to get the maximum amount of food they can in a given time, or do they attempt to spend the least amount of time they can to get a given amount of food?

A brief, quantitative overview of Barí subsistence presents means and ranges of figures that need to be examined.

Summary Overview

The Barí feed themselves by a combination of shifting agriculture (strictly speaking, their small-scale, digging stick cultivation ought to be called horticulture), fishing, hunting, and gathering. The order of the list reflects the importance of the activities in supplying food. Mean daily individual food intake (fresh, edible portion, averaged over all seasons, both sexes and all ages) is around 1,500 g of crops (Beckerman 1975: 323, 328–329); 300 g of fish (Beckerman 1980a: 104); 100 g of game (Beckerman 1980a: 104); and a few grams of wild plant material, mostly palm fruits (Beckerman 1977). Crop consumption is relatively constant around the year and among longhouses, but fish and game consumption vary markedly with season and location, and gathered resources make an erratic contribution. Despite the substantial differences in the mean caloric content of a gram of a food procured by each of the four major subsistence activities, the differences in amounts consumed are great enough that the weight ranking also indicates the ranking by caloric contribution.

Caloric importance in the diet does not, however, reflect time and labor demands; indeed, the rankings are somewhat inverted. In general, men spend a variable 100–400 hr/yr in subsistence horticulture, depending largely on whether they are cutting new fields that year; women spend a more consistent 150–200 hr/yr. Men dedicate 500–600 hr/yr to fishing, women around 350–450. Most men also allocate 750–1,000 hr/yr to hunting. Women do not hunt. Women expend, on average, something over 100 hr/yr of their time gathering, with most of this effort directed at nonfood items. The average man probably gathers for 50 hr/yr or fewer. Women also spend about 1,000 hr/yr cooking and other food preparation (men do very little food preparation), although this high figure is somewhat deceiving, as explained below. Time expenditures in subsistence activities (except cooking and the harvesting component of horticultural labor) vary with season, location, and, for horticulture and hunting, the recency of occupation of the longhouse site.

Subsistence activities follow the weather but not rigidly. Men often prefer to cut new fields so as to take advantage of the January–March dry season for drying the slash. Fields are accordingly often planted in March or April, which makes them ready for a first weeding around July or August—if anyone is in residence at the longhouse to which the field pertains during those months. Subsequent weeding takes place as needed, usually just after each reoccupation of the longhouse. Harvesting is essentially continuous, after the maturity of the manioc, during each period of occupation of the longhouse, but ceases when people migrate to the next longhouse.

Fishing and hunting are in complementary distribution. The average male spends 125 hr/mo in the sum of these activities (Beckerman 1983b) with the emphasis following the weather, fishing dominating in dry months, hunting in wet months. Women accompany men on most fishing expeditions and participate actively, but they stay home when men hunt.

Gathering is a sporadic activity, driven by demand for raw materials as well as by fruiting schedules of wild plants. Men's gathering of wild palm fruits is often a response to an unsuccessful fishing or hunting trip. Women's gathering expeditions are normally more deliberated and show a notable tendency to complementary distribution with women's agricultural labor.

Agriculture

Overall Characteristics

The Barí are model swidden horticulturalists. The great majority of Calories in the diet comes from crops, and all traditional longhouses are located
in the middle of a cultivated field. Virtually all longhouses also have associated with them more distant, subsidiary fields. Questions about Barí
subsistence begin with cultivated plants.

Although there is some tendency to seasonal concentration in time and
effort devoted to horticultural chores, the contribution of the fields to the
diet is effectively constant around the year. In geographical terms, however, indications are that higher elevations are less productive and require
greater agricultural labor investments to assure a constant crop supply.
Because migrations tend toward seasonal alternations between uplands
and lowlands, this evidence suggests that temporal variation in agricultural investment is ultimately driven by elevational differences. Hence the
stress in this section is on geographical rather than seasonal variation in
agricultural parameters.

CROPS

In their fields the Barí plant a curiously small inventory of traditional cultivars (R. Lizarralde 1968: Table 4.1; Beckerman 1983a, 1987; M. Lizarralde 1997). Of these, the twenty-one *Musa* (banana and plantain) varieties and three *Saccharum* (sugarcane) varieties are Old World crops,
acquired at least as long ago as the period of the first pacification (see
chapter 3) and fully integrated into the agricultural repertoire. All other
crops are, as far as anyone knows, old American cultivars.

The two major crops are manioc or yuca (*Manihot esculenta*, Euphorbiaceae), the staple of the Barí diet, and plantains and bananas (*Musa bal-
bisiana* x *acuminata*, Musaceae).

The Barí have four traditional varieties of manioc (M. Lizarralde 1997:
42), all of them "sweet"—that is, without significant amounts of prussic
acid (HCN) in the flesh of the roots. (There is some question as to how
traditional two of these four varieties are.) They do not need or know the
elaborate processing techniques of peoples who cultivate "bitter" manioc.
All the traditional varieties take over a year to grow to harvestable weight
and can be left in the ground for well over two years without rotting. The
Barí speak with some disdain of the manioc strains grown by the homesteaders encroaching on their land, which begin to rot in less than a year

(Beckerman 1987: 66), although they do appreciate the taste of the "red" variety of homesteader manioc.

A single planting of manioc produces an average of at least 5 kg of roots (fresh weight), the roots making up about half the weight of the whole plant. In terms of nutritional and agricultural attributes

> the dietary value of manioc is in its starch. Typical figures (there is not much variation) for raw peeled roots are about 62% water, 35% carbohydrates (almost all starch), 1% fiber, 1% ash; 0.8% protein, and 0.2% fats; calories run around 150/100g (Montaldo 1973: 21, 25).

> Manioc gives one of the highest yields of calories per unit land per unit time of any cultivar, but perhaps its greatest advantage for tropical forest swidden agriculture is not its productivity but its tolerance. It will grow in soils that are poor in nutrients and of such acidity and high levels of available aluminum ions that most other crops would find them toxic. (Beckerman 1987: 67)

The only crops besides manioc that make a more than sporadic contribution to the Barí diet are the various cultivars of bananas and plantains.

> Bananas are broadly similar to manioc in their dietary value, the following rounded figures being typical: 75% water, 22% carbohydrates (mostly sugar rather than starch), 1.2% protein, 1% ash, 1% fiber, 0.8% fat; calories are about 90/100 g.

> Bananas and plantains share many of the diagnostic characteristics of root crops. They are propagated by vegetative parts, not seeds; the edible part is high in carbohydrate and low in protein. They are not seasonal, but are ready a given amount of time from the moment of planting. An important difference, however, is that the *Musa* spp. cannot be stored on the living plant. Parrots, in particular, are fond of the ripe fruits and will destroy them even before they begin to rot and fall to the ground.

> Bananas and plantains are considerably more demanding of soil conditions than is manioc. In particular, they prefer soft, deep, well-watered alluvial soils and do not do well in hard or shallow soil. (Beckerman 1987: 67)

FIELD ARCHITECTURE

Most fields are dominated by manioc. Indeed some subsidiary fields on colluvial soils are pure stands of manioc. In contrast, some subsidiary fields in alluvial pockets are exclusively *Musa*; and a few fields are dedicated entirely to arrow cane (*Gynerium sagittatum*).

However, the most typical subsidiary field has in its productive phase a central core of manioc surrounded by a double-file ring of *Musa* spp. This kind of field is found primarily on alluvial soils. Some subsidiary fields, mainly those made by only one or two men, have a good deal of sugarcane in them. In general, the structure of the subsidiary field is simple, a matter of monocropping or concentrically zoned duocropping.

The crop inventory and the architecture of the house-surrounding field are considerably more complicated. In 1961 Lizarralde prepared a sketch map of the house-surrounding field at Karibaigdakaira (Map. 4.1), the largest Barí longhouse we know of. Because this house was rather new at that time (and was soon abandoned), its field never developed the full complement of crops found associated with more mature longhouses. It was rather a manifestation of a minimally complex house-surrounding field.

Later, drawing on observations made in the early 1970s, one of us described the mature house-surrounding field "in terms of an ideal pattern that is sometimes fairly well realized" in order then "to discuss real house-surrounding fields in terms of modifications of that pattern":

> An ideal house-surrounding field . . . has an outer ring of bananas, in with which may be mixed a few other tall plants: achiote, avocado, *bakora*, *buera*, and sugar cane. In all the cases I have observed, the full list of these additional cultivars is never represented in a single field. . . . In the great majority of cases, only one or two minor cultivars are present in the outer ring, and those are manifested by only a few individuals.
>
> The middle ring of a house-surrounding field is composed almost entirely of manioc. Mixed in with the manioc may be a few pineapples and (known from only a single observation) *karikairobera*, a fiber plant [*bii*, another fiber plant is also sometimes found among the manioc plantings]. Other plants often grow along the radial trails leading through this ring to the jungle beyond, but these trails and the crops that sometimes line them are most accurately thought of as extensions of the innermost ring with which they connect and whose microenvironmental properties of unobstructed sunlight and wide diurnal temperature range they share.
>
> The inner ring of a house-surrounding field is the location of most minor crops. It can be thought of as a concatenation of many small kitchen gardens—one for each household inside the longhouse—that happen to be aligned in such a way as to produce a closed, oval curve. Even

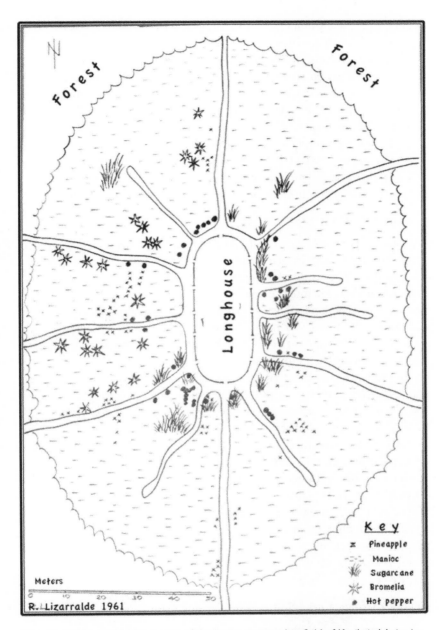

Forest

Forest

N

Longhouse

Key

✕ Pineapple
--- Manioc
🌾 Sugarcane
✳ Bromelia
● Hot pepper

Meters

0   10   20   30   40   50

R. Lizarralde 1961

Map 4.1. R. Lizarralde's sketch map of the house-surrounding field of Karibaigdakaira in 1961. This field was exceptional for its reduced inventory of crops, probably as a result of the short time it was cultivated. Its lack of an outer ring of bananas and plantains may also have been due to the "hardness" of the soil on which it was located.

here, where many different cultivars are sown in close proximity, there is a certain tendency to zonation. The very innermost sub-ring tends to be composed of one or more of the three ground-crawling vines: squash, yams, and sweet potatoes. Next often comes a more or less continuous sub-ring of *bakira*, the Barí barbasco, and the outermost sub-ring is usually composed of triplet clumps of sugar cane, cotton, and [both sweet and hot] chile peppers. If tobacco is present, it will be found here also.

The overall proportion of land devoted to various crops—and this proportion is actually fairly well represented in many individual fields as well as in the aggregate for all fields—is 70–75% in manioc, 20–25% in bananas, and 0–5% in all minor crops. (Beckerman 1983a: 90–91)

STAGES OF FIELD LIFE

Over two generations ago, Conklin (1961) noted the sequence of swidden agricultural activities in his outline for the study of shifting cultivation. The swidden farmer (or farmers) must determine where and when to make a new field. He must decide how big the field is going to be. He must elect to clear the field alone or with others (if the latter, which others?) and with greater or lesser fastidiousness. He must then decide how long he is going to let the field dry before he burns it. The burn itself requires labor decisions parallel to those made in clearing. The farmer must next choose the crops to plant and the arrangement in which they are to be planted. Then planting, cultivating, weeding, and harvesting all demand choices as to when and how and with whom they are to be done, how much time is to be invested overall, and how this labor is to be scheduled. The preharvesting steps and the timing of harvesting are major factors determining the productivity of the field. Replanting, usually an aspect of harvesting, can be continued for several harvests, or discontinued; and the crops chosen for replanting can be the same as those just harvested, or different. These latter decisions effectively sum to the farmer's broader choice about when to abandon the field and how abruptly to do so. Once the field has been abandoned, the farmer can choose to reuse it or not. If he so chooses, he must decide how much time needs to elapse before it is ready to be cleared again.

LABOR COSTS

Labor costs are associated with these stages in the life of a swidden field. The cost of finding an appropriate site is difficult to distinguish from the general acquisition of environmental knowledge. The Barí monitor their surroundings constantly and are acutely aware of the most minute characteristics of the landscape. Much, if not most, of the investigative cost of finding a suitable field site is piggybacked on continuous observations of the environment incidental to fishing, hunting, visiting, and migration from one longhouse to another.

When a field location is chosen, the forest is cut down, a strictly male activity. For fields not made entirely by a single individual, all the men involved work together through the whole area to be felled, without respect to the sections they will later plant and cultivate individually. They first sweep through with machetes, brushing out the low-hanging vines, understory vegetation, and saplings. Then, the ground cleared for working, they return with axes and take down the large trees. The "driving tree fall," in which several trees, tied together by vines in the canopy, are notched so that when the giant of the group is cut down it drags the others with it, is regularly used. The work is hard and dangerous. In 1972 a man was killed by a falling tree while clearing a field under contract to a homesteader, and similar deaths are described from pre- and postcontact times in our field notes. Observations of clearing (with iron tools) from Beckerman's 1970–1972 fieldwork indicate that it costs an average of about 31 man-hours per hectare (mnhr/ha) to brush out a field and 55 mnhr/ha to fell the large trees (Beckerman 1975, 1983c).

Unlike house-surrounding fields, which are always cleared by all the adult men planning to inhabit the longhouse to be built in the middle of the field, subsidiary fields may be cleared by a labor force varying from a single man to a party of two or a few men up to all the adult males in the house. Fields cleared by one or two men are often smaller than those cleared by all the male members of a local group, but there is no fixed relation of field size to size of labor force.

After clearing, a field is typically left to dry for a month or two, then burned. In our experience, the firing of a Barí field is a casual affair, often delegated—as is the custom with jobs considered undemanding drudgery—to a teenaged boy. The boy ambles to the field with a palm splinter torch and spends less than an hour poking flames into a few of the denser heaps of branches and dead leaves on the upwind side of the cleared area. No piling or stacking of the dried slash takes place before the fire is set. As a result, the Barí get a conspicuously incomplete burn, even though some larger logs may smolder for days. Not even all the leaves are consumed, and virtually none of the branches over a few centimeters in diameter suffer more than a scorching. Although this perfunctory firing leaves it difficult to traverse the tangle of trunks and branches left covering the field and deposits considerably less fertilizing ash than could be obtained from a more complete burn, it is not without possible agronomic benefits. The dead slash continues to disintegrate for years, releasing a supply of nutrients into the field as it decomposes. The partially burned field also serves as a source of firewood for longhouse hearths, sometimes for years.

Barí fields are usually planted immediately after firing, as soon as the women have gone through the cleared area and pulled up the scorched small weeds that sprouted between clearing and burning. Indeed, the fire may still be smoldering in a few places when planting starts. It is at the planting stage that women begin their agricultural role.

Each man with the aid of his wife (or another close female relative, if he is unmarried) plants only his individually apportioned section of the field. Thus the stage at which women take up their agricultural chores is also the point at which labor ceases to be communal and becomes restricted to the hearth group. The way a typical communal field—either house-surrounding or subsidiary—is planted was described by Beckerman:

> Women bring baskets packed with manioc stems, which have been cut from plants they already have growing in another field. As the men work through their individual sections of the field, excavating shallow holes with machetes (or occasionally with the traditional digging stick), their wives and children work alongside them, pulling up the vines and other volunteer weeds that sprouted during the drying period between the felling and the burning, piling them on mats, and carrying them to the edge of the field. In each hole the man puts five or six pieces of manioc stem, with the "eyes" facing down, at a shallow angle. Men also plant the bananas and plantains around the circumference of the field. (Beckerman 1987: 77)

From this time on, the farmer and his wife will recognize the plants he has set in the ground. It is the plants, rather than the ground they grow in, that belong to them (strictly speaking, they are his, but she may use them freely for household purposes). In the circular to elliptical house-surrounding field, the section of the field holding a man's plants is shaped like a wedge pointing at his hearth position inside the longhouse. Because the wedge cuts across all the rings, it contains individuals of all the different cultivars planted in the field. Subsidiary fields may be partitioned similarly into wedges but may also divided into stripes running roughly parallel to the long axis (like the streaks on a watermelon) or in more idiosyncratic patterns.

Mean per hectare labor investments for the planting phase (Beckerman 1975, 1983a) are also available from the 1970–1972 fieldwork. They are drawn mainly from the planting of a single traditional subsidiary field. It costs about 20 mnhr to cut from a preexisting field enough manioc stems to plant a hectare; this labor is performed by both men and women. It costs a woman about 98 mnhr to do the preliminary weeding of a hectare her husband is going to plant; and it costs a man about 75 mnhr to plant a just weeded hectare. (In practice, the areas weeded and planted by a couple in a single house-surrounding field are much less than a hectare.)

A new manioc field typically needs only one weeding, two to four months after planting, before the manioc forms such a dense, closed canopy that it shades out potential competitors. Older fields, in which the manioc canopy has been thinned and broken by harvesting, require more attention. Both men and women weed, often accompanied by their children. Although the actual labor of weeding is individual or collaborative within the hearth group only, it is often the case that a decision by one individual or couple to spend some time weeding a field will inspire others to do the same, presumably to enjoy one another's company during this boring but necessary work. Barí say that in precontact times, when a local group migrated to a longhouse it tried to stay there long enough to weed the active fields. More than once we have seen, just after the reoccupation of a longhouse, a shared enthusiasm for weeding that led the whole group to go off, as close to simultaneously as Barí ever leave a longhouse, to work on a major active field. At the field, however, people weed only around their own crops, in their own areas. After a longhouse has been occupied for several weeks and the major active fields are in tolerable shape, weeding tends to be a less coordinated, more individual affair.

Labor investment in weeding is highly variable, depending on (among other things) soil type, altitude, age of field, density of crops, and time since the last weeding. Mean weeding labor cost is around 400 mnhr/ha (Beckerman 1983a). However, this figure covers enormous variation.

> The labor (of weeding) might descend to only 100 manhours per hectare for a field weeded exceptionally early and blessed with exceptionally docile weeds. On the other hand, I once observed a man spend time totaling an entire hour . . . to clear no more than a single square meter of

a dense *Bactris* stand in a manioc patch surrounding the house, an experience which projects to an incredible 10,000 manhours for an entire field so endowed. (Of course in practice any field so afflicted would simply be abandoned.) (Beckerman 1975: 348)

It must be pointed out that weeding is not a single event like cutting or first planting. Rather it takes place a variable number of times over the life of the field. Thus the per hectare cost of weeding needs a temporal dimension when used for some comparative purposes. Barí typically weed a given field less often than once a year. We estimate that, discounting for the proportion of cultivated land that is weeded in a given year, the Barí actually spend between 75 and 150 mnhr/ha/yr weeding (Beckerman 1987: 79). That is, of field area in active production, only about a quarter is weeded each year.

One year to fifteen months after first planting, the manioc in a field is large enough to eat (Beckerman 1983a). Harvesting is done a bit at a time, with each woman taking only enough roots to feed her hearth group for the next three days to a week. Replanting is part of harvesting. With her machete, the woman cuts down the aboveground parts of several manioc plants, except for 20–30 cm of stem that she uses as a handle to rip the roots from the ground. Other pieces of stem are chopped from the felled plant and casually reinserted in the hole left by the removal of the tubers. The harvested roots are separated and packed in baskets. Larger roots may be tied together with a strip of bark and carried home, unpacked, on this line.

A woman harvests individually, or with her daughter(s) or unmarried sister(s). Sometimes her husband accompanies her. Frequently, several women do their harvesting simultaneously; when they have finished packing their carrying baskets, they help each other to their feet, necks and foreheads straining against tumplines holding baskets weighing up to 40 kg. Their daughters carry smaller loads, according to their ages. Even girls as young as three help their mothers and carry home a few roots.

Because wrenching the large roots from the ground (and probing the hole with hands and machete for remaining tubers) is such hard work, harvesting-replanting is the most labor-expensive agricultural chore on a per area basis. A woman works at an average 570 mnhr/ha in this activity, although the actual amount of time she spends in a single harvesting replanting episode is almost always less than an hour, and the area harvested is a tiny fraction of a hectare.

The decision to fallow a field does not cost any labor; rather it is a choice to suspend labor investment in a particular field. Barí do not typically set out special "successional crops" when they decide to fallow a field, as some tropical forest peoples do. However, *Musa* cultivars may take over a fallowed field on their own (see below).

FIELD SIZES

House-surrounding fields commonly have an area of near 0.7 ha, a typical figure for lowland South Americans (Beckerman 1987: 69). The variation of this average figure over the last few decades before pacification is discussed in the Appendix.

Subsidiary fields are usually larger than house-surrounding fields, often about 1.0 ha in extent, but they are more variable in size as well. This variation and its change over time is also discussed in the Appendix.

CROP PRODUCTIVITY

MANIOC   A conservative estimate (Beckerman 1983c: 97 n.) for the mean annual tuber production of a manioc field in active use is 18 t/ha/yr, fresh weight. Production may run as high as 25 t/ha/year (cf. Beckerman 1975: 326), especially where new, faster-maturing varieties of manioc have been adopted in recent years. Assuming a water content of 60 percent for the tubers, these fresh weight figures convert to a dry matter production of 11–15 t/ha/yr.

MUSA   Our best estimate is that one of the most common of the Barí musaceous crops, a small banana they call *chirira*, produces a bit over 4 t/ha/yr (Beckerman 1983a: 98 n.). At a water content of 75%, this fresh weight figure works out to a dry matter production of about 1 t/ha/yr.

FIELD AREA PER CAPITA

Combining manioc consumption figures and maturation times given above with productivity and planting density figures developed below (a minimum of 5 kg edible root per planting and a density of about 5,556 plantings/ha) allows the calculation of a minimum per capita requirement for productive cultivated land. If the average person eats 1.76 kg of manioc each day (Beckerman 1975: 323; this figure for fresh, unpeeled weight of the roots translates to about 1.40 kg/day of edible portion), then he consumes the equivalent of 0.35 plantings/day. If each planting requires an average of 1.8 m^2, then daily individual consumption uses the product of 0.63 m². In a year's time, an individual consumes the manioc grown on 230 m² (= .023 ha). For a local group of fifty members, this requirement translates to 11,500 m², or a little over 1 ha.

AREA UNDER CULTIVATION PER
PERSON AND PER LONGHOUSE

At any given traditional longhouse, land in active production, that is, garden land under mature crop, available for current harvesting seems to range from 0.025 to 0.05 ha/person or a little more. Total land under crop, that is, the sum of land planted but not yet producing, land in active production, and land in early fallow but still bearing potentially harvestable crops, runs roughly between 0.05 and (at least) 0.1 ha/person for a Barí longhouse. These figures are developed in detail in the Appendix.

All but one of the local groups whose fields provided the data for these estimates had more than one longhouse in their migration cycle (and that one small house [Ashtacacayra] had the highest per capita area of land actually bearing mature manioc). Thus the amount of cropped land available to these local groups was two to five times that of any one of their longhouses. The evidence thus points strongly to the conclusion that the Barí maintain considerably more land under crop at any point in time than is necessary simply to meet their daily consumption requirements. They appear to be deliberately overproducing, as if to ensure a cushion of surplus. In agriculture, the Barí give evidence of buffering—indeed, of keeping several times as much land under crop as they need.

One result of this overproduction is the ability to host visitors for extended periods. As described in Chapter 6, whole local groups of traditional Barí often visit other such groups for a singing and gift exchange ritual. These visits can last for a month or even two or three. Marriage possibilities are usually explored during these visits.

This buffering need not be as labor-expensive as it might seem at first blush. Because of the multiyear life of most Barí fields, once a local group has built up a surplus of planted land in excess of its consumption needs people can maintain that reserve indefinitely just by planting in replacement in any given year only what they have actually used up in that year. That is, once the initial investment is made, it is no more expensive to maintain a cushion than it is to produce at the level of bare subsistence.

Variation in Agricultural Productivity

By Location

Evidence presented above indicates that agricultural productivity (amount of food produced per unit of labor) decreases with increasing altitude, as one moves toward the western and southern borders of historical Motilonia, up from the alluvial flats of the Maracaibo Basin, and into the foothills of the enclosing cordilleras of the Andes.

The reason is a matter of physical geography. Because streams at high altitudes are small and fast flowing, they usually transport rather than deposit sediments—sediments that also tend to be less plentiful upstream than after the accrual of contributions of additional streams downriver. Also, because these higher streams are fast flowing and the topography of their V-shaped valleys is steep, their watercourses tend to be more or less direct, without meanders. The result is that alluvial pockets, typically deposited on the inside bank of a river meander where the water moves slower than on the outside bank, become fewer and smaller with increasing altitude.

The Barí declare that the very best soil for all their crops is a brown, sandy alluvium they call *bírida*. In addition to their assertion of an advantage in ease of working the soil and its greater production, aerial photographic evidence discussed below suggests that fields planted in alluvium have mean life spans several times longer than those sown in shallower, erosional soils. Thus Barí claims of less planting and harvesting labor and more food per unit of soil for alluvium are augmented by photographic evidence of lower demands for clearing of new fields where alluvial soils are used.

By Season

Although there is experimental evidence that manioc gains little root weight during dry periods and may even lose weight (Mayobre et al. 1982a, 1982b), the climate of Motilonia has a dry season short enough and damp enough that we have never heard Barí comment about seasonal deficits in manioc production.

Variability in Agricultural Decisions and Activities

Labor Time

Subsistence agricultural labor requirements can be estimated from the figures developed above for minimal and actual land area under cultivation. If the average person consumes the product of about 0.025 ha/yr in manioc, then ensuring a steady manioc supply requires the creation or replanting of that much new field per person per year. In addition, if the actual figure for land in active production is closer to 0.05 ha/person for each house in the migration cycle, then in order not to lose ground, that much land per longhouse, multiplied by the number of longhouses belonging to the local group, must be maintained each year on average. The evidence presented above suggests that 0.1–0.2 ha/person, distributed among the full suite of longhouses owned by a local group, is the ordinary area of land kept in active production.

Usually, about half the inhabitants of a longhouse are in their mid-teens or older (Lizarralde and Lizarralde 1991)—old enough to be expected to pull their weight in agriculture. The sex ratio of these people is usually close to one, with a slight bias toward excess males. It follows that a typical married adult has a minimum of three dependents: two or more young children who do little or no agricultural work and a spouse or other member of the opposite sex who does complementary agricultural labor. We thus expect each adult to do enough agricultural work to support at least four people—himself (or herself) and three or more dependents. This amount of labor will prepare, maintain, and harvest a minimum "individual consumption area" of $(40)(0.025) = 0.1$ ha/yr. (This estimate is based on population average consumption and ignores age- and sex-based differences in amounts consumed.) In addition, the evidence of field measurements and other estimates suggests that the active crop area requiring maintenance (but not preparation or harvesting for that part in excess of the "individual consumption area") is generally at least $(4)(0.1) = 0.4$ ha/yr and may be as high as $(4)(0.2) = 0.8$ ha/yr. Here again is evidence of buffering.

The exclusively male tasks of clearing, burning, and first planting cost a man about 170 hr/ha (taking the male contribution to the preparation of manioc stems for first planting as half the total expenditure for this task). The shared task of preparing manioc stems and the (almost) exclusively female tasks of weeding for first planting and harvesting-replanting cost a woman about 680 hr/ha.

The question of how much weeding is required while the field is under crop, which is needed for this calculation, is not straightforward. On the one hand, new fields ought to be weeded in their entirety during their first year, but sometimes they are not. Simply splitting the 400 mnhr/ha average labor cost of this activity evenly between men and women adds 200 mnhr/ha to each sex's investment.

However, in addition to the replacement land that is newly planted, there is the larger area of actively producing "surplus cushion" land, some of which is also weeded during the year. The best estimate is that the weeding demand of all active agricultural land over the course of a year comes to 75–150 mnhr/ha, discounting for the substantial proportion of actively producing land not weeded in a single year (Beckerman 1987: 79). The mean is close to 110 mnhr/ha.

Estimated agricultural labor requirements follow from this line of reasoning. Men are expected to spend at least 170 + 200 = 370 hr/ha × 0.1 ha preparing replacement land and an additional 110 hr/ha × 0.4 ha weeding "cushion" land. The total is 37 + 44 = 81 hr/yr. Simply dividing by 365 yields a quotient of mean daily agricultural labor of 0.22 hr/day.

Women are expected to spend 680 + 200 = 880 hr/ha × 0.1 ha preparing replacement land and an additional 110 hr/ha × 0.4 ha weeding cushion land. The female total is 132 hr/yr. Its daily equivalent is 0.36 hr/day.

These estimates can be compared to actual observations of agricultural labor, but the latter are not without their difficulties.

One alteration of traditional subsistence that complicates the following discussion was the tentative, missionary-encouraged initiation of commercial agriculture, sometimes with new crops such as maize and beans, and ranching that began almost immediately after contact. In some locations, men cleared land for fields and pastures intended for market production. (Plantains and cattle were the most popular products.) Work invested in these activities was to some extent in addition to labor expended in traditional, purely subsistence agriculture. On the other hand, the new mercantile clearings were also harvested for food for immediate consumption; and much of the money earned from them was intended to be spent on new, "exotic" foodstuffs, such as rice, spaghetti, brick sugar, and cooking oil. To some extent, then, the time spent in commercial agriculture was a replacement for, rather than an addition to, time spent in traditional subsistence agriculture.

Compounding the problem is the scheduling of male swidden agricultural labor in particular, "a drizzle punctuated by cloudbursts" (Beckerman 1987: 85). Because much male labor (especially clearing and first planting) is expended in continuous stretches of full workdays concentrated in a few weeks of the year, it is difficult to distinguish traditional from transitional labor patterns without a longer and more evenly distributed observation period than either of us achieved. The episodic nature of male labor creates a serious sampling problem. Female labor (harvesting in particular), mainly occurring in snatches of an hour or two more or less evenly distributed over the year, can be better sampled from our records.

The male sample from 1970–1972 comprises fourteen men and teenaged boys observed for a total of 554 man-days. Three of these men were observed for a total of 91 days each, ranging over four months. All but two of the others were observed for much shorter periods, ranging from 19 to 25 days, in a single stretch each.

The female sample is made up of nine women and teenaged girls observed for a total of 311 woman-days. Two of the women were observed for 91 days each, and the others for shorter periods, as in the case of the men.

Dealing first with subsistence agriculture alone, the records show that in the two most traditional longhouses, Antraikaira and Culebritaskaira, with no commercial agricultural activities, two men observed for 25 days (in February-March 1971) in the former averaged 0.9 hr/day in agricultural activities, while five men and boys observed for 19 days (in May-June 1972) in the latter spent no time in agriculture.

In the small and traditional but acculturating longhouse of Ashtakakaira, the five men and boys—only three of them resident for the whole 91 days of observation (in October-November 1970, January-February 1971, August 1971, September 1971)—averaged 0.4 hr/day in traditional subsistence agriculture. Over the same period of observation, they averaged 1.0 hr/day in commercial agricultural activities—preparing a field intended mainly to produce plantains for sale.

In the semitraditional longhouse named Shubakbarina, two men observed over 24 days (March 1972) spent no time in traditional agricultural activities but averaged 3.5 hr/day clearing land on which to pasture cattle promised them by a missionary.

Summing for traditional subsistence agriculture exclusively, in 554 man-days of observation, 186 mnhr of this kind of labor were recorded. The quotient is 0.33 mnhr/day, a figure 50 percent higher than the minimal requirement estimated above on the basis of consumption demands and field areas.

Commercial agriculture adds 508 mnhr to the labor total for the 554 man-days of observation, giving a total male agricultural labor investment of 690 mnhr and a daily average of 1.24 mnhr/day.

Turning to female labor in subsistence agriculture, in the two most traditional longhouses we find less of a disparity than exhibited by the men. In Antraikaira two women and a teenaged girl observed for 25 days each averaged 1.1 mnhr/day in agricultural labor; while in Culebritaskaira two women observed for 19 days each averaged 0.9 mnhr/day. Over the 91 days in which Ashtakakaira was observed, the two women who were resident for the entire period averaged only 0.33 mnhr/day in strictly traditional agricultural labor; adding in their slight efforts in commercial agriculture brings the figure up to only 0.37 mnhr/day.

Overall, women were observed to invest an average of 0.43 mnhr/day in traditional agriculture, a figure that rises to only 0.46 mnhr/day when commercial agriculture is added to the traditional variety. The mean observed female labor expenditure, then, is higher than but rather close to the predicted 0.36 mnhr/day.

It should be added that because women's harvesting-replanting labor happens in brief and frequently solitary episodes, often when the men of the longhouse are occupied in some other activity, it is easy for a male ethnographer to miss. These figures for female agricultural labor are minimal and probably undercount the time.

Both the male and the female agricultural labor figures indicate that the Barí budget more time to agriculture than would be needed just to replenish the depletion of fields by crop consumption and field abandonment. The implication again is that in this aspect of subsistence the Barí are not aiming to maximimize the rate of crop production per unit labor, or to minimize the time spent in agriculture.

Nor are they attempting to maximize the amount of food they produce, since they clearly have substantial additional time they could invest in agriculture if they chose. What they are doing, these data suggest, is maintaining a substantial "buffer" of cultivated plants that will probably never be eaten in order to eliminate even the possibility of a shortfall.

It needs to be reiterated that in addition to buffering their own agricultural reserves, the Barí of a given local group are providing for visitors from other groups who may come to sing and exchange with them, often staying for months at a time. The obligations of hospitality and the reproductive opportunities it enables are another motive for maintaining a buffer supply of crops in the ground.

Labor Scheduling

SEASONAL

As mentioned, the best time to clear a field is early in the major dry season, in order to get a good burn at the end of the drying period. Nevertheless, given the Barí's habitual acceptance of an incomplete burn, a tolerance echoed in their major crops, it is possible to clear a field at virtually any time of year. R. Lizarralde recorded a field cleared in May, at the height of the minor rainy season.

Burning and planting tend to be concentrated at the end of the major dry season and the beginning of the rainy season. But, again, they may take place at other times of the year

Weeding and harvesting, the latter especially, occur around the seasons as needed.

DIURNAL LABOR

Agricultural labor takes place in both the morning and the afternoon, without the concentration on one or the other that we note below for fishing and hunting.

MIGRATION

The first two or three weeks after reoccupying a longhouse in the migration cycle are commonly dedicated to getting its garden in shape. Weeding occupies a lot of people's time just after their return. Clearing and planting of a new garden, if one is to be made, are also activities that often take place just after a longhouse is reoccupied.

OTHER SUBSISTENCE ACTIVITIES

In general, agricultural labor fills in around other subsistence activities such as fishing and hunting, which are given priority according to the presence of favorable conditions (e.g., low rivers, clear water) and actual observations of prey animals. However, when people begin to work on a major agricultural project such as clearing or planting a new field, they generally dedicate themselves to that activity until it is completed—unless, of course, a tapir or a herd of peccaries is spotted wandering by. Another exception is the initial weeding of the field of a just reoccupied longhouse, which seems to absorb people's attention for several days after their arrival—unless, of course, a tapir or a herd of peccaries is spotted wandering by.

Labor Costs by Crop

Different crops are typically planted in different episodes of work, on different days. Manioc is usually the first crop planted in a new field. *Musa* is often second, or essentially simultaneous, if planted in the outer ring of a manioc field. The planting episodes for each of these crops fill at least one full workday.

MANIOC

Manioc grows from bits of stem; a Barí farmer plants these at an average density near 0.5 plantings/m² — with a range of only 0.3 plantings/m² to 0.8 plantings/m², in the dozen spots in the half dozen fields where these figures were obtained. (To picture these densities, visualize holes about 10 cm deep, spaced 1.5 to 2 m apart, each containing about half a dozen lengths of stem [Beckerman 1983a: 97]. Plantings in holes up to 40 cm in diameter, and as deep as 30 cm have been observed, but they were quite unusual.) The densest planting occurred in a plot described in field notes as having "bad, very sloping red soil," and may have reflected an attempt to mitigate erosion with compact ground cover. A well-designed, extensive survey of manioc planting densities might find systematic differences with respect to soil type and field age, but such distinctions do not emerge from the small and opportunistic sampling reported here.

BANANAS AND PLANTAINS

Bananas and plantains grow from suckers cut away from the roots of a mature plant. The Barí plant each sucker individually, usually at a density between 0.1 and 0.2 plants/m², that is, with 3 m or more between one plant and the next (Beckerman 1983a: 98). As a *Musa* plant matures, it puts out new suckers around its base, each of which will eventually grow into a mature plant after the original stalk fruits and dies. Thus bananas and plantains both propagate themselves and increase their density in the absence of human attention. The second feature is undesirable, because closely packed *Musa* produce little fruit.

OTHER CROPS

Minor crops include pineapples, sweet potatoes, yams, squash, cotton, onoto, avocado, and *Tephrosia*. These are distributed within a field as described above.

Variation in Field Characteristics

Field Ownership

Individual Barí sometimes make private fields. Motives suggested include a shortage—current or anticipated—in the production of the man's current section(s) of the communal field(s) associated with a longhouse, an assertion of social independence from other members of the local group, and a test of the productivity of the soil in a new area.

The Relationship between Location and Number of Fields

In deciding where to put a field, Barí farmers need to take into account the locations of other features of the landscape: the soils, the longhouse, the other fields, and the rivers (Beckerman 1987). Each longhouse has a set of fields that belong to it—that is, fields its inhabitants clear and tend while they are residing there. (We are not aware of any fields that belong to more than one longhouse in this sense but have not established that such fields never exist.)

SOILS

The major field belonging to every longhouse is the one in the center of which the longhouse stands. Because longhouses are usually built on a rise or spur, the house-surrounding field is typically planted in a thin upland (*terra firme*) soil such as an erosional Tropept or Orthent. Subsidiary fields may be as close as a two-minute walk from one of the longhouse doors or as far as a half day's trek. They occur prominently on the alluvial pockets of Tropaquepts and Eutropepts on the inside turns of river meanders. Nevertheless, a significant number of subsidiary fields are cut in forest growing on upland soils. Pedological mapping and laboratory analysis relating traditional field location to soil type, particularly with respect to colluvial soils, remains to be done. It is clear that the Barí have a sophisticated appreciation of soil differences.

> The Barí recognize many different soil types, but prefer a small set of them for agriculture. *Birida*, a brown alluvial soil with considerable sand, is considered best for all crops. Lacking sufficient *birida*, bananas and plantains may also be planted in *kungbangbaitana*, a wet, less easily worked soil described as "black," although the color is actually a sort of brick-grey. Manioc will rot in *kungbangbaitana*, however, and the second-

ary soil choice for that crop is *bongkita*, a reddish, clayey colluvial soil with small stones in it. (Beckerman 1987: 74)

LONGHOUSE

The distance from the longhouse to its subsidiary fields is variable. Some fields are under 200 m from the nearest longhouse door. The farthest ones surely associated with a house appear to be no more than 4.5 km away, a distance notably less than the 7 km often cited as the maximum distance tropical South Americans are willing to walk to a field (Beckerman 1987: 69). Aerial photographs also record several "secluded" fields with no house visible within 10 km or more. These isolated fields may be distant cultivations of a known house or may represent anticipatory clearings intended to serve a projected longhouse planned to be built close by. In a few cases they may appear to be isolated only because of photo gaps.

In six aerial photographic series shot between 1937 and 1960 and including both the Colombian and Venezuelan parts of Barí territory, seventy-two longhouses and their associated subsidiary fields can be observed, twenty-four of them at altitudes above 200 m and forty-eight at or below that level. The mean distance from the longhouse to the farthest subsidiary field for the lowland houses is 2.18 km, while the mean distance for the highland houses is 2.53 km.

This difference leaves open the possibility that the Barí sometimes deal with decreasing availability of desirable soil at higher altitudes by increasing the distance they are willing to walk to their fields, enlarging the agricultural circumference around the longhouse. However, the small divergence between lowland and highland houses (in some of the photo series there is no significant difference) also suggests that this strategy is often not necessary.

OTHER FIELDS

Subsidiary fields are also located with respect to other subsidiary fields. In this regard, there is a striking difference between fields on alluvial soils and those on erosional soils.

Aerial photographs reveal that alluvial fields typically abut one another, with the border of one forming the beginning of the next, so the complex of fields packs an alluvial pocket on the deposit bank of a river meander. Fields on upland soils almost never display this pattern; in fact, they are usually not even close to each other. Even when they are close, there is always, as far as our observations go, a border of uncut forest between one field and the next. The tall trees presumably serve as a passage for deep forest animals and as a source of seeds and other propagules for re-growth of the field after its abandonment, in addition to providing leaves and other debris to enrich the thin soil of the terra firme agricultural plot.

In the aerial photographic series mentioned above, the average maximum distance from each other reached by the subsidiary fields associated with a given longhouse is 3.5 km in the 1937–1939 series and 3.9 in the 1958 series, both of which cover the Colombian part of Barí territory. In three Venezuelan aerial photographic series, the mean distances between farthest fields is 3.5 km for the 1947 coverage, 3.2 for the 1949 flights, and 3.4 for the 1954 series. In the 1958 Colombian series, which covers the largest number of longhouses, the mean of the maximum distances is 3.6 km for the lowland longhouses and 4.3 km for the highland longhouses, perhaps reinforcing the observation made above that an increased agricultural radius is one means of coping with decreased availability of alluvial soil at higher altitudes.

RIVERS

The distance of subsidiary fields from major rivers is also highly variable. Fields on alluvial soil are perforce adjacent to rivers at most locations in areas where there is significant relief. In flatter regions (now abandoned for decades) alluvial soils are less confined because channel movement and sheet flooding have laid down alluvium in many places distant from current streambeds. Fields on upland soils are similarly untethered to water-courses; traditionally the Barí have not relied on riverine transport to move goods.

ALTITUDE

Barí responses to geographic differences in agricultural productivity (i.e., those stemming from the scarcity of agriculturally desirable soils at higher altitudes) can be discerned in the aerial photographic evidence from Colombia. In this record, there are seventeen longhouses that appear in photographs taken two years or more apart. These longhouses, known thereby to be at least two years old at the time of their appearance on the more recent photographs, reveal a directional relationship between altitude and number of associated subsidiary fields (Beckerman 1976). The houses range in altitude from under 100 m to nearly 600 m, and the mean number of subsidiary fields per longhouse is 8.1.

As expected, the higher the altitude, the greater the number of subsidiary fields associated with a house, suggesting again that as pockets of alluvium become smaller and sparser at higher altitudes it is necessary to plant more nonalluvial fields—fields that have shorter lives and lower productivity than alluvial ones and must therefore be more numerous to maintain a similar supply of cultivated food. The linear equation for the relationship is

$$Y = 0.021X + 2$$

where X is the altitude of the longhouse in m, and Y is the number of associated subsidiary fields, $r^2 = .49$. This relationship, with altitude accounting for half the variance in field number, obtains even though houses built specifically to serve as bases for hunting tend to have fewer fields than others and hunting houses are usually located at higher altitudes.

This evidence suggests, again unsurprisingly, that Barí achieve a steady supply of cultivated food in the face of geographical variation in soil quality simply by increasing their labor investment at higher altitudes.

Size of Fields

HOUSE-SURROUNDING FIELDS

The size of house-surrounding fields can be measured for eighty-eight such fields visible on aerial photographs from numerous series flown over Venezuelan and adjoining Colombian Motilonia at various dates between 1936 and 1964. The house-surrounding fields had a mean area of 0.7 ± 0.43 ha (mean ± standard deviation) and a modal area of 0.6 ha. This issue is discussed in more detail in the Appendix.

SUBSIDIARY FIELDS

In addition to the omnipresent house-surrounding field, traditional long-houses acquire subsidiary fields at various distances. Aerial photographic evidence suggests that the house-surrounding field, by itself, is almost never found to be entirely adequate. Of seventeen longhouses appearing on two or more series of aerial photographs two or more years apart, and thus known to be over two years old, only one had only its house-surrounding field. (When a longhouse reaches the end of its useful life—and that of its house-surrounding field—if it is replaced with another longhouse constructed nearby, then this new longhouse of course is initiated with subsidiary fields already associated with it.)

Although their size is quite variable, a longhouse's subsidiary fields tend to be larger than its house-surrounding field. In aerial photographs taken between 1936 and 1964, the 452 subsidiary fields associated with traditional longhouses ranged between 0.01 and 4.4 ha. Mean size was 0.82 ± 0.74 ha; median was 0.6, and mode was 0.5. These figures are developed in more detail in the Appendix.

Life Span of a Barí Field

Some time after first planting, a Barí field is fallowed. Replanting ceases, all but the most casual and occasional harvesting ceases, and the land is allowed to begin its return to forest. The years between clearing and fallowing are highly variable and difficult to enumerate adequately. It is clear that there are substantial differences in mean life span between house-surrounding and subsidiary fields and between subsidiary fields on alluvial soils and those on nonalluvial soils. Longitudinal data are scarce and ambiguous, however.

The clearest cases are the house-surrounding fields. Aerial photographic evidence, as well as statements from Barí and mission personnel (who tend to be more quantitatively oriented than the Barí themselves), suggest that house-surrounding fields remain in production for the length of occupation of the longhouse: about a decade. There are even a few cases of a longhouse built on the site of a previous longhouse, in the middle of the old house-surrounding field. This field life, markedly longer than the three or four years typical of lowland South American swidden (Beckerman 1987: 71), is due primarily to two unusual features of Barí agriculture. First, the semisedentary Barí harvest their fields only when resident in the longhouse to which the fields pertain. Thus any single Barí field is harvested and replanted at no more than half and perhaps as little as a fifth of the rate endured by a field maintained and utilized by year-round residents. Traditional Barí manioc can, the Barí proudly assert, remain in the ground for over two years without rotting or becoming too fibrous to eat. These considerations, a low rate of harvesting combined with strongly competitive staple crop varieties that remain comestible for years, apply to all Barí fields and primarily concern the matter of weed invasion, one of the two major reasons for the fallowing of swidden fields. It is also the case that because people must pass through the house-surrounding field every time they leave or return to the longhouse, constant monitoring and frequent casual weeding are very easy.

Second, and applying only to the house-surrounding field, is the issue of soil nutrient depletion, the other primary motive for fallowing a swidden plot. Because people are actually living and sleeping in the center of the house-surrounding field, that land receives all their garbage and most of their excreta. Garbage includes ashes from the hearth (often carefully deposited on the hearth group's triplet clumps of sugarcane cane, cotton, and chili peppers) as well as leftovers from meals and the *Heliconia* leaves on which the meals were eaten (this garbage is tossed into the hearth group's wedge of the field with less discrimination). Tergas and Popenoe (1971: 684–688) note that *Heliconia* leaves are rich in phosphorus. Excreta include the products of virtually all the urination and defecation of the women and children resident in a longhouse, and probably about half that of the men. Using standard figures for the weight and composition of human waste products and supposing that fifty people reside in a longhouse for three months of the year, the 0.4 ha house-surrounding field yearly receives over a metric ton of feces and over 60 kg of nitrogen, mostly in the form of urea (Beckerman 1983a). This ongoing fertilization appears to be the way the Barí hold soil nutrient depletion at bay for a decade or more, even in the poor and shallow erosional soils of the house-surrounding fields.

In March 1971 Beckerman spent some time in a highly traditional longhouse, Antraikaira, whose house-surrounding field was, people complained, nearly played out. Most manioc came from a subsidiary field about half a kilometer away. While he was there the inhabitants finished cutting a new subsidiary field on the deposit bank of a river, only 200 m from the longhouse. They allowed it to dry, burned it, and planted it in under a month. When he returned to that location in December 1972 the original longhouse had been burned and sugarcane had been planted on its spot. A new longhouse, complete with new house-surrounding field already bearing mature manioc, had been constructed a few hundred meters away. Aerial photographic evidence reveals that Antraikaira was at least seven years old when it was abandoned.

Subsidiary fields have more variable life spans than house-surrounding fields. The Tropaquepts predominant in the alluvial deposits supporting many subsidiary fields appear in some cases to be able to sustain cultivation for a very long time—perhaps even permanently. Beckerman (1975: 338) once estimated an average life span of fifteen years for alluvial fields in Colombia. Lizarralde observed a similar figure for an alluvial field complex in Venezuela. Even if approximately accurate as a mean, this figure must cover an enormous variance.

For subsidiary fields on nonalluvial soils, Beckerman estimated three years from planting to fallow, with even more variance.

> I have seen fields of this . . . type that were cleared but never planted,
> thus giving a time from establishment to abandonment of 0; I have also
> identified, on aerial photography, fields apparently in colluvium, that
> seem to have been maintained for over 20 years. (Beckerman 1975: 338)

When the Barí abandon a field, they do not plant the elaborate set of tree crops that allows some swidden peoples to extend the useful life of a fallowed field for decades (cf. Denevan et al. 1984, on the Bora of Peru). On the other hand, "plantains and bananas, in particular, will continue putting out new shoots, and new bunches of fruit, until they are choked out" (Beckerman 1987: 71); and the "typical subsidiary field tends . . . to see a gradual centripetal encroachment of new suckers from the [surrounding ring of] bananas after the manioc canopy is broken by harvesting, so some pure stands of bananas may have begun life as fields of manioc surrounded by rings of bananas" (Beckerman 1983a: 90).

Even so, abandoned stands of bananas tend to grow so thick that fruit production rapidly decreases. Barí continue to harvest the available bunch of *Musa* when passing by an abandoned field at an opportune moment (bananas are rapidly consumed by parrots if not promptly harvested), but this exploitation of the fallow stage is casual and infrequent. The same applies to other crops that may survive for a few years into the fallow cycle.

The cases of extraordinarily longevous upland fields are probably occurrences of self-propagating—but dense and largely fruitless—stands of bananas.

Fishing and Hunting: Overview

Although the crops described above supply abundant food calories to their cultivators, that energy is almost all in the form of starch and sugar. As far as anyone knows, the Barí never had beans or equivalent vegetable protein sources among their aboriginal cultivars, although they may have cultivated maize early in the twentieth century (see chapter 3). Animal protein is a necessary complement to their agricultural staples. Three quarters of the animal protein in the Barí diet comes from fishing, the rest from hunting.

With respect to the incentives that guide people's behavior with respect to fishing and hunting, an obvious issue is the benefit of producing a surplus. In this respect, fish and game differ from manioc. The difference is spoilage. Manioc can be preserved in the ground for over a year after maturity. The Barí are able to preserve both fish and game for only a few days, by smoking them. One-day-old smoked fish is delicious, as are most kinds of game. But after three or four days of nightly resmoking, fish take on the consistency of cardboard. The Barí still eat them as long as they do not smell too bad and may also boil these remains before eating to re-hydrate them, but they are no more appetizing than one might think old boiled smoked dried fish would be. Insufficient smoking leads to rotten fish, which the Barí do sometimes eat, after boiling. Although they claim to like the taste, or at least not to mind it, we have noticed that they never go out of their way to prepare rotten fish.

Game can be preserved by nightly smoking for a couple of days longer than fish, perhaps nearly a week. Eventually, it too becomes either stiff and dry or rotten. Sometimes dry smoked meat is boiled to soften it, but rotten meat is often just eaten as is — frequently with consequences that include late-night dashes out of the longhouse.

The upshot of these observations is that more fish or game than can be eaten in four or five days is effectively useless. This circumstance may be one reason that, as we discuss below, jackpot game kills are widely shared within the longhouse, even if accomplished by just one man, and the most skillful fishermen sometimes stop work early.

As mentioned at the beginning of this chapter, fishing and hunting are in complementary distribution. If one computes the mean number of hours spent per man per month in the sum of these activities, averaged over all the adult male members of the hearth group, the figure works out to 125 ± 20 hours, irrespective of month or altitude or location (Becker-man 1983b: 289–292). Nevertheless, the proportion dedicated to fishing versus hunting changes dramatically with month and location, as detailed below.

It is a feature of Barí subsistence that although there is no prohibition against combining traditional fishing and traditional hunting on the same trip, the two do not often take place in the same stretch of time, and when they do the bag from the hunting component is usually small. In our most complete run of hunting and fishing data, for the small lowland long-house of Ashtakakaira (November 1–30, 1970; January 24–February 21, 1971; August 14–29, 1971; and September 4–17, 1971), thirty-four tradi-tional fishing expeditions took place. Of these, five were also occasions on which game was taken, although in no case did the game weigh more than a single kilogram. In the highland longhouse of Antraikaira (Febru-ary 28–March 23, 1971) there were four fishing expeditions, one of which also brought home game. In the lowland longhouse of Shubakbarina (September 7-9, 1970; September 28-October 17, 1971; March 2-27, 1972) there were fourteen fishing expeditions, one of which also took game. In the mission settlement of Sapakdana (February 15-28, 1972) there were six fishing trips, none of which included hunting. In the highland longhouse of Culebritaskaira (May 20-June 7, 1972) there were seven fishing trips, none of which involved hunting. Only the one combined trip made from Antraikaira brought home any substantial amount of game. The fact that 90% of all animal protein acquisition trips are either fishing or hunting but not both simplifies the analysis below.

However, a comparative complication emerges when the question of individual versus group returns is raised. A Barí fisherman pools his catch with that of the other members of his hearth group, both male and female, everyone contributing his or her own catch. It is our shared impression that these individual catches tend to be rather similar in size, at least among married men. Clearly, some men are better fishermen than others. Nevertheless, the better fishermen often appear to work shorter hours than the less skillful, particularly when the fishing is good and the catch abundant. Most fishing trips are collective expeditions, and all the men usually start fishing at the same time. But toward the end of the episode it is common to see some men relaxing on the bank while others remain in the water with their spears. (It may be that because of preservation issues described above, there is little point in taking home more fish than can be eaten in four or five days.)

The great majority of traditional fishing expeditions are collective trips, involving all the adult males (and usually most of the adult females) in the longhouse. Individual and small-group traditional fishing does take place, but it is not common. Summing across the times and locations above, of 62 traditional fishing trips recorded, 16 involved only one or two men, but 13 of those 16 took place in the unusually small longhouse of Ashtakakaira, where they involved a notoriously difficult man who began to have problems getting along with the other residents soon after he moved into the house, over a year after it had been established. His private fishing trips and the small fishing trips of the other men in which he did not participate, were a declaration of his social distance from the other inhabitants. Eventually, he moved out.

The upshot of the usually collective makeup of fishing trips and the similarity of the catch from one man to the next is a leveling that makes it reasonably straightforward, in calculating fishing yields, to project up from the catch of one or two men to that of the entire fishing group. The situation is different for hunting.

There are hunting trips of all sizes, from collective expeditions involving every adult male in the longhouse to individual forays. The distribution of game among hunters is considerably less uniform than that of fish and depends on several considerations. Large quantities of game taken at one time are distributed on return to all the hearth groups in the longhouse, whether hunted by one man or several. Thus a tapir, two or more peccaries, or several spider monkeys find their way to everyone—although it must be said that kills of this magnitude are usually made by an expedition involving multiple men.

On the other hand, even in a joint hunting trip involving every man in a longhouse, if the take is small—say, one or two capuchin monkeys or a single guan—then the prey remains with the man who shot it and is consumed by his hearth group only. Likewise, individual hunting trips, except on the very rare occasions when a single hunter manages a jackpot kill, produce food for that man's hearth group only.

It is not always easy to classify hunting trips by the number participating. Two or three men may leave the longhouse together but return hours apart. Even when they return close together, one man may have no game while the other carries, say, a guan and a spider monkey.

All these considerations make it problematic to project individual or small-group hunting yields to the level of the entire longhouse, as we have done with fishing yields. Our analyses of hunting yields are mainly made with reference to individuals or hearth groups, not whole longhouses.

In the discussions below, only traditional fishing and hunting are analyzed. Fishing with hook and line and with cast nets and hunting with firearms, recent introductions to Barí subsistence, are mentioned only in passing. At the time of Lizarralde's early fieldwork, in the early 1960s, these innovations were still so rare as to be inconsequential. By the time Beckerman began work in 1970, their effect was beginning to be noticeable, although it was still local in time and space.

For instance, when Beckerman arrived at Ashtakakaira on November 1, 1970, he gave away large quantities of fish hooks and fishing line. For the rest of the month the residents took advantage of this windfall. In November, traditional fishing occupied 122 mnhr and produced 28 kg of fish (cleaned weight). Hook and line fishing occupied 71 mnhr and provided 25 kg of fish. However, by the following February traditional fishing at Ashtakakaira occupied 113 mnhr and provided 229 kg of fish, while hook and line fishing had fallen to 23 mnhr and provided only 10 kg of fish. Similarly low contributions for hook and line fishing occurred at the same longhouse in August and September of the same year (Beckerman

1983b: 283–286), indicating that the falling-off was not just a seasonal adjustment, but a lasting decline. The novelty had worn off, and the hooks and line were no longer superabundant.

A similar pattern was observed with the introduction of firearms. When a longhouse first acquired a shotgun, either by means of the visit of a man who already owned one or by means of its acquisition by a regular resident, shotgun hunting occupied a lot of time and produced a lot of game, because a shotgun is a much more effective weapon than a bow. (In Ashtakakaira, in the months enumerated above, traditional hunting with bow and arrow yielded about 70 g of game per mnhr; shotgun hunting yielded 536 g per mnhr.) However, shotguns were still rare in the 1970s, and shells were expensive enough that after the first excitement of possessing firearms hunters who still had shells left were unwilling to use them on anything weighing less than about 1.5 kg and were often reluctant to take them out of the longhouse at all unless there were evidence of substantial game in the neighborhood. Most of our hunting data were gathered in situations where shotguns were absent, but even when present they often went unused. For instance, in the eighty-nine days of observation in Ashtakakaira, a shotgun was used on only eight days and was not even present for 60 percent of all the days. Over the eighty-nine days, traditional hunting produced 41 kg of game, and the single shotgun also produced 41 kg, but 34 kg of the latter were hunted in the first six days after the shotgun owner moved into the house. He rapidly became abstemious with his ammunition. None of the other sites mentioned above had shotguns present except for brief visits by nonresidents.

A note on the quantity and quality of the data in this section is necessary. None of the data we use here were collected with the current analysis in mind. Originally, R. Lizarralde planned to write a general ethnography, but the rapid changes occurring in the 1960s between each visit and the next forced him to focus on settlement pattern and the changes it underwent, as well as Barí history. Beckerman intended an energy flow study emphasizing agricultural activities. These subjects took much if not most of our field time. Thus, although the occurrence of fishing and hunting trips was regularly recorded in our field notes, we often did not accompany these trips or weigh or count the fish and game they produced.

We are aware of two potential biases that resulted, one systematic and one concerning sampling. In terms of fishing returns, there are fewer quantitative data after the first two years in the field for each ethnographer—after 1963 for Lizarralde's Venezuelan notes and after 1971 for Beckerman's Colombian notes. (But the latter's 1983 notes did record quantitative fishing and hunting data.) Also, our time in the field was not distributed evenly or randomly but depended on the academic calendar, funding availability, the plans of other people (both Barí and non-Barí), and competing activities. As shown below (Tables 4.1–4.3), there are data gaps for several months. As far as we know, these gaps and the other deficiencies in our data are not systematic with respect to altitude, location, and so on.

Fishing

A general description of traditional Barí fishing follows.

> The most common kind of Barí fishing expedition involves the building of two stone dams from the upstream and downstream ends of an island to adjacent spots on the shore, and the spearing of the fish trapped between. Less common is the use of spears and sometimes arrows in an undammed stretch of water, often one which has a natural constriction of some kind at one end. This kind of expedition almost always works its way upstream. Rarely used techniques include blocking off muddy puddles with large leaves in order to get fry with *Tephrosia* [a barbasco], and building a substantial pole and palm frond dam across a small tributary in order to get large catfish that try to return to the main river at night, with spears. Except for puddle fishing with *Tephrosia*, all these techniques require clear water, and are greatly favored by low water as well.
>
> Women as well as men participate actively in most fishing expeditions. When dams are constructed, the women build the downstream member of the pair. They also collect a good many loricarids and a few crabs, by guzzling under rocks, and they clean and usually scale all the bocachico taken, on the spot. . . . Some fishing trips are not accompanied by women; and women occasionally make fishing trips of their own, on which they collect whatever aquatic creatures they can grab by hand. (Beckerman 1980a: 76)

Species Taken

By far the most important fish taken by the Barí using traditional methods is the bocachico (*Prochilodus reticulatus*, family Prochilodontidae), accounting for about 70% of the total weight of fish in the diet, whether one computes by whole weight, cleaned weight, or edible portion of cleaned weight. An adult bocachico is about 25 cm long and weighs around 270 g after it is gutted and scaled. The mean yearly per capita consumption (again averaged over both sexes and all ages) of edible portion of bocachico is about 83 kg (which corresponds to a weight in whole, uncleaned fish of about 118 kg [Beckerman 1975: 303; 1980a: 83]). Bocachico consumption averages to about 227 g/day/person, although it varies so greatly from month to month and place to place that we hasten to add that average daily consumption figures are useful only as an index of overall contribution to the diet and convey no information about individual nutrition on a particular day or even a particular month.

Next in importance are various genera and species of the family Loricaridae, the armored catfish, which account for about 20% of the fish eaten, around 65 g/day/person, edible portion (Beckerman 1975: 303; 1980a: 86) and again show considerable temporal and spatial variability— although less than the bocachico. Some Loricarids are about the size of a bocachico or even a little larger, but in rainy months in particular the Barí also collect large numbers of fry-sized Loricarids, smaller than the last two joints of a man's finger.

Smaller contributions to the diet are made by various catfish (family Pimelodidae), which contribute on average about 17 g/day/person, edible portion. Catfish range in size from about 10 cm to as large as a man's calf. There is also a small fish, probably of the genus Piabucina (which is sometimes considered synonymous with the genus Lebiasina) in the family Lebiasinadae that provides about 10 g/day/person; and the tigerfish (*Hoplias malibaricus*, family Erythrinidae), which is about the size of the bocachico and provides about 6 g/day/person (Beckerman 1975: 303; 1980a: 90–91). These fish also show variable availability in time and space.

Even smaller yearly contributions come from fishes such as rays (*Potamotrygon magdalanae* and *P. yepezi*, family Potomtrygonidae) and knifefish (four species in the family Sternopyginae) which can be up to 1 m long.

Places Fished and Techniques Used

Each longhouse has associated with it a number of known, named fishing spots, places in a river where people habitually build the double weirs that characterize the most common and productive kind of Barí fishing. The great majority of these traditional fishing spots are places where the river parts around an island and one arm can be cut off between a pair of weirs. People also sometimes build lateral weirs that fence off a shallow area adjacent to the riverbank, in the absence of an island. The number, proximity, and area of these weir sites vary with altitude and with the specific location of the longhouse. There are also stretches of river unsuitable for weirs that are known for being productive for open water fishing. These places, too, vary according to altitude and longhouse specifics.

A more detailed discussion of fishing techniques than given above may be useful. Traditional Barí fishing is done with spears, arrows, and hands. Spear fishing is the most common and most dramatic technique. A Barí fish spear is a flexible wand of black palm wood, pointed at one end, 2 to 4 m long, occasionally fitted with a handle when it becomes shortened from repeated resharpening. It is as thin as a woman's finger, only a little over 1 cm in diameter.

Holding this spear toward the middle, palm upward, poised at his side, a Barí fisherman stalks the shallow, sunny water of a river. Spotting a bocachico, he makes a rapid thrust, immediately followed, if he makes a hit, by two or three more thrusts to run the fish up the spear so it cannot wriggle off. It is difficult to describe the skill, speed, and grace involved. A bocachico is a fast-swimming, scaly fish only about 25 cm long. Unless it is speared in its center of gravity—a spot smaller than a quarter—the spear will flip the fish around but not penetrate its scales. With the point of a flexible spear as much as 3 m from his hand, adjusting for the refraction of the water, the fisherman must hit a spot a little larger than an nickel on what is often a moving target. Beckerman claims the movement is so fast that it took him a year just to be able to see it correctly.

Boys accompany their fathers and attempt spear fishing as early as six or eight years old. They do not achieve competence until their early or middle teens. Men in their twenties appear to be most skillful, and by their late thirties their reflexes are clearly not what they once were. Older men, and younger men who are not feeling well, often use a bow and fishing arrow (essentially a short fish spear hafted in a piece of arrow cane,) stalking for hovering fish and then letting the spring of the bow provide the speed that is no longer in their arms.

Two rare fishing techniques take advantage of special conditions. Rivers on the northern edge of Motilonia where rainfall is least, such as the río Negro, may be reduced to hardly more than a series of large puddles linked by a trickle at the end of the dry season. These puddles, though dark and muddy, can be fished by constructing a platform over them and then stabbing blind from the platform into the opaque water. Big bottom-dwelling fish can be taken this way. Farther south there is a time of year at the end of the minor dry season when large catfish swim upstream into small creeks and then descend at night. One can dam the small streams with poles and leaves and then spear the catfish by torch-light as they try to get back downstream.

A third major traditional fishing technique uses nothing more than the human hand. Called "guzzling" in Appalachia, it is the art of mov-ing the hand underwater very, very slowly toward a stationary fish, then suddenly grabbing it. Women use this technique more than men, but it is used by both sexes. Loricarids both large and (especially) small are often taken this way, as are other fish who present themselves opportunistically. Freshwater crabs and turtles also succumb to guzzling from time to time.

In the pursuit of Loricarids and other fish that tend to hide in crevices, either spearing or grabbing may be accompanied by the use of a barbasco (fish poison), *Tephrosia sinapu* (Leguminoseae). The roots of this culti-vated plant are pounded between rocks and then stuck into the cranny where the fish has taken refuge, where the sap oozes into the water. The fish is not stunned, as is usual in the use of barbasco, but is disturbed enough that it flees its niche and makes itself available to a spear or a hand.

The same barbasco is sometimes used to poison puddles in tiny streams, particularly where there is a concentration of *Piabucina*. The puddles are completely dammed off with *Heliconia* leaves, and in this case the barbasco actually stuns the fish, which can then be collected. This kind of fishing is a rare fallback technique, used when larger streams and rivers are opaque and unfishable.

It is crucial to realize that all these fishing techniques (with the excep-tion of the blind stabbing in the río Negro) require visual contact. Except under the most extraordinary conditions, one cannot spear or grab a fish one cannot see. Normal Barí fishing is possible only when the rivers are clear—that is, when it has not rained for at least a day.

A Barí man goes fishing about one hundred days out of the year, usually accompanied by his wife and children. (Women and children accompany double weir fishing trips consistently, although for any given trip some women in a longhouse may opt out, and women may absent themselves entirely from open water expeditions). These fishing trips, with or with-out the construction of weirs, last an average of about six hours, with trips to more distant locations of course taking longer.

The part of a fishing trip when people are actually in the water, spear-ing or grabbing fish, begins around noon or late morning at the earliest, although if the fishing spot is a distant one people may have to leave the longhouse early in order to reach it by noon. We suspect there are two reasons for this timing. Waiting until midday allows the river time to clear from nocturnal rainfall upstream. (Rivers clear quickly in northern Motilonia because of the steep slope of the river courses there; lower gradient waters to the south take longer.) Also, vertical light is best for seeing into the water.

An inevitable question is why the Barí fish using these techniques and patterns. Certainly not all lowland South American peoples follow these methods. In many other societies, harpoons are important traditional fishing tools. In some, palm fiber nets are employed and may have been used in pre-Columbian times. Very often, barbasco is used to stun the fish so that they float to the surface of the river. In most lowland societies fishing is typically done from canoes. Yet the Barí have no harpoons (except for harpoon arrows that are used only for terrestrial game, never for fish), no aboriginal nets, and no canoes. Their barbasco is used as an irritant, to make fish flee their hiding places, not to stun them.

In many other lowland societies, the typical fishing trip involves one man, or two men in a canoe. Barí fishing is usually a group activity. Furthermore, the characteristic method of Barí fishing, the double-weir spear fishing trip, although known from other parts of lowland South America and the world, is not particularly common.

We believe that the distinct Barí fishing kit of artifacts and labor organization is best explained by the nature of the rivers and the fish in their homeland. The watercourses of Motilonia are for the most part relatively shallow, fast flowing, stony bottomed, clear-water rivers. They provide multiple locations where a man can stand in a stream shallow enough that his eyes can look directly down into the water and his spear arm can whisk through the air. And the rivers in those locations are often crystal clear, their beds strewn with cobbles and boulders suitable for building a weir.

Complementarily, the major fish taken by the Barí, the bocachico, are herbivores that graze on the sun-loving algae encrusting cobbles in shallow, sunny stretches of water. Because the algae do not grow well in deep water where sunlight does not penetrate fully, the feeding ecology of the bocachico obliges them to spend a lot of time in the shallow river locations where they are vulnerable to double-weir spear fishing. Furthermore, the bocachico is a schooling fish, so when they are present they are typically present in abundance, although they are individually small.

This situation presents two incentives for group fishing. First, building the weirs requires considerable man-hours. A single individual could not get them built during daylight hours and still have enough time to fish (Beckerman 1983c). Second, it is likely that having many men fishing in the same spot improves the rate at which fish are speared, because the latter have to expend effort in constant evasion and tire quickly (Beckerman 1991a). As a young fisherman explained the course of a double weir fishing trip, "At the beginning, the bocachico move nimbly, but later they get sort of slow and stupid."

The final piece of the puzzle is that there are no really big fish in Motilonia (nothing to compare with the 3 m pirarucú of the Amazon, for instance). The largest are knifefish, up to a meter in length but slender and slow, and the few big catfish, some of which may approach a meter; both are found only in large, deep rivers. Both are scaleless and not so big that they cannot be taken with a slender Barí spear. There is nothing in the waters of Motilonia that requires a harpoon or offers a big reward to an individual fisherman.

Distribution of Fish

All the members of each hearth group contribute their fish to a common pool. The young married men and older teenaged boys usually make the biggest catch, followed by older men, young boys, and women. This ranking is accurate for most trips (when bocachico, other fast-swimming fish, and the larger Loricarids are the main prey), but women's contribution sometimes equals or passes men's when the catch is dominated by the smaller Loricarids.

Fish are not often shared outside the hearth group. However, close examination of this issue is obnubilated by Barí practices of courtesy. Gifts of food are made with exquisite discretion. In the middle of a meal, while all the people in the house are gathered around the *Heliconia* leaves set between each hearth and the hammocks of the people who use it, a small child is sent to carry a portion of food — sometimes wrapped in leaves — from one hearth group to a specific individual in another. The name of the recipient is whispered to the child, who trots silently off and hands over the package without a word; it is the height of bad manners to stare at or comment on the gift. Unless the child comes from or goes to an immediately adjacent hearth, it is usually impossible to observe both ends of the transfer without being more boorish than either of us was willing to be. We are certain that interhearth group gifts of fish are considerably less common than transfers of game, but as to their absolute frequency or the magnitude of the quantities involved, we confess ignorance.

Variation in Fishing Productivity

OVER THE DECADES

The data on variation in fishing returns by season and by altitude must be considered in the context of a conspicuous decline in fishing returns over the decades since the 1960 peaceful contact with the Barí (Fig. 4.1). In fact, by the 1990s we were afraid that the bocachico was near extinction in the Maracaibo Basin. As mentioned in chapter 2, an average of about 8 million bocachico a year were reported caught commercially in the southwestern corner of Lake Maracaibo in the years 1967–1971, and the harvest continued and probably increased in subsequent years. This southwestern population was the one exploited upstream by the Barí. Compounding commercial overfishing was the draining of the swamps where the young fish developed and riverine pollution due primarily to agricultural runoff. Bocachico were rare to absent in Motilonia in the

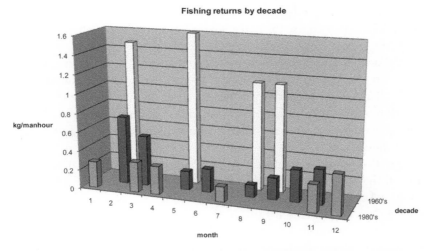

Fig. 4.1. Decline in traditional fishing productivity over the decades. Returns in kg/mnhr are distinguished by decade, 1960s, 1970s, and 1980s, but are averaged between lowland (≤ 200 m) and highland (> 200 m) longhouses in each decade, for the months of May in the 1960s and March in the 1970s. Disaggregated returns are given in Tables 4.2a, 4.2b, and 4.3. The data for the 1980s include two (of three) fishing trips in March in which a motorized canoe was used, reducing travel time; in addition, casting nets were used on those trips, increasing the rate at which fish were taken. The decline in return is clear, despite the inclusion of these data for technologically enhanced fishing.

1990s. Nevertheless, recent observations by M. Lizarralde suggest that the bocachico may now be making a comeback in the region.

SEASONAL AND ALTITUDINAL VARIATION

As the rivers rise and fall, muddy and clear, and as the bocachico migrate back and forth from the swamps and the lake, the productivity of fishing varies significantly. The Barí respond by adjusting the amount of time they dedicate to that activity.

To determine how fishing productivity varies seasonally, it is necessary to control for altitude since fish size and abundance vary significantly with stream size. In order to keep samples as large as possible, we have chosen to make only a bipartite division between lowland houses (at or under 200 m altitude) and highland houses (above 200 m). It is also necessary to control for channel distance from Lake Maracaibo, because it is to be expected that the presence and abundance of bocachico will be more seasonal on the upstream borders of its migratory range than it will be near the river mouths and swamps that are the center of the range. Distance from the lake is an independent variable, conceptually unrelated to altitude, although of course the two are correlated in this roughly semicircular basin.

Although it is the migratory bocachico that show the greatest seasonal variation (Table 4.1, Fig. 4.1), the issue of greatest nutritional importance to the Barí is the productivity of fishing as an activity and not the composition of the catch. Fishing for Loricarids and other nonmigratory fish flattens to some extent the oscillations caused by the comings and goings of the bocachico.

Month-by-month data for overall fishing productivity, bocachico and all the other species combined, collected over the years for lowland (Tables 4.2a, 4.2b) and highland (Table 4.3) longhouses, reveal this pattern. When the lowland data from the 1970s (the only really substantial data set) are aggregated for better statistical control and compared with the mean numbers of days per month that the Barí go fishing (Table 4.4), a pattern emerges. Barí fish most when fishing returns per manhour are highest. Spottier lowland data from the 1960s accord with this pattern (Table 4.5), although they imply a greater investment in fishing overall, a finding consistent with the greater yields recorded for fishing in the 1960s (see Fig. 4.1) before commercial exploitation and the draining of the swamps around the mouth of the Catatumbo had seriously depleted the bocachico population. Similarly spotty lowland data from the 1980s show the same pattern (Table 4.6).

Table 4.1. Bocachico fishing returns, kg/mnhr, for longhouses visited in 1970–1972 (adapted from Beckerman 1980a)

	Culebritaskaira alt. 350 m	Shubakbarina alt. 100 m	Ashtakakaira alt. 100 m	Sapakdana alt. 80 m
January			0.49	
February			0.63	1.00
March		0.52		
April				
May				
June	0.27			
July				
August			0.38	
September		0.11	0.23	
October		0.08		
November			0.12	
December				

Note: These figures pertain only to fishing trips that were targeted primarily at bocachico and whose catch was mostly bocachico. They exclude fishing trips in which other species were the sole or main quarry.

Data for the higher altitudinal zone during the 1970s are too spotty to be more than suggestive (Table 4.6,) but they do not contradict this pattern. There is only one record from a highland longhouse during the 1960s: in an observation period of four days, the people of Ohbadyá made two fishing trips, one of which yielded a return of 0.89 kg/mnhr; the catch for the other was not quantified.

The upshot of the way the Barí adjust their time investments to the seasonally varying generosity of the rivers is that a man concentrates nearly half the roughly hundred days per year he goes fishing in the months of January through March, the major dry season. A bit less than a quarter of those fishing days fall in October through December, the major rainy season. Of the remaining fishing days, about a fifth fall in April-June, the minor rainy season, and the smallest number in July-September, the minor dry season. It will not do, nevertheless, to insist on this distribution as comprehensive and constant. It was reckoned largely from data from lowland settlements. Insofar as a local group of Barí moves between lowland and highland longhouses—a common pattern—or occupies only highland settlements, it is to be expected that the numbers will change somewhat. However, we have no evidence that contradicts the general

Table 4.2a. Traditional fishing returns by month, counting labor of both men and women, for lowland settlements in the 1970s and 1980s

	Jan.	Feb.	Mar.	Apr.	July	Aug.	Sept.	Oct.	Nov.
Ashtakakaira	.52	.72				.13	.23		.37
alt. 100 m	1971	1971				1971	1971		1970
175 km	n=5	n=17				n = 2	n = 1		n = 4
Sapakdana		1.00							
alt. 80 m		1972							
150 km		n = 1							
Phatuikaira				.21	.16				
alt. 150 m				1983	1983				
200 km				n = 2	n = 2				
Shubakbarina			.72				.05	.34	
alt. 100 m			1972				1971	1971	
150 km			n = 4				n = 1	n = 3	
Shubakbarina			.62						
alt. 100 m			1983						
150 km			n = 1						

Note: Left column, top to bottom, identifies the name of the settlement, its altitude, and its approximate distance from the lake edge swamps. Each cell contains (top to bottom) the mean return in kg/mnhr, the year in which the observations were made, and the number of fishing expeditions contributing to the mean. The mean is a time-weighted average, the total weight of fish acquired by an individual fisher in the observed trips divided by the total number of hours s/he spent on those trips. Only months in which fishing data were collected are shown.

pattern: the majority of effort is concentrated in the most productive times of the year (Table 4.7).

Implications

This pattern speaks to three of the five questions about Barí subsistence raised at the beginning of this chapter. In concentrating their fishing efforts when they are most productive, the Barí deal with temporal variation in fish abundance by adjusting their own time investments. They also reveal the relative affluence provided by their environment and subsistence practices. If the Barí, like some tribal peoples, were constantly on the edge of hunger, they would have to work the longest hours during the

Table 4.2b. Traditional fishing returns by month, counting labor of both men and women, for lowland settlements in the 1960s

	Feb.	Apr.	May	Aug.	Sept.
Otaká		.66	2.00		
alt. 160 m		1963	1964		
175 km		n = 6	n = 2		
Ikiakaira			1.52		
alt. 120 m			1965		
150 km			n = 1		
Catalaura				1.13	1.13
alt. 50 m				1966	1966
150 km				n = 2	n = 1
Kirongdakai	1.47				
alt. 60 m	1966				
50 km	n = 1				

Note: Left column, top to bottom, identifies the name of the settlement, its altitude, and its approximate distance from the lake edge swamps. Each cell contains (top to bottom) the mean return in kg/mnhr, the year in which the observations were made, and the number of fishing expeditions contributing to the mean. The mean is a time-weighted average, the total weight of fish acquired by an individual fisher in the observed trips divided by the total number of hours s/he spent on those trips. Only months in which fishing data were collected are shown.

months when fishing was the worst in order to get enough to eat. The question of whether they are food maximizers or time minimizers cannot be definitively answered by these data, but an indication does emerge.

In studies of animal behavioral ecology, the food maximizer versus time minimizer question is resolved experimentally. One enriches the environment, thereby increasing the rate at which the foraging animal obtains food. If the animal increases the amount of time it forages in response to this enrichment, it is a food maximizer; if it decreases its amount of foraging time, it is a time minimizer.

Anthropologists do not perform experiments, of course, but if we take the seasonal variation in fishing productivity as the natural equivalent of

Table 4.3. Traditional fishing returns by month, counting labor of both men and women, for highland settlements in the 1960s and 1970s

	Mar.	May	June
Ohbadyá		.89	
alt. 300 m		1966	
		n = 1	
Culebritaskaira		.20	.25
alt. 350 m		1972	1972
275 km		n = 3	n = 4
Antraikaira	.12		
alt. 600 m	1971		
200 km	n = 2		

Note: Left column, top to bottom, identifies the name of the settlement, its altitude, and its approximate distance from the lake edge swamps. Each cell contains (top to bottom) the mean return in kg/mnhr, the year in which the observations were made, and the number of fishing expeditions contributing to the mean. The mean is a time-weighted average, the total weight of fish acquired by an individual fisher in the observed trips divided by the total number of hours spent on those trips. Only months in which fishing data were collected are shown.

an experimental manipulation, then it follows that the observation that the Barí fish most when the fishing environment is richest is consistent with their being food maximizers.

Also consistent with this inference (although based on a data set too small to be conclusive) is a calculation made on records from the lowland Colombian longhouses visited in the 1970s, the lengthiest data run we have for fishing trips where we know the duration of each phase of the trip. In the nine timed fishing expeditions that took place in January–March, the fishing season with the highest returns, the segments of the trips that consisted of actual fishing, discounting travel time and dam building time, averaged 228 minutes. In the four timed fishing trips that took place in October–December, the season with the lowest returns, the actual fishing time averaged only 129 minutes.

A comparison of Tables 4.2a and 4.2b with 4.3, and of 4.4, 4.5, and

4.6 with 4.7, suggests but does not definitively demonstrate an answer to another question. It seems that the Barí deal with spatial variation in fish abundance by fishing less when they are in high altitude longhouses—houses whose neighboring rivers are smaller and farther from the swamps than those near the lowland settlements. Taking all these conclusions together, the remaining question, the matter of whether there is buffering, appears to be answered in the negative. There is no evidence that the Barí sacrifice any fraction of the efficiency of fishing in order to increase its reliability. The implication appears to be that they do not feel that fishing is an activity with high risk attached to it.

Table 4.4. Fishing returns per man-hour and mean fishing days per month for lowland houses in the 1970s, aggregated by three-month season

	Jan.–Mar.	Apr.–June	July–Sept.	Oct.–Dec.
Mean return, kg/mnhr	0.62	no data	0.14	0.36
Mean number fishing days/month	15.5	6.1	4.8	7.5
Observation days	71	20	57	53
Fishing trips observed	36	4	9	13
Trips with weighed catch	27	0	4	7

Note: Mean number of fishing days per month is calculated by multiplying fishing trips observed/observation days by 30.5.

Table 4.5. Fishing returns per man-hour and mean fishing days per month for lowland houses in the 1960s, aggregated by three-month season

	Jan.–Mar.	Apr.–June	July–Sept.	Oct.–Dec.
Mean return, kg/mnhr	1.47	1.06	1.13	no data
Mean number fishing days/month	16.3	10.6	9.0	10.3
Observation days	15	45	27	6
Fishing trips observed	8	14	8	2
Trips with weighed catch	1	3	3	0

Note: Mean number of fishing days per month is calculated by multiplying fishing trips observed/observation days by 30.5.

Table 4.6. Fishing returns per man-hour and mean fishing days per month for lowland houses in the 1980s, aggregated by three-month season

	Jan.–Mar.	Apr.–June	July–Sept.	Oct.–Dec.
Mean return, kg/mnhr	.30	.25	.16	no data
Mean number fishing days/month	9.2	4.4	3.2	no data
Observation days	10	21	19	0
Fishing trips observed	3	3	2	0
Trips with weighed catch	3	3	2	0

Note: Mean number of fishing days per month is calculated by multiplying fishing trips observed/observation days by 30.5. Two of the three fishing trips made in Jan.–Mar. used a motorized canoe to reach the fishing spot and include some fish (in both cases less than half) taken with casting nets. The mean return in kg/mnhr for these months would be somewhat lower if it were adjusted for these nontraditional practices, but we have refrained from convoluted tinkering with these data.

Table 4.7. Fishing returns per man-hour and mean fishing days per month for highland houses in the 1970s, aggregated by three-month season

	Jan.–Mar.	Apr.–June	July–Sept.	Oct.–Dec.
Mean return, kg/mnhr	.12	.23	no data	no data
Mean number fishing days/month	6.6	11.2	no data	no data
Observation days	23	19	0	0
Fishing trips observed	2	6	0	0
Trips with weighed catch	2	6	0	0

Note: Mean number of fishing days per month is calculated by multiplying fishing trips observed/observation days by 30.5.

Reliability

Other data support this inference. Despite its predictable seasonal oscillation, fishing is a rather reliable activity. In our database of ninety-five traditional fishing trips recorded between 1961 and 1983, there was only one trip that produced no fish at all, and it was short. Even minimal returns were relatively rare. Of the seventy-two trips at all locations from

1961 to 1983 for which the recorded data permit a calculation of the individual hourly return rate, the maximum was 1.93 kg/mnhr and the mean was 0.51 kg/mnhr (standard deviation = .44).[1] When these figures are compared with parallel calculations (below) for hunting, the relative reliability of fishing stands out.

Hunting

All traditional Barí hunting is done with bow and arrow. The blowgun is unknown and spears are used only for fish. (Once in a while someone scares up a lapa in the course of a fishing expedition, and the rodent, true to its semiaquatic habits, dives into the river. It may then be stabbed with a fish spear.) There are two kinds of bows and six kinds of arrows, specialized for particular kinds of prey (Beckerman 1994).

Barí participate both in planned hunting trips and in spontaneous hunts that erupt when someone spots game in the course of another activity (travel, gathering, garden work, etc.) that has taken a man or men into the forest. Women do not accompany planned hunts. If women are present when a spontaneous hunt erupts, they sit by the side of the trail and doze until the men get back.

Spontaneous hunts are much less common than planned ones. We have found it useful to divide the latter into three rough classes, although the Barí do not make this distinction, and not all hunts fit unambiguously into the classification.

One kind of hunt we call the "early morning jaunt." The most frequent participants are teenaged boys and younger men. They slip out of the longhouse before dawn, carrying bow and arrows. Sometimes just one leaves, but often several depart at nearly the same time. They usually return independently, however. Usually they return home an hour or so after sunrise but sometimes hours later. Unless they are very late, the other members of the hearth group hold breakfast for them.

The express purpose of the early morning jaunt is to pick off night-roosting birds before they fly away for the day and to try one's luck with nocturnal mammals such as the agouti as they return to their dens. However, our impression is that these forays are as much scouting expeditions as full-fledged hunting trips. They seldom bring in a significant amount of meat, but an occasional consequence of the early morning jaunt is a full-scale hunting trip later the same day in response to a sign of game spotted before dawn. It may also be that for people such as the Barí, who were hunted for centuries as if *they* were game, a predawn patrol for enemies was a wise precaution.

Another type of hunt is the individual or small-group foray that takes place anytime after breakfast, including the hours around sunset. Men seldom leave the longhouse together for these excursions, but they may join forces later. (The Barí are superb trackers. It is no more a challenge for a Barí hunter to find another in the forest than it is for an American undergraduate to follow Mapquest instructions to a shopping mall.) Various motives may inspire these forays, ranging from hunger to a desire to impress potential in-laws to boredom. These hunts, like the early morning jaunts, may also serve as scouting expeditions. If a tapir or a herd of peccaries is spotted, it is likely that someone will sprint back to the longhouse to alert the other men, who will then join the hunt.

The third kind of hunt is one that involves all the men in the house and is often planned and to some extent directed by the *istoashina*, the younger "chief," of the longhouse. It may be initiated because game has been spotted earlier or may be a response to a lack of meat in the house, irrespective of whether anyone has seen tracks or spoor recently. It usually begins in midmorning and almost always begins before midafternoon—unless word comes back to the longhouse that large game has just been glimpsed, in which case all the men tear off at a dead run no matter how few hours of daylight are left. On these hunts men often leave the longhouse within a few minutes of each other and return almost simultaneously.

Species Taken

Hunting is an activity in which you never know what you are going to get. The return for a day's work may be a jackpot kill but more often is nothing. Even so, there are regularities over the long term. Four families of warm-blooded animals provide over 80% of hunted meat: Tayassuidae (peccaries), Cebidae (monkeys), Dasyproctidae (agoutis and lapas), and Cracidae (guans). However, the most common single species taken by the Barí is the local squirrel, *Sciurus granatensis* (see Table 2.1).

Below we rank the major bird and mammal prey species, as we did with the fish, in terms of their contribution to the diet. However, because of the smaller overall quantity and more pronounced variability of hunting returns, in this case we add the warning that this ranking, extrapolated from Beckerman's 1970–1972 fieldwork, is not drawn from a sufficiently long run of observations as to inspire confidence in its statistical reliability.

We estimate that the average Barí, the same sexless teenager perching in the center of gravity of the population pyramid who was invoked above, consumes more meat from peccaries than from any other birds or mammals—about 27 g per day, averaged over decades. There are two species in Motilonia, the collared peccary (*Pecari tajacu*, Tayassuidae) and the white-lipped peccary (*Tayassu pecari*). The former is smaller than the latter (about 14.5 kg butchered weight, on average, vs. about 16 for the individuals observed, which include juveniles) and runs in smaller herds that range less widely.

The Barí eat four species of monkey. In order of contribution to the diet, these are the spider monkey (*Ateles hybridus*), the howler monkey (*Alouatta seniculus*), the capuchin monkey (*Cebus albifrons*), and the owl or night monkey (*Aotus griseimembra*). Together, they provide something like 24 g of meat per day.

There are two large rodents that make a considerable contribution to the diet: the agouti (*Dasyprocta punctata*, Dasyproctidae) and the lapa or paca (*Cuniculus paca*, by some authors included in the Dasyproctidae, by others given its own family, Agoutidae). Their average joint contribution in grams per day is probably close to that of the combined primates.

There are a good number of South American relatives of the turkey with an honored place in Barí cuisine. Hilty (2003), in the standard book on the birds of Venezuela, notes six that are well documented in Motilonia: the rufous-vented chachalaca (*Ortalis ruficauda*), the band-tailed guan (*Penelope argyrotis*), the crested guan (*Penelope purpurascens*), the wattled guan (*Aburria aburri*), the yellow-knobbed curassow (*Crax daubentoni*), and the northern helmeted curassow (*Pauxi pauxi*), all in the family Cracidae. Together (and perhaps joined by less well attested species) they contribute about 16 g of meat per person per day.

Squirrels (*Sciurus granatensis*, Sciuridae), although they are the most common single game species taken, weigh so little that their input to the diet is only on the order of 2 g a day.

The most desirable game from the point of view of the Barí is the tapir (*Tapirus terrestris*, Tapiridae), the largest mammal in South America (about 150 kg) and one of the tastiest. However, this solitary animal is taken so rarely that it barely figures in our records of successful hunts.

Other game animals—and there are dozens more—are either so small (e.g., parrots) or so infrequently taken (armadillos, brocket deer, iguanas) that their average contribution to the diet as an individual species is also minimal, although taken together they make a significant contribution.

Places and Techniques

For all three types of foray and for most species of prey, the activities of the hunt are drawn from the same repertoire. Like most active foragers, the Barí divide their time behaviorally into searching and pursuing (which includes killing). Until a prey animal is actually sighted, a Barí hunter moves quietly through the woods, which he reads like a detective novel. A few husks of fruit on the forest floor indicate that a troop of spider monkeys was feeding in the canopy two days ago. A dead leaf pressed into the soil reveals that a brocket deer crossed the trail earlier in the day. A distant buzz is the call of a wattled guan. A faint sulfurous smell signals the recent passage of a herd of peccaries.

When luck combines with skill, the hunter spots the prey and the pursuit begins. The hunter focuses his attention on a single animal—or a single troop or herd, as the case may be—and ignores the other signs of the forest. The strategy of the pursuit depends on the animal. With arboreal game, the trick is to get in position for an unobstructed shot. Monkeys move rather slowly through the treetops, even when they fleeing for their lives. They can be followed, but if they are clever enough to remain high and to keep leaves and branches between themselves and the hunters' arrows, they are reasonably safe. Guans, which are often at about the same tree level as monkeys, present a similar challenge—obliging the hunter to keep his eye on the prey while maneuvering around the forest floor to find his shot.

With peccaries, in contrast, the trick is to turn the herd and scare it into milling around in a panic. If peccaries stampede they are fast enough that they may get clean away; if they turn on the hunters, they are dangerous. With the solitary tapir, the idea is for some men to drive this very fast, very strong beast into an ambush set up by other men. Just trying to chase it down almost never works.

Game can be taken anywhere. It is not terribly rare for a bird or a squirrel to blunder into the immediate vicinity of a longhouse. On the other hand, for serious hunting, one ought to travel to a place unblemished by recent human presence—one reason for the cycling of the local group around its various bohíos.

Some informants have told us that the conceptual wedge of property whose apex is at a man's hearth within the longhouse and whose arms extend outward to encompass the hammocks of his hearth group and the slice of the house-surrounding field where his crops grow runs farther into the rain forest to take in an area of forest that is his personal hunting ground. Others have said that one may hunt wherever one wishes. Everyone agrees that once game has been located, a man may follow wherever it flees.

Distribution of Game

As is the case with fish, all the members of each hearth group contribute their small game to a common pool, and there it stays. In the case of large game or abundant medium-sized animals such as several of the larger monkeys, the meat is shared outside the hearth group. If a collective hunt takes down half a dozen spider monkeys, for instance, or a couple of peccaries, the meat is divided on the trail, and each hunter carries his portion home to his own hearth. If large game is taken by an individual, the hunter himself distributes his kill on arrival at the longhouse to all the hearths, handing a cut to each woman cooking for her group that night. Although this distribution is made quickly and silently, without any ostentation, it is not as cryptic as the distribution of cooked food, and one is aware of a quiet pride on the part of the hunter and occasional admiring glances from the women.

Variation in Hunting Productivity

OVER THE DECADES

Although our data are insufficiently abundant for statistical reliability on this point, a comparison of Tables 4.8 and 4.9 suggests that there was a decline in traditional hunting productivity, analogous to but not as steep as the decline in fishing productivity from the 1960s to the 1980s.

Seasonal and Altitudinal Variation

Again, the data are inadequate for statistical confidence. The 1970s data (Table 4.8) are consistent with the proposition that hunting is more productive at higher altitudes, which we believe is correct. However, the sample sizes are small, and there are no high altitude data from the 1960s (Table 4.9) to support or undermine this proposition.

With regard to whether the amount of effort dedicated to hunting

Table 4.8. Traditional hunting returns by month in the 1970s

Location	Jan.	Feb.	Mar.	May	July	Aug.	Sept.	Oct.	Nov.
Ashtakakaira	.03	.15				.07	.05		.07
alt. 100 m	n = 2	n = 7				n = 11	n = 10		n = 22
1970–1971	d = 8	d = 21				d = 16	d = 14		d = 30
Shubakbarina			.12					.14	
alt. 100 m			n = 8					n = 8	
1971–1971			d = 26					d = 17	
Sapakdana		.14							
alt. 80 m		n = 2							
1972		d = 14							
Antraikaira			.27						
alt. 600 m			n = 12						
1971			d = 23						
Culebritaskaira				.20					
alt. 350				n = 5					
1972				d = 12					

Note: Left column, top to bottom, identifies the name of the settlement, its altitude, and the year(s) in which the observations were made. Each cell contains (top to bottom) the mean return in kg/mnhr, the number of hunting expeditions contributing to the mean, and the number of days of observation in the indicated month. The mean is a time-weighted average, the total butchered weight of game acquired by an individual hunter in the measured trips divided by the total number of hours he spent hunting. Both lowland and highland settlements are represented. Because of the high variability of hunting returns, only observation runs of at least eight days, with multiple hunting trips, are included here. Only months in which hunting data were collected are noted in column headings

varies with altitude, the situation is again inconclusive. In twenty-three days in March 1971, the highland longhouse of Antraikaira (600 m) recorded hunting at a rate that projects to 15 days/mo, while the lowland longhouses in that season around that date averaged 9.7 days/month (Table 4.8). In nineteen days in May and June 1972, the highland longhouse of Culebritaskayra (350 m) recorded hunting at a rate that translates to 12.8 days/mo, compared to 13.9 for the lowland houses in that season in the early 1960s (Tables 4.8, 4.10).

The evidence is a bit more convincing on the question of seasonal variation. The data do not suggest regular seasonal variation, only high overall variability (Table 4.10). This suggestion is bolstered by an analysis of day-to-day hunting returns. Of the 176 individual and collective hunting trips from 1964 to 1972 for which we have both game records and hunting times, 84 produced no game at all. The maximum hourly rate of return, 4.96 kg/mnhr, was achieved by a hunter at Shubakbarina, who took down two white-lipped peccaries while the rest of the men in his longhouse were fishing. His was an exceptional trip. The mean bag for all 176 hunting trips was only 0.22 ± 0.56 kg/mnhr (mean ± standard deviation). These figures compared with the fishing mean of .51 ± 0.44 kg/mnhr. There is little doubt that overall hunting is less reliable than fishing.

Although the Barí do not experience seasonal fluctuations in hunt-

Table 4.9. Traditional hunting returns by month in the 1960s

Location	Mar.	Apr.	May	July	Aug.	Sept.
Otaká alt. 160 m 1963		.22 n = 4 d = 12				
Otaká alt. 160 m 1964			.20 n = 9 d = 19			
Ikikaira alt. 120 m 1964			.16 n = 4 d = 8			
Kirongdaka alt: 60 m 1967				.67 n = 4 d = 10		
Catalaura alt: 50 m 1966					.32 n = 5 d = 17	.02 n = 5 d = 10

Note: The locations (left column, top to bottom) identify the name of the settlement, its altitude, and the year(s) in which the observations were made. Each cell contains (top to bottom) the mean return in kg/mnhr, the number of hunting expeditions contributing to the mean, and the number of days of observation in the indicated month. The mean is a time-weighted average, the total butchered weight of game acquired by an individual hunter in the measured trips divided by the total number of hours he spent hunting. Because of the high variability of hunting returns, only observation runs of at least eight days, with multiple hunting trips, are included here. Only months in which hunting data were collected are noted in column headings.

Table 4.10. Mean hunts per month for lowland houses in the 1960s and 1970s, aggregated by three-month season

	1960s			
	Jan.–Mar.	Apr.–June	July–Sept.	Oct.–Dec.
Observation days	8	59	31	6
Observed hunts	1	27	8	5
Hunts/month	3.8	13.9	17.7	25.4

	1970s			
	Jan.–Mar.	Apr.–June	July–Sept.	Oct.–Dec.
Observation days	69	0	44	47
Observed hunts	22	0	26	31
Hunts/month	9.7	no data	18.0	20.1

Note: Mean number of hunts per month is calculated by multiplying observed hunts/ observation days by 30.5. The data displayed here summarize all observation days, including visits too short to be used in the hunting returns averages.

ing productivity that are sufficiently pronounced to show up in our data, they do display seasonal changes in the amount of time they dedicate to hunting (Table 4.10), with a pattern that appears rather stable over the decades. If the returns for hunting do not vary notably and reliably with season, why does hunting effort do so, and why does it follow this pattern?

Hunting and Fishing Revisited

There are essentially two parts to the question of why hunting effort varies and why it follows the pattern it does. Why do the Barí increase their hunting effort in the rainier months, and why do they not let it fall to zero in the drier months? The first is easily answered. The seasons when hunting dominates subsistence effort are the times when fishing is worst. It is not so much that hunting improves during these months as that fishing goes to hell: hourly returns decline dramatically, and on many days the rivers are muddy and traditional fishing is impossible. We emphasize this point. It is seasonal variability in per manhour fishing returns and the increasing removal of even the possibility of successful fishing that drives the rainy season increase in hunting, *not* a seasonal change in hunting returns.

There was more to be drawn out of this comparison when we looked more closely at the variability of fishing and hunting returns. Previously published records (Beckerman 1983b: 283–284 [Tables 9.1 and 9.2]) showed daily fishing and hunting returns for a small, traditional bohío in November 1970 (the rainiest month, when the fishing is worst) and late January-February 1971 (the driest months, when the fishing is best). The thirty days of November witnessed twenty-two hunting trips by one or more of the men in the longhouse (there were four men until November 23, when a fifth arrived). These hunts produced 17.25 kg (butchered wt.) of game, for an average of 0.78 ± 1.24 kg/trip (mean ± standard deviation). The largest take on a single hunt was only 4.0 kg, and eight hunts produced no game at all. The coefficient of variation was 1.59.

The same month saw six fishing trips. (There were only six because only on those days did the inhabitants of this bohío judge the waters to be clear enough to be worth fishing.) They produced 28.25 kg of cleaned fish, for an average catch of 4.71 ± 3.01 per fishing trip. (The largest catch was 8.50 kg, the smallest 1.50.) The coefficient of variation was 0.64. It is to be underlined that November is the rainiest month, when fishing is worst, and would be expected a priori to show some days with a pitifully small catch, leading to a high coefficient of variation.

Less than two months later, in a data run from January 24 to February 21, the men of this bohío (now reduced to only three) made nine traditional hunting trips, netting 5.55 kg of game. (Two of these hunts brought home no game at all, and the biggest bag was only 3 kg.) The mean was 0.62 ± 0.96 kg/hunt, and the coefficient of variation was 1.55.

Over the same period, the inhabitants of the bohío carried out twenty-one traditional fishing trips, spearing 173.65 kg of fish. (The biggest catch was 31.0 kg, and on two trips nothing was caught.) The mean was 8.27 ± 8.96 kg per fishing trip. The coefficient of variation was 1.08.

In both the wettest and the driest months, the coefficient of variation for hunting was conspicuously higher than that for fishing. The lesson was clear: Hunting, no matter how good or bad the fishing, was inherently a more inconsistent way of obtaining animal protein.

When fishing was good, animal protein was abundant and reliable. When fishing was bad, animal protein was often scarce (although occasionally superabundant) and highly variable. This latter period was subsistence crunch time for the Barí, the season when a nutritional shortfall was a possibility. It was hunting that carried them through the depth of the rainy season, the only time when meat hunger might have become an issue. Thus hunting, even though it supplied far less meat than fishing on an annual basis, was in a sense more crucial than fishing. Every year at the height of the rainy season it was the defense against potential undernutrition. It is impossible to believe that the Barí themselves did not recognize the greater variability of hunting over fishing as a source of animal protein. Hence, we believe, the Barí admiration for a good hunter and his desirability as a husband and son-in-law (see chapter 6).

The second part of the question, why the Barí hunt at all during, say, January through March in the lowlands, when average fishing returns are about three times higher than average hunting returns, is less straightforward to answer. (Even considering the possibility that men may look at women's labor in fishing as a free resource does not reduce the return advantage of fishing over hunting in this season to less than about two to one.) Three possible answers were proposed by Beckerman (1983b): (1) it is advantageous to hunt on the way to and from a fishing spot, and this opportunistic hunting may account for some dry season fishing; (2) one of the activities of hunting trips may be to reconnoiter for good fishing spots, surveying the rivers for the presence of schools of bocachico; and (3) even in the driest months there are rainstorms that prevent fishing for a day or two, and these days are when most hunting takes place.

Later research has not been kind to these propositions. It is true that a bit of hunting does go on during travel to and from fishing spots, but, as noted above, this sort of hunting occurs on only about 10% of fishing trips and even when it does take place hardly ever produces an appreciable amount of game.

Questioning of Barí informants produced emphatic denials that scouting for locations of fish is one of the goals of hunting. In fact, some people said that one does not even look before beginning the construction of the weirs. (This statement speaks loudly to how well the Barí understand their environment. They don't have to look; they already know.)

The idea that even in the drier months rain can prevent fishing, or decrease its expected returns to below what hunting may bring, and that these days are when most hunting takes place may have a little more to recommend it, but even here the evidence is weak. A review of dry season weather records and dry season hunting does not reveal a strong tendency for hunting trips to occur on the day following a rainstorm.

A related possibility arises from the observation that most dry season hunts are early morning jaunts, typically brief. Barí are definite that one of the motives for these hunts is to scout for signs of game. They are information-gathering expeditions, not about fish, but about game. A lengthier hunt, later in the day, often follows an early morning jaunt that has discovered promising signs of game. Given the greater variability of hunting returns with respect to fishing returns, it pays to stay alert to the possibility of a jackpot kill. A troop of spider monkeys or a herd of peccaries offers a return per manhour higher than anything that can be expected from fishing even in the best months.

With this explanation we have reached at least a tentative answer to one of the five questions posed at the beginning of this chapter. On the one hand, the Barí deal with temporal variation in hunting returns—variation that is not regular and seasonal but random and day-to-day—by frequent monitoring of the environment and flexible responses to what they discover on their scouting trips. They also deal with the regular, seasonal variation in fishing returns by focusing their hunting effort in seasons when fishing is worst.

Insofar as how the Barí deal with spatial variation in hunting returns, we have only inconclusive evidence that this variation exists (we believe it does) and similarly inconclusive evidence that they manage it by decreasing their fishing effort (see Tables 4.4–4.7) and increasing their hunting effort (see Table 4.8) at higher elevations (we believe they do, but the case is far from closed).

With regard to the other three questions, there is no direct evidence from hunting as to whether the Barí are time minimizers or food maximizers, but the amount of effort they put into fruitless hunting trips is perhaps more consistent with the latter strategy. That said, it remains clear that the Barí are not hungry in the sense of ever being near famine. There are over 5,000 daylight hours in a year ($365 \times 14 = 5,110$), and a Barí man spends only about 1,500 of them in fishing and hunting combined (with a maximum of another 400 in gardening). The amount of daytime that men spend lying in their hammocks contemplating the roof of the longhouse when they could be out on the food quest argues again that these are people who are in no way destitute.

The question of buffering is interesting in the context of hunting. The Barí may well enhance the reliability of their hunting, perhaps at some sacrifice in efficiency, by increasing the number and duration of early morning jaunts and other zero return hunts. This issue resolves to whether a reduction in the number of man-hours spent in such primarily scouting hunts would increase the overall efficiency of hunting in kg/mnhr while also increasing its variance. It is a question that cannot be decided by our data but one that we believe reveals a potentially important difference between fishing and hunting, not only among the Barí, but among many peoples with subsistence economies embracing both activities.

Gathering

Gathering is a minor activity among the Barí, both in food produced and in time invested. It is essentially an individual activity, although it may take place in the course of a group hunt or fishing trip. Only two practices that might be considered special techniques are involved. They are described below in the sections dealing with the individual species appropriated by gathering.

Species Taken

The most important gathered foods for the Barí are the fruits of five species of palms, the first four closely related: *Oenocarpus bataua* [= *Jessenia bataua*, *J. polycarpa*, etc.], *OE. mapora*, *Euterpe oleracea* and *E. karsteniana*, and *Attalea butyracea*. The first makes by far the largest contribution to the diet. *OE. bataua* fruits are a little larger than jumbo olives, purple-black ovoids 3 to 4 cm long by about 2 cm in diameter. They have to be cooked slightly before eating. Putting them in a pot with water and heating it just hot enough to make it uncomfortable to the hand is sufficient. The edible part is the oily mesocarp between the outer skin (exocarp) and the nut. To eat them, "the proper technique is to ease the whole pericarp off the nut in two or three large pieces, then scrape the mesocarp from the exocarp with the thumbnail. The pasty pulp that collects on the nail tastes slightly like Brazil nuts" (Beckerman 1977: 149). The same cooking and eating practices are used with the smaller *OE. mapora* fruits, but the blueberry-sized *Euterpe* fruits are just chewed and the inedible parts spit out.

   The mean weight of a bunch of *OE. bataua* fruits brought home to a given hearth is around 4 kg, about 15% of which is the edible mesocarp. (Mean weight for a bunch of *OE. mapora* fruits is about 3 kg and for both *Euterpe* spp., around 2 kg.) In broad terms, about 10 percent of the wet weight of the mesocarp is fat, in the form of an oil whose composition is chemically similar to olive oil (Balick 1986); about 5 percent is protein. It is thus not surprising that the Barí use it as a meat substitute. Beckerman (1977: 150) observed, "It is a common occurrence, when a hunting expedition is on its way home empty- or light-handed (or on the rare occasions when a fishing expedition is in the same lamentable situation) for it to stop for a moment on the trail and send a boy or young man up an Oenocarpus . . . tree to pluck a bunch of fruit. The hunting party seldom has to go more than a few meters from the trail to find a suitable tree."

The Barí climb trees the way many tropical peoples do, with the hands clasped around the trunk and the feet joined by a loop of vine. It is an efficient and dangerous way to climb a relatively slender tree without branches below the canopy.

A large number of other wild fruits are eaten when encountered (cf. M. Lizarralde 1997). Our favorite is *Spondias mombin* (Anacardiaceae), a purple-flecked bright yellow fruit about the size of a Kalamata olive with a delicious tart flavor. It is usually eaten where found in the forest and seldom brought home to the longhouse.

A gathered animal associated with palm trees is the larva of the palm weevil (*Rhynchophorus palmarum*). This insect infests the crowns of many different species of palms, but the Barí harvest it mainly from the deliberately felled trunks of *OE. bataua*, whose pith becomes honeycombed by larvae within two or three months after cutting. One splits the trunk with an ax and extracts the larvae by carving away the pith with a knife. The grubs, about the size of the last two joints of a man's little finger, can be eaten steamed (a heap of larvae is wrapped in a leaf and put over the fire), raw, or alive. The texture is like biting down on a tiny balloon filled with toothpaste, and the taste is something like rotten walnuts.

Occasionally picked up in the course of fishing expeditions, especially those that concentrate on plucking Loricarids from the rocky bottoms of rivers and streams, is the large riverine snail *Pomacea exima*. These mollusks, about the size of a man's fist, are solitary. A fishing trip rarely brings home more than one or two.

Considerably more abundant is the land snail, *Strophocheilus oblongus*. It is about the size of a child's fist and can occur in densities of up to one snail every two or three square meters, especially in riverside stands of *Heliconia*. Eating one is like chewing on a bicycle tire, except that it does not taste like rubber; it tastes like dirt. Only children will eat it.

Turtles are picked up when encountered in the forest. Viloria and Calchi La C. (1993) list six species known from the Barí region. One of them, *Rhinoclemmys diademata* (Emydidae) is the most common in our experience; it is 15–20 cm long by 10–12 cm wide. It is tied into its shell and boiled alive. Turtle eggs are dug out of sandy riverbanks when people observe the tracks in the sand. Iguana eggs are similarly gathered.

Other gathered materials are nonfood items such as strips of bark and palm frond petioles for mats and lengths of vine for basketry (cf. M. Lizarralde 1997).

Places and Techniques

Gathered foods are mostly widespread; palms in particular are very abundant. There must be differences in abundance related to differences in altitude and rainfall, but no one has yet mapped them. The only procedures related to gathering that might qualify as special techniques are tree climbing to obtain palm fruits and tree trunk splitting to harvest palm weevil larvae.

Distribution of Gathered Foods

All gathered foods remain within the hearth group, as far as we are aware.

Variation in Productivity

There are no good data on the geographical variability of either palm trees themselves or the abundance of their fruits. (It is likely that the *Oenocarpus* species do not thrive much above 600 m.) With respect to seasonal variability, consumption records suggest that one or more of the four species have at least some trees bearing fruit somewhere in the Barí area nearly year round but that there is a peak of fruiting, especially for *OE. bataua*, in March through June or July.

Gathered foods are largely incidental to the Barí diet, with the exception of the palm fruits, which clearly do serve to ameliorate brief shortfalls of fish and game. In that sense, they are used to buffer the variability of the protein supply.

People and Resources

As described in chapter 3, the evidence suggests that for most of their history the Barí have lived at population densities of well under one person per square kilometer, densities more characteristic of hunters and gatherers than of many slash-and-burn cultivators. These low densities are surely a major reason that the rain forest natural populations that fed the Barí continued to thrive throughout the centuries. As shown in this chapter, an examination of Barí traditional subsistence reveals no evidence of the aboriginal human population depleting its food resources. Only when the Venezuelan and Colombian national economies accessed the region did resources come under threat. Variations in resource abundance that did occur in traditional times were local and seasonal and were successfully dealt with by mobility and by routine switching between alternate resources.

On the other hand, as we show in chapter 6, this historically low population density cannot be attributed to any sort of restraint on reproduction. The Barí are a natural fertility population among whom the mean number of pregnancies experienced by a postmenopausal woman is around eight. Their limited population is the result of high mortality, not birth control. The causes of mortality and the preventive strategies with which the Barí confronted these causes are the subject of the next chapter.

Note

1. A single aberrant fishing trip is omitted from these figures. One afternoon in 1970, in the small (nine inhabitants) Colombian longhouse of Ashtakakaira, the five men went to a small stream with a muddy bottom where they constructed a weir of poles and palm fronds rather than stones and *Heliconia* leaves. They left a large opening in this weir and went home, ate dinner, and went to sleep. They woke and returned around midnight with torches and closed the weir. Within minutes catfish nearly a meter long began throwing themselves against it. After these brutes were run through, the men continued up the stream, spearing bocachico as they went. They returned home after dawn with so much fish that most of it spoiled and had to be thrown away. (They had tried to salt it but, new to the process, were too stingy with the salt.) The take from this unique trip was 2.44 kg/mnhr. How they knew that on this night the catfish would migrate downstream we have never learned.

CHAPTER 5

Protection

Obtaining an adequate, regular supply of nutrients is necessary but not sufficient for the maintenance and reproduction of life. The world is full of dangers—and the tropical rain forest has its share, some of which are illustrated in Tótubi's biography in chapter 1. Every society owns a set of strategies whereby its members try to protect themselves and their loved ones from the hazards of their place and time. We deal with the dangers of Motilonia and the responses of the Barí under three broad headings: accidents, disease, and homicide. There is no general theory in ecology that encompasses all these threats, so for each type of hazard we begin the discussion by posing questions about how people protected themselves from that specific kind of danger.

In 1988 and 1989 we interviewed fifty-nine Venezuelan Barí who were old enough to have lived a substantial part of their lives before modern contact—people estimated to have been born before about 1943. These people constituted about half the estimated size of this cohort among the Venezuelan Barí at that time. Lizarralde took genealogies and elicited the cause and approximate date of death, when known, for all deceased members of the informants' families. In 1996 he completed forty additional genealogical interviews with elderly Barí, also noting causes of death when mentioned by the informant. The combined database records 238 precontact deaths with specified causes. A large number of additional people in these genealogies are known to be dead, but their causes of death were not recorded. They are not considered further. It is likely that accidental deaths and homicides are overrepresented among the deaths with specified causes because of the psychological salience of these calamities, while deaths from disease, attributed by the Barí to the quotidian working of death spirits, are underrecorded.

Our discussion of disease is also complicated by a feature of Barí culture suggested in chapter 1. When you ask the Barí for the cause of someone's death, unless the death was caused by an obvious trauma such as shooting or drowning, you usually get the name of the death spirit held responsible. The description of circumstances and symptoms is largely incompatible with the categories of Western science. Our treatment of disease is filtered through this incongruity in ideology.

Accidents

There is no overarching theory that deals with the various misfortunes we have grouped under this heading. The main question to be asked is simply, What do the Barí do to protect themselves specifically from this or that danger? The principal dangers are several and varied.

In the first place, human beings are not the only predators in the rain forest. Of the 238 precontact deaths with reported causes recorded in Lizarralde's genealogies, three were of men killed by jaguars. To protect against jaguar attack at least one armed man accompanies any trip that goes a substantial distance into the forest. Barí are explicit that jaguars are the main reason that someone always brings a bow when people go off to fish or clear a new field.

Men and boys sometimes fall from trees when they climb to pluck fruits or to retrieve arboreal game or the arrows they have shot at it. This hazard is sex-specific. Women and girls do not climb trees. In the same sample of 238 deaths from known causes, five male deaths were attributed to falls—four from trees and one down a pit while exploring a cave. Because teenaged boys do a great deal of the tree climbing, it is likely that due caution is often not taken.

Drowning is a customary danger for people who spend as much time fishing and crossing rivers as the Barí. In the sample, eight people are recorded as having drowned, five males and three females, the latter including a mother-daughter pair.

In the Barí interpretation, all these people were dragged under by *taibabioyi*, water spirits. Insofar as precautions taken against drowning, all Barí over the age of about six know how to swim. (Men do a sort of trudgeon crawl, changing to a sidestroke when they have to carry their weapons in one hand, out of the water. Women and children dogpaddle.) In addition, mythology mandates respect for the taibabioyi, who are believed to live inside large rounded rocks in the rivers—rocks shaped roughly like a longhouse. One proscription forbids a fisher groping for Loricarids from putting a hand too far under a large rock; to do so would be to violate the world of the taibabioyi. Whatever the supernatural virtues of forbidding this activity, the advantage of avoiding a behavior that might leave a fisher caught with his or her head underwater is obvious.

Snakebite is a peril about which the Barí are concerned whenever they are on the trail. The fer-de-lance is not rare in Motilonia. In Lizarralde's genealogies, no fewer than twenty people are noted as having died of snakebite. The sex ratio, 15 men to 5 women, is probably a reasonable index of the relative amounts of time that men and women spend in the forest.

The total figure for snakebite deaths may actually be too low. Eight people (five children and three adults) are recorded as having been lost in the woods, or as having "gone off to live with the *ihchingbarida*" (spirit people who inhabit the forest and sometimes take Barí away to live with them). All these people who disappeared into the woods and were never seen again are presumably dead. Some substantial fraction of them likely died from exposure, perhaps combined with a trauma, such as a broken leg, that prevented them from getting home. But some of them were almost certainly hit by poisonous snakes or even killed by jaguars.[1]

There is little barefoot people can do about snakebite except to remain constantly vigilant. Both authors have stories about the times on the trail when we were grabbed and held by the Barí just as we were about to step on a poisonous snake. When a poisonous snake is found near a longhouse or a field or fishing spot, it is killed immediately. Finally, the Barí fear and avoid going out in the forest at night, largely because of the danger of stepping on a poisonous snake in the dark.

Disease

Disease ecology is a well-developed field of human biology. However, the limited data available for the Barí do not allow the deployment of this body of theory. The important question that our data address is the identification of those features of Barí culture—settlement locations, residence architecture, migratory patterns, and supernatural beliefs—that ameliorated the threat of disease among the precontact Barí, whether by design or by unintended consequence.

The epidemiological history of the Barí is obscure. We know that malaria has been present in the general region for centuries. Leishmaniasis is chronic in Motilonia, and probably has been for a long time. The usual intestinal parasites of the tropics have certainly been present for ages. We know that yellow fever, typhus, and influenza were reported as major public health problems in surrounding nonindigenous populations at various times in the first half of the twentieth century, as noted in chapter 2, although there is no evidence as to whether they reached the Barí, and if they did, where, when, and to what effect. We know that a series of devastating measles epidemics nearly finished the Barí in the 1780s, 1790s, and again in the 1960s, when the disease entered as a consequence of regular contact with criollo populations. But even for the more recent of the two series of measles epidemics, which was met by the resources of modern medicine, the record of infection and mortality is partial and defective. We intend to describe those postcontact epidemics elsewhere, along with the other major modern threats to Barí health, tuberculosis and hepatitis.

Here we discuss the major diseases known or suspected to have been a threat to the Barí in precontact times. Malaria and Leishmaniasis are prominent among them.

Malaria is an infectious disease caused by a single-celled parasite transmitted by the bite of a mosquito. The parasite attacks the red blood cells and causes chills followed by high fevers; it can kill an infected individual in several ways, including fatal damage directly to the blood and secondarily to the kidneys, the liver, and the brain, among other organs. Worldwide, it is still the case that in most years about a million people die from malaria.

There are five species of the parasite that naturally infect humans: *Plasmodium malariae*, *P. vivax*, *P. knowlesi*, *P. ovale*, and (the most lethal) *P. falciparum*. Most common in Barí territory is P. *vivax*; P. *falciparum* is a relatively recent arrival. The parasite has a complicated life history, linked to that of its vector, mosquitoes of the genus *Anopheles*. The parasite alternates between sexual and asexual reproduction.

When a female *Anopheles* mosquito (only the females drink blood) bites an infected person, the blood it withdraws contains both male and female *Plasmodium* gametocytes, which in the insect's stomach join to produce a gamete, which then produces a zygote, which in turn becomes an oocyst. The oocyst crosses the intestinal wall and releases multiple sporozoites throughout the mosquito's body cavity. These asexual, free-swimming sporozoites eventually reach the mosquito's salivary glands, where they are ready to infect the next person bitten by the insect.

Once injected into the blood of the next victim of the mosquito, the sporozoites travel to the liver, where they divide, transform into another life stage, and pass into the bloodstream. In the blood, this *Plasmodium* life stage invades the red blood cells, divides into multiple cells of another life stage called a merozoite, and in effect explodes the red blood cells, producing the characteristic malarial fever. This latest life stage can divide to produce more merozoites (which invade still more red blood cells) and can also transform itself into male and female gametocytes carried in the bloodstream, ready to resume the cycle when sucked up in the next mosquito bite. A possible weak link in this chain of infection is the mosquito bite. We discuss how the Barí shelter themselves against insects below, after the description of another insect-borne disease, Leishmaniasis.

Leishmaniasis takes two forms, muco-cutaneous (attacking the skin and mucous membranes) and visceral. Both are caused by flagellates of the genus *Leishmania*. As far as we are aware, only the muco-cutaneous form occurs among the Barí. This infection usually produces a skin lesion, a wet ulceration that looks like leprosy. In addition to appearing on the skin, the lesion can form in the nasal mucosa. In that site it sometime mimics the nose-destroying effects of syphilis, which is not present among the Barí.

Although usually self-limiting, muco-cutaneous Leishmaniasis can be fatal. Old Aishgdora, wisest and kindest of men, had multiple lesions on both his legs in 1970. Cured by a missionary, Bruce Olson, he suffered a relapse or reinfection a decade later and died around 1984. Ashimbia, whose nasal mucosa were ravaged by Leishmaniasis in his old age, died in 1991.

Leishmaniasis is carried by sand flies of the genus *Phlebotomus*. Humans are an important reservoir, and in some places dogs are as well. Sand flies are attracted to the wet lesions and carry the infection to the next person they bite. As with malaria, a possible weak link in the chain of infection is the insect bite. That observation leads us to an examination of the Barí longhouse.

A longhouse is dark inside. It has doors at each narrow end and may have from zero to three doors on each long side, but these openings are only about a meter and a half high. The light from the cleared ring surrounding the house penetrates only weakly beyond the door.

Outside, the ring of cleared and swept earth around the house receives unobstructed sun; on a clear day, it blazes. The contrast between the ring and the inside of the house is such that it takes a while for one's eyes to adjust upon entering.

This contrast is not lost on the insects. Sand flies are creatures of bright sunlight (e.g., riverbanks, hence their name). Lying in a hammock inside a longhouse, one can see the sand flies dancing hopefully in the puddle of light just inside each door. But they can come no further. For whatever reason of insect physiology or insect psychology, they are unable to enter the deep shade of the house interior.

Mosquitoes are a more complicated story. Although there may be as many as a dozen different species of *Anopheles* in Motilonia (Service 1993), it appears likely that one of them, *A. nuneztovari*, is the major culprit for malaria transmission there (Rubio-Palis and Zimmerman 1997; Kiszewski et al. 2004.) The abundance of *A. nuneztovari* changes dramatically with the season, in response to rainfall and humidity, with abundance of the former promoting the creation of still-water breeding sites and high levels of the latter favoring adult survivorship (Rubio-Palis and Curtis 1992). It may be significant that the rainy season, when the mosquito is most abundant, is also when the Barí tend to be in their upland longhouses, where there are fewer pools of standing water than at lower altitudes. Throughout the year the Barí practice of building longhouses mainly on the tops of spurs, with the ground sloping away in all directions, tends to distance their dwellings from the spots where large swarms of this mosquito emerge from the larval state.

A. nuneztovari feeds from dusk to dawn, with the feeding peak taking place around midnight (Rubio-Palis and Curtis 1992). The traditional Barí are usually inside the longhouse, with the doorways closed off by substantial bundles of tightly tied palm fronds, by dusk or shortly thereafter. On only the rarest occasions are they out of the longhouse around midnight.

A physician and professor of tropical medicine at the Universidad del Zulia, Adolfo Pons, led a team of four doctors who examined one hundred Barí, both regular residents and visitors, in the large longhouse Karibaigdakaira on December 13, 1960, and January 21, 1961, before the postcontact epidemics arrived (Pons et al. 1962). They reported an absence of splenomegaly and negative results from finger stick blood slides, which led them to conclude there was no malaria among the inhabitants of this house or their visitors. To the best of our knowledge, malaria arrived in Barí territory around March 1961, via the Tukuko mission, to which it had been introduced earlier by Colombian workers.

The Pons expedition also found four cases of Leishmaniasis among the people examined, confirming the precontact presence of this disease among the Barí.

A finding that has yet to be explained was their assertion of the widespread presence of leprosy among the Barí. A single man was in fact taken away from his people and confined to a leper colony where he eventually died. But the finding of additional cases was never reproduced, and no later medical work with the Barí mentions leprosy. It is likely that these investigators confused one or more advanced cases of Leishmaniasis with leprosy.

Some cases of carate were also reported by the Pons team. Carate is a benign cutaneous infection, essentially confined to Latin America, that produces patches of unpigmented skin but has few other effects. It is caused by a microorganism that looks like the syphilis spirochete but is not transmitted sexually and does not infect any part of the body except the skin.

No venereal diseases were found, nor was tuberculosis. However, tuberculosis had become the major killer of older Barí by the 1990s and remains so.

Also to the point are the parasitological reports this team worked up from fecal samples taken from twelve Barí who visited a mission station where the doctors were staying. They found eggs of the intestinal parasites *Ascaris* (roundworm), *Trichuris* (whipworm), and *Necator* (hookworm), but none of them abundant. These intestinal worms can be problematic, especially in small children, but in low numbers are usually not a major health threat.

A similar situation was found with the microorganisms that cause dysentery. All twelve Barí displayed *Trichomonas* spp. and *Giardia lamblia* in their stool, and two of them had cysts of *Entamoeba histolytica*. Again, most of the infections were at a relatively low level.

The medical team was impressed by the prevalence of conjunctivitis and corneal ulcers, which they attributed, no doubt correctly, to the Barí custom of plucking out not only the eyebrows but also the eyelashes.

The medical profile of the pericontact Barí, then, was one that has often been reported for newly contacted native peoples of the neotropical forest, before they are crushed by the inevitable Old World epidemics: universal but light infestations of intestinal parasites, both worms and single-celled organisms; and a moderate prevalence of usually chronic diseases such as Leishmaniasis and carate. Aside from these ills, the people were generally in good health.

There are several features of Barí culture, in particular, matters relating to settlement pattern, that must have aided substantially in sustaining this relatively positive health profile. First, being at war with the rest of the world, the Barí maintained a no-man's-land between themselves and their enemies. And it was their enemies who were the host populations for malaria, yellow fever, influenza, typhus, and so forth. Some

Anopheles mosquito species have been observed to fly as far as 10 km from a release point, but they typically disperse over shorter distances (Kaufmann and Briegel 2004). The Barí probably were beyond the range of normal dispersal.

Aside from the border of empty land between themselves and the reservoirs of the major pathogens, the Barí presented other obstacles to infectious disease. Local populations of Barí were small and widely dispersed, and visits between one local group and another were not frequent but were generally formal affairs typically concentrated in, if not confined to, the dry season. Acute infectious diseases must have had a hard time of it. A longhouse had far too small a population to maintain an acute infection such as measles. The entire Barí population was segregated into separate groups to such a degree that for most of the year an infectious disease would be unlikely to be able to travel from one local group to another in a human host.

The consequence of this settlement pattern must have been a sort of unintended quarantine of the infectious diseases that did enter Motilonia. It was reinforced by a feature of Barí culture mentioned in Tótubi's life story. When they get sick, most Barí seem to consider their illness embarrassing if not actually shameful. They take to their hammocks in discomfiture and stay there. In contrast to many other lowland South American peoples, who deal with sickness by fleeing (and thereby transmit the disease to the settlements in which they take refuge), the Barí generally stay put.

One other feature of Barí settlement is likely important in health terms, in a minor way: the semisedentary pattern of residence in their longhouses. We suspect that the low intestinal parasite burden that the contact-era Barí revealed is related to their regular migrations. An absence of several months from a longhouse site allows excreta deposited in the house-surrounding field to decompose and the eggs of parasitic organisms contained therein to be subjected to erosion, sheet wash, wetting and drying cycles, and similar processes that cannot be favorable for maintaining a large population of parasite eggs and cysts. Thus the Barí appear to have avoided the heavy intestinal parasite burdens that are common among fully sedentary people, who are obliged to live where their own wastes are present in constantly renewed abundance to reinfect them.

Another practice that may have had some effect in keeping the intestinal parasite load low among Barí children in particular was based in beliefs concerning a variety of supernatural beings, the *shungbaraba*. These spirits are dwarfs who live in and move through the earth the way fish move through water. At night especially, they reach up and grab children, who then die, as reported in Tótubi's biography. They concentrate on children who have misbehaved; conspicuous among the behaviors that arouse their anger is throwing food on the earth floor of the longhouse or eating food that has fallen on the ground. Children are of course cautioned against such practices.

All in all, the settlement practices of the Barí appear to have been their most important defense against the diseases that battered them so mercilessly when the barrier against contact with the Old World was removed, although other traditions may also have aided in keeping them relatively healthy.

Homicide

In August 1989 we interviewed Ramón Arikang (his real name), an elderly man now deceased. He lived off-reservation at Ishkandakaira, a small settlement of Barí clinging to a tiny piece of land beside a huge property that an hacendado named Cecilio Hernandez had stolen from them years before.[2] He was ancient and shaky; his eyes wandered, and his voice sometimes trailed off. Eventually, we asked about the attack on the longhouse named Baku-agyá, where we knew he had been living at the time of a massacre. He was quiet for a moment, and then he looked at the horizon; his eyes steadied and his voice firmed. It was clear he could still see it. It had taken place, we calculated, more than thirty years earlier.

Part of the local group at a bohío named Turibakaig had separated temporarily from the rest and were residing at another of their longhouses, Baku-agyá. Arikang was out hunting white-lipped peccary with the other five able-bodied men at Baku-agyá. They had left just after breakfast. The women were in the longhouse, having stayed to weed the fields. They got tired around midday and came home to rest in their hammocks. The Indian killers, Colombians, the Barí were sure, came up the trail to the bohío shortly after noon. A woman named Akashi (all the wounded and murdered people in this account are identified by their real names) saw through the thatch that someone had passed. She went to one of the doors to look. She was shot through the left forearm, just above the wrist. She ran out another door and hid down a slope behind the longhouse.

Another woman, Akbaingshibabió, had a two-year-old son. She ran from the house with him in her arms. They shot her in the arm, and she dropped the boy, still alive. One of the Indian killers picked him up; another came over with a knife and slashed him upward from the navel to the heart. His mother was shot in the back four times as she tried to get over a log in the house-surrounding field. The shot that killed her hit her upper spine.

Arikang's wife was named Atraktaka. She was behind a post in the longhouse, hidden from the door where Akbaingshibabió had fled, but a killer came to another door, behind her, and shot her in the back. The bullet came out through her right breast.

Then the killer entered the house for the first time. He picked up Atraktaka and Arikang's six-month-old daughter and dragged her dead mother outside. He put them both in the cleared ring just outside the bohío, the mother lying on her back. He disemboweled the little girl, navel to heart, and put her face down on her mother's body. Then he and the other killers spread the dead woman's legs and shoved a pole into her vagina.

Then they killed a mentally disabled man who had been left in the house when the other men went off. He was shot in the side, by the door, then dragged outside to the cleared ring. His younger brother, Akbadú, ten or twelve years old, was shot in the back as he fled. They dragged him back and put him beside his brother.

There was a little girl named Arokbá who was playing in the house-surrounding field. She was about eight. When she heard the noise she ran back to the longhouse. She was shot between the eyes, twice.

Then the Indian killers set fire to the house.

Three women and two boys escaped the massacre unharmed. (Akashi, the first person shot, eventually recovered.) One of the surviving women ran after the men and told them what had happened. They got back to the burned longhouse around 4:00 P.M. They did not chase the Colombians immediately. They made a lean-to for sleeping while one of the men ran off to tell the rest of their local group at Turibakaig what had happened. Some men from Turibakaig arrived the same night, and many more the next day. Then they went after the Indian killers.

They chased them all the way to the río Negro but did not catch them. Two days later the six men who had been in Baku-agyá returned to the site to bury their dead.

As far was we are able to judge, the Barí have been the objects of atrocities such as this for most of the past five hundred years. One cannot know them without giving due attention to the homicides that have marked their lives.

The first thing to know about homicide and the Barí is that all killing was external. Internally, the Barí have enjoyed an unbroken civil peace for as long as anyone remembers. In fact, it was only after there were grown-up, mission-raised Barí that either of us ever heard a Barí adult so much as raise his (or her) voice to another person. Traditionally, if two people were not getting along the problem was solved by distance: one of them simply moved to another local group.

The situation with non-Barí could not have been more different. As discussed in chapter 3, violent attacks on the Barí by European peoples began in the sixteenth century and were probably preceded in prior centuries by indigenous raiding and slaving. There was a brief surcease from violence during the first pacification (1772–1818), but that respite was marked by catastrophic infectious disease mortality.

In terms of the ecological issues that arise with respect to these horrific events, one set of questions deals with the way that the Barí arranged their settlement and mobility patterns to deal with foreign attack. One of us (Beckerman 1991b) has argued, on theoretical grounds, that the settlement strategy most likely to be successful in preserving a population under attack bifurcates on the question of relative strength: If you are, or can assemble to become, more numerous than the enemy, aggregate. If you are irreversibly outnumbered, disperse. Below we see evidence that the Barí employed both these strategies, as well as others.

Another set of questions turns on the means of compensating for disproportionate losses in one part of the population pyramid. As we will shortly see, adult males were the segment most at risk from outside attack. How did Barí survivors deal with this loss of husbands and fathers?

As noted below, the Barí implemented various novel options in their responses to the increasing external violence that beset them in the twentieth century, in addition to deploying ongoing defensive features of their culture that had been in use for centuries.

After the discovery of oil in the region in the second half of the nineteenth century but especially from 1914 on with the arrival of foreign oil companies, attacks on the Barí became more frequent and increasingly brutal. For the score of years before modern peaceful contact, the pace increased even more. The instigators were

> international oil companies (largely U.S. and British-Dutch), particularly on the Colombian side of the border, and Venezuelan cattle ranchers. Land acquisition and the desire to be relieved of Barí raids were the major motives for state-level war on the Indians. There is good reason to believe that most of the killings were carried out by hired Indian killers, so-called *pájaros*. . . .

Their major tactic was to fall upon a Barí longhouse at dawn, set it afire, and shoot the occupants as they fled. People unable to flee (small children, the wounded) were hacked to death with knives or machetes. If the killers encountered Barí before they could fire the house they began shooting at once. Thus Barí were also killed when found on the trail, while fishing, and during their own raids on oil-camp and hacienda tool sheds. (Beckerman and Lizarralde 1995: 498)

But professional Indian killers were not the only culprits. Another source (R. Lizarralde 2004) describes in detail the assaults on two Barí longhouses, one in 1941 and the other in 1958. The first was carried out by an armed group organized by Venezuelan ranchers and the second by a small band of ranch hands.

The mortality from these assaults on the Barí was of considerable magnitude. In our 1988–1989 interviews with Venezuelan Barí who had lived a large part of their lives in precontact times, we heard direct testimony from survivors of twenty-seven mortal incidents, "mortal incident" being defined as an attack in which one or more Barí lost their lives (Beckerman and Lizarralde 1995). These incidents took place between the early 1940s and 1961. (Despite the peaceful contact in 1960, killing of Barí continued for another year.) They encompassed at least 72 deaths: 37 adult males, 10 adult females, 13 boys, 8 girls, and 3 infants, as well as one child whose sex was not remembered. At least 5 more children were stolen and presumably given to criollos to be raised by their families in the region. The disproportion of the sex ratio of the slain adults must be largely a result of the way the Barí men fought to protect their women and children, confronting the killers and allowing some of the more vulnerable people to escape. Another factor in the preponderance of adult male deaths was the greater exposure of men while they were hunting or otherwise away from the house. In at least two cases, the shot that killed a hunter was heard in his longhouse and warned the residents, including his wife, to flee.

There is every reason to believe that these loss numbers are far from the full total of murdered Barí during those years. The cited figures included only individuals mentioned as being killed in mortal incidents to which our informants were eyewitnesses. A search for all cases of homicides recorded in our life histories, including all reports of violent deaths, brings the total to at least 125.

From frequent newspaper reports in the 1950s about criollos shot and killed by Barí arrows (but never about criollo retaliations) we can assume that counterattacks occurred regularly during this decade.

Another piece of evidence as to the magnitude of Barí deaths by homicide occurs in a 1962 article, three of whose coauthors were missionary priests of the Capuchin order. It contains a not very veiled reference to massacres they evidently knew about that may not be fully included in the tabulations from our interviews:

> From 1947 to our days the invasion of these lands by way of Perijá by so-called civilized people has risen again, provoking bloody clashes with the Motilones. This occurrence took on the form of tragedy during the years 1958 and 1959, in which, in an organized way and with entirely speculative intentions, groups of men, in their majority undocumented [an indirect way of referring to illegal Colombian migrants] without the scruples of conscience, imitating the Welzers [a German banking house that financed brutal pillaging expeditions in western Venezuela in the sixteenth century] and other *conquistadores*, have dedicated themselves to burning longhouses and assassinating Motilones without regard for age or sex, pillaging their lands and gardens, that they then fenced in large areas to sell to the highest bidder. (Pons et al. 1962: 17–18; our translation)

The steps the Barí took to protect themselves from these attacks (and previous assaults going back centuries) were varied. In fact, the entire Barí pattern of settlement and migration may be seen for the most part as an adaptation to external attack.

It is clear that semisedentism, the practice of maintaining multiple houses and migrating among them, made people difficult to find. There were two aspects here. The first was just having many houses, some of which were in places difficult to locate—or to get to, even if the locations were known. According to interviews we conducted in the 1980s, of the twenty-four Venezuelan longhouses in current use at the moment of peaceful contact in 1960, six had been sited primarily because these locations were believed to be so remote that the ranchers and oilmen, and their hired killers, were unlikely to attack there.

The second protective aspect of semisedentism was the actual migration among the various longhouses. Even if all the longhouses belonging to a local group were known and accessible, there was only one chance in two (or three, or four, or five) that the people would be in residence when the killers arrived. Such was the experience of the local group that occupied the longhouses Shisabai and Senikaig (Lizarralde 2004). The killers first reached the unoccupied Senikaig and only later found and attacked Shisabai.

One additional advantage of multiple longhouses was succinctly set out by a Spanish colonial officer in 1755. Experienced in previous military expeditions against the Barí, he had been invited to lead another. He replied:

> I cannot refrain from offering that the general expeditions, the more they are practiced with good fortune, end with more expenses than benefits, and instead of containing the Indians, they let them know our weakness; for possessing a territory of more than two hundred leagues of land in which without doubt they must have many houses, and being unable (because they are not known) to be attacked all at once, as soon as they see themselves confronted in one place, they abandon it and go to another until the withdrawal of the people of the expedition restores the first to them: which is what they have always done. (Quoted in Beckerman 1980b: 540–541)

The point here is that even when semisedentism failed as a means of preventing an attack, it remained useful as a way of surviving and recuperating from one.

Other aspects of Barí settlement may also have aided in their defense against their human enemies. Whatever the initial reason for the somewhat unusual custom of putting the longhouse in the middle of a cultivated field, one result of this arrangement was the elimination of adjacent forest cover for a potential attacker. The elimination of cover may even have been implicated in the arrangement of crops in such a way that the lowest plants were located closest to the longhouse.

The Barí also responded with innovations in settlement pattern as the pace of raiding increased in the 1950s. These responses were in the direction predicted by Beckerman (1991b). The extremely large longhouse of Karibaigdakaira was built to hold the combined residents of several local groups, probably with the joint intention of sheltering all of them in a remote area and amassing enough adult males to repulse an attack if one occurred. Shortly after Karibaigdakaira was built, its people decided that concentrating so many people in a single longhouse was not a good idea, given the disparity in firepower between bows and firearms. The residents of at least one local group of those who had built Karibaigdakaira then deliberately spread themselves among all the longhouses in their annual round, an unusual disposition of population, thinking that, as one informant told us, "That way they couldn't kill us all."

Informants also told us about other, more occasional defensive practices related to longhouses. They mentioned a dummy longhouse that had once been built to mislead enemies into believing that Barí were in a place that they never occupied. And, as mentioned in Tótubi's biography, individual families could and sometimes did hide their children at night in the house-surrounding field when they anticipated a raid.

Apart from practices of location, settlement, concealment, and mobility, Barí society had a number of social institutions that may have helped people, especially children, survive the loss of a parent—a father in particular. (Recall that most massacre deaths, and most accidental deaths, were men.)

Our reproductive histories show that in traditional times a woman had roughly one chance in three of being widowed while she still had young children (Beckerman et al. 2002). Almost all these bereaved women remarried. An observation that impressed both of us was how thoroughly the new husbands adopted the children of the deceased man; Barí men were exemplary stepfathers. In fact, some children never knew until we interviewed their senior relatives in their presence that the men who had raised and fed them had married their mothers only after they were born.

Another custom that probably helped children survive the death of a father is discussed in more detail in the next chapter. It is the idea of partible paternity, the belief that every man who has intercourse with a woman around the time she became pregnant with a particular child, or at any time during the pregnancy, shares the biological paternity of that child.

These secondary fathers had acknowledged obligations to the mother and her child. Among them was the obligation to make gifts of fish and game. Some men honored these obligations and some, whether because they were living in another local group or because they were slackers, did not. Nevertheless, we believe that allowing his wife to take a lover who would become the secondary father of one or more of his children was the closest thing to a life insurance policy that a Barí man could acquire. It meant that in the event of the death of the mother's husband, there would be another adult male with at least some sense of obligation to feed the child until the widow remarried.

Puzzlingly, our data do not indicate a tendency for widows to remarry with men who were their lovers and the secondary fathers to their children by an earlier husband. In all our marriage records, we know of only one such case.

Another way in which secondary fatherhood probably helped children to survive was illustrated in Tótubi's biography. Even if a woman's lover were a member of another local or even territorial group and the woman never saw him again after a brief affair, his other children were still considered the siblings of her child. They were in the category of the most reliable and trustworthy sorts of people one knew, linked by bonds of brotherhood. It was appropriate for them to make common cause in times of adversity.

In sum, partible paternity, whatever its other advantages, also helped to ameliorate the absence of husbands and fathers lost to women and their children as a result of the murders perpetrated on the Barí by their neighbors.

Notes

1. A search of all our notes, life histories as well as the genealogies to which the figure of 238 deaths from known causes pertains, reveals at least 18 Barí reported to have been lost in the forest and never seen again. Ten of these people were children under the age of ten—six girls, including two *arikbas* (mentally disabled people), and four boys. The other eight, five men and three women, were over the age of sixteen.

2. This man had already burned the fields and houses of the people living at Ishkandakaira and had threatened them with calling down his workers and the National Guard to attack them.

CHAPTER 6

Reproduction

If it is true that people, like all organisms, take in nutrients and defend themselves from dangers in order to live, in the ultimate biological sense they live in order to reproduce. The Barí, like all peoples, reproduce largely in the context of the peculiar human institution of marriage. To the ordinary anthropological understanding of marriage they add a system of sanctioned extramarital affairs that contributes to the health and survival of their children. These matters have to be understood not only in the contexts of the Barí natural and social environments but also within the framework of Barí social organization and Barí life history.

This chapter is organized in five sections. The first is a brief sketch of the general features of Barí social organization that are immediately relevant to their marital and reproductive behavior. The second focuses on the specifics of that behavior; it is organized around the reproductive part of the traditional life cycle of a Barí woman. The third is a selection of brief matrimonial histories chosen to illustrate the on-the-ground workings of the marriage system. The fourth section is an exploration of some demographic parameters of the Barí insofar as they can be inferred from our data, organized to highlight their relevance to issues in human evolutionary ecology. The fifth is an examination of what may be the most interesting aspect of Barí reproductive behavior: their elaboration of the ideology of partible paternity.

The theoretical questions on which the demographic and partible paternity data bear are elaborated at the beginning of the fourth and fifth sections, where the data are presented and analyzed. Here we confine ourselves to a brief appreciation of the issues for which sections one, two, and three serve as background to the explorations in sections four and five.

There are two families of issues dealt with in section four. These are questions pertaining to characteristics of the Barí population in general (fertility, birth spacing, sex ratio, variances in male vs. female offspring number) and questions pertaining to differences within the population, in particular, differential reproductive success and the reasons for it (ecological setting, sex of first child, superior hunting and fishing abilities).

In section five we present our latest findings on partible paternity. Recent research (Walker, Flinn, and Hill 2010) has shown how old and common this practice is in lowland South America, strengthening the disconfirmation of the standard model of human evolution that stressed the "naturalness" of sexually faithful monogamy in humans (Beckerman and Valentine 2002).

Social Organization

Overall, most Barí marriages were monogamous, but there was no bar to polygyny, and there were regions where during some years most men were polygynously married. The proportion of polygynous men varied widely with the region and time period under consideration. We know of no cases of polyandry, although, as discussed below, married women often had affairs with men who were not their husbands.

Both marriages and affairs were regulated by a strict canon of who was sexually available and who was not. Although the Barí had no descent groups, they married—to a first approximation—as if they were divided into two exogamous patrimoieties. For every Barí, male and female, the social universe was divided into two categories of people, *sagdodyira* and *okdyibara*. The words correspond rather well to the standard anthropological distinction of kin and affine, respectively.

Sagdodyira was the category that focally included one's father, one's siblings, and one's children if one were male. Relations were ideally easy and familiar, and the incest taboo precluded all sexual contact. Okdyibara was the category that focally included one's spouse, one's brother- and sister-in-law, one's father-in-law, and one's children if one were female. It also included one's mother. Relations (except for the mother-child relationship) were potentially edgy, although there were cases of extraordinary devotion too—most obviously between mother and children but sometimes also between son-in-law and father-in-law. All okdyibara of the opposite sex were potential mates, with the exception of a man's own mother, who was of course covered by the incest taboo.[1]

It is important to underline the point that only okdyibara were legitimate sexual partners. All sagdodyira were prohibited from any sexual contact whatsoever, in principle including even verbal references to sexual topics while in each other's company.

The sagdodyira-okdyibara classification of the primary, secondary, and tertiary relatives of a male and female ego (Figs. 6.1, 6.2) illustrates the way in which these assignments appear to be consistent with the premise that there were two implicit exogamous patrimoieties underlying the categorization of these relatives.

One inherited one's classification of people to whom no genealogical tie could be traced from one's father, who was classified as one's sagdodyira. Thus both men and women in principle—and overwhelmingly also in practice—classified the social universe in the same way as their fathers. This rule required that one's classification of others be the exact opposite of one's mother's, because one's mother and father had to be okdyibara to each other.

In principle this system ought to have assigned all Barí to one of two implicit, sociocentric, intermarrying patrimoieties, such that one was sagdodyira to everyone else in one's own moiety and okdyibara to everyone in the other moiety. But in fact it did not. First, such moieties did not exist as named groups, and there was no evidence of their presence as implicit categories. Second, they *could* not have existed, even as covert categories, because the system contained a few "mistakes."

One's classification of another person was supposed to follow one's father's classification of that person. But what happened if the person was a stranger, if one had no known genealogical connection with that person, and one's father had no preexisting classification of him or her?

In such a case, the Barí first had recourse to a chaining rule. If there were intermediate people who had an established classification for both oneself (or one's father) and the target stranger, then the proper classification of the people at the ends of the chain could be worked out. Four implicit rules generated the proper classification of any two people connected through other people who knew their own classification with respect to their adjacent links:

The sagdodyira of my sagdodyira is my sagdodyira.

The sagdodyira of my okdyibara is my okdyibara.

The okdyibara of my sagdodyira is my okdyibara.

The okdyibara of my okdyibara is my sagdodyira.

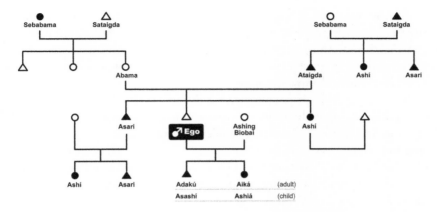

Fig 6.1. Barí kinship terms, male speaking. The solid figures indicate individuals classified as sagdodyira and the outline figures indicate those classified as okdyibara, from the point of view of Ego.

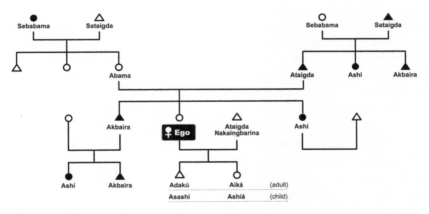

Fig. 6.2. Barí kinship terms, female speaking. The solid figures indicate individuals classified as sagdodyira and the outline figures indicate those classified as okdyibara from the point of view of Ego.

Given these rules, if it were possible to trace known links between any two people, their proper classification for each other could be established (see Fig. 6.2). Both authors have heard conversations in which links were traced in this way to establish the correct classification of people who were previously unknown to each other.

But what if the two people were so distant, both genealogically and geographically, that the links connecting them were unknown? In that case the classification was usually decided so as to maximize marriage possibilities. Here was the point at which the "mistakes," that is, inconsistencies that prevented the emergence of moieties even as covert categories, entered the system. Once any two people had decided that they were, say, okdyibara, when in order to be consistent with the rest of the system they should have been sagdodyira, then they had opened the opportunity for another pair of people, tracing their relationship through the "mistaken" pair, to make their own relationship the opposite of what it "ought" to be.

We want to emphasize that such instances were remarkably rare and could occur only where there was no known connection between the people involved. It would have been quite impossible, for instance, for parallel first cousins to reclassify themselves as okdyibara or for a granddaughter and her maternal grandfather to decide to become sagdodyira. But the existence of such "mistakes" established the point that Barí classification of others as marriageable or nonmarriageable was at base a matter of dyadic ties and not of the workings of hidden moieties.

The matter was vital, because all people recognized by the community as sagdodyira to each other, regardless of whether they had known genealogical connections, were covered by the incest taboo. In over fifty years of ethnographic investigation, Lizarralde recorded only three cases in which people married someone classified as sagdodyira—all postcontact and all resulting in the couples being driven out of their territorial group (Lizarralde and Lizarralde 1991). These cases are examples of how seriously the generally live-and-let-live Barí took the matter of incest, which posed a grave danger to everyone in the community. An old man once observed to Beckerman, as they watched the sun rise in a sky polluted by distant refinery smoke, that the sun rose dirty in these days because young people were having sex with their sagdodyira.

Now if all okdyibara of the opposite sex, except mother and son, were potentially marriageable, whom did the Barí marry? It is important to note at the outset that the Barí were somewhat unusual among tribal peoples worldwide in that their marriages were not necessarily prearranged by the parents of the bride and groom. A girl's parents might promise her to a particular man (e.g., her MBS or her MB), but if the girl flatly refused the match, then it was usually called off.

Instead of relying on parental negotiation, an aspiring husband often had to find an okdyibara girl and court her. Then her parents had to approve the match. In almost all cases, both the girl and her parents had a veto over any potential husband for her. (There were a very few cases in which girls were married against their wishes, but if a girl's objections were strong enough she always had the option of running away.)

Like a great many tribal peoples, the Barí considered a bilateral cross cousin a model of the proper kind of spouse. However, as typically happens when an ideal marriage type is specified, few marriages were of the ideal type. In a universe of 282 marriages pulled from our genealogies (all cases that met the criterion that all four parents of the marrying couple were known), only nine were actual first cross cousin unions—four marriages of a man to his MBD and five of a man to his FZD. An additional four marriages were of a man to a woman with whom the first cross cousin connection was through a stepparent—three marriages to a MBWD and one to a FWBD.

As is not uncommon among lowland South American peoples, uncle-niece marriages were also favored. Due to the rules of the sagdodyira-okdyibara system, these matches could only occur with the cross sibling, between a man and his ZD. Our sample contained nine such marriages, plus five that might be considered genealogically congruent, two with the FDD, two with the FWDD, and one with the MHDHD.

We found no cases of aunt-nephew marriage, although a woman's marriage to her ZS would technically meet the requirements of the sagdodyira-okdyibara system.

The Barí had short genealogical memories. There was formerly a taboo on naming the dead (now mainly honored in its absence), and in general people recalled only ancestors with whom they had been personally acquainted. As a result, it was difficult to speak with assurance about second cousin marriages. Our genealogical sample included four documented FFDD marriages. Surely there were many additional second cousin matches among these 282 marriages, but our genealogies did not extend far enough back to uncover them.

It was common for a man to marry his wife's sisters, particularly her younger sisters as they matured, although sometimes a man married sisters simultaneously. Our genealogical sample includes twenty-eight men who were married to two sisters or half sisters and three men who were married to three sisters or half sisters. In the great majority of these cases, the wives were full sisters.

Overall, in the 282 marriages, there were 47 in which there was a previous affinal link between the husband and wife, not including the cases in which a man married his wife's sister(s).

Kin and affinal connections were only one constraint on marriage. In addition to the strict rule that one must marry an okdyibara and the idea that a first cross cousin was the best kind of mate, the traditional Barí had clear preferences as to the group affiliation of a potential spouse. Both men and women but men in particular preferred a spouse from their own local group. However, the conflicting pressures with respect to this preference illustrated the complexities of reconciling the various people who had a voice in a marriage.

The reason for preferring marriage within the local group was clear-cut. Most first marriages were uxorilocal: The husband joined the hearth group of his wife and worked for and under the authority of her father. As long as the wife's parents were both alive and in good health, the wife's father seems usually to have been in a position to insist on this arrangement if he wanted it—which he usually did. A young man wanted a father-in-law he knew well and got along with well—and of course he also wanted the continuing company and support of his own nuclear family of origin.

In this desire to marry within his local group, a young man was often supported by his prospective mother-in-law. Thinking ahead, the mothers of marriageable girls looked to the time when their husbands would die or become feeble and the son-in-law, as the fishing and hunting breadwinner, would gain the upper hand. They wanted to be sure that their sons-in-law did not eventually take their daughters to live in their own local groups of origin—as in fact did happen with some frequency with "foreign" sons-in-law. Nevertheless, given the small size of Barí local groups, the limitation of potential spouses to people classified as okdyibara, and the practice of polygyny, it was common for a young man to be unable to find an eligible bride in his local group (Lizarralde and Lizarralde 1991).

And there was yet another reason for young men's frequent inability to obtain wives in their own local groups. If the prospective husbands—and the mothers of the young women they hoped to marry—usually preferred a marriage within the longhouse, the girls' fathers often wanted "foreign" sons-in-law, those without close kin living in the same space. That way they could have uncontested authority over their sons-in-law, avoid potential conflicts between themselves and the in-marrying husband's parents, and preclude trouble between a daughter and her husband's mother.

In view of these considerations, it was not surprising that in many life histories men recounted visiting other local groups with the specific intent of finding a wife. The festivals in which people from different local groups visited, sang together, and exchanged arrows and skirts provided one vehicle for such visits. Most common was a festival in which both men and women came as visitors. But there were also occasions on which male-only groups, with bachelors prominent among them, came to sing. A young man on either kind of visit might attach himself to a hearth group of the hosting local group and remain there for courting purposes when the rest of the visitors from his local group returned home. A wife from another local group within the same territorial group was generally preferred to a wife from a different territorial group, but there was no bar to marrying between territorial groups. In traditional times, about 25% of marriages joined a husband from one territorial group to a wife from another (Lizarralde and Lizarralde 1991).

It also happened sometimes that a women-only group went to sing at another longhouse. It is possible that the search for husbands was one of the motives of such trips.

There were also age preferences for a spouse. Overall, Barí husbands were on average about four years older than their wives (Lizarralde and Lizarralde 1991). There were, however, no rules forbidding departures from this tendency, and there were marriages of young men to women twice their age and of teenaged girls to old men. Our impression was that the former were generally successful, but the latter often ended in the young woman leaving her elderly husband for a younger man.

A first marriage generally began with an affair between a young man of eighteen or twenty and a girl around thirteen to fifteen, although some people delayed sexual activity considerably longer. The girl was usually living in the hearth group to which her nuclear family of orientation belonged. (Only if she were an orphan would she be living elsewhere.) The boy might be a member of the same hearth group (when brothers-in-law formed a single hearth group, their children were cross cousins), might be from another hearth group in the same longhouse, or might be a wife-seeking visitor from another local or territorial group. If the last, he usually attached himself to some other hearth group in the longhouse, not to that of the girl he was wooing.

As long as the couple were okdyibara to each other, their sexual relations were nobody's business but theirs, and sometimes these affairs went on for quite a while. Indeed some unmarried girls carried on simultaneous affairs with more than one boy, although that was rare. Marriage, however, was very definitely the concern of people other than the young lovers.

The Barí made a clear distinction between people who were married and people who were only having an affair. The difference was that a woman who was married had been "turned over" to her husband by her parents or (if her parents are dead) by her brother. We examine this process in subsequent sections of this chapter.

Reproduction in the Life Cycle

The usual course for a description of the life cycle is to start at birth and finish at death. Here, because the emphasis is on a woman's reproduction, we begin around the time a girl reaches puberty and continue only to the marriages of her daughters.

In common with a number of other tribal peoples in lowland South America, the Barí generally said that first intercourse brought on menstruation, although a few of the women in our life histories mentioned that they had their first periods and went through their puberty rites (always motivated by the occurrence of a girl's first period) a good while before they had sex for the first time. We suspect that the Barí would argue that first intercourse was sufficient but not necessary; it brought on menstruation in a pubescent girl, but menstruation would eventually happen without it.

First intercourse was not a subject we specifically investigated in taking life histories, but a number of women mentioned their experiences in passing. Sometimes the first partner was an older man who approached a girl and asked her if she wanted to have sex with him. In other cases the first sex partner seemed to have been a boy only a little older than the girl. In all cases the man or boy and the girl were okdyibara.

As soon as it was clear that a girl had started her first period, her mother made a small enclosure of mats inside the longhouse and put her in it. She stayed there until the bleeding had stopped, deemed dangerous to other people, especially men, and to crops. She observed food taboos (variable but usually including pineapple, palm fruits, and peppers) and in some cases was not allowed to drink water for a day or two, lest she develop a big belly. Her father, or sometimes her mother on her father's behalf, rubbed her body with saliva and/or peppers filled with salt and saliva to protect her against skin diseases. Her mother entered the enclosure to talk to her about becoming a woman.

Once the bleeding stopped, the girl left the mat enclosure, bathed with her mother, received a new skirt, and began life as an adult. She could now sing and exchange skirts, she was expected to take adult responsibility, and she could have sex freely.

There were two common routes to first marriage. The necessary final step in both was the permission of the bride's parents; their consent was what made a marriage out of an affair. (The boy's parents' consent seems to have been less important or even unimportant, at least in the majority of cases, although we have not investigated the topic sufficiently to be certain.) In one route the boy and girl decided that they wanted to marry, and he then approached her father and asked permission. The father seldom responded immediately. Instead, he asked his daughter privately if she really wanted to marry the boy, and he consulted his wife.

Lizarralde recalls that because his informants emphasized the importance of gaining the permission of the potential bride's father, he believed during his early years with the Barí that a girl's father was the dominant figure in the decision to turn her over as a wife. In later years, however, after the accumulation of more in-depth information about more marriages, he came to the conclusion that typically it was the girl's mother who had the final say. Her father was more a mouthpiece than a decision maker.

If the girl's parents decided that the proposed marriage was acceptable, then weeks or months after the potential groom had pressed his suit, often when the local group migrated from one of its longhouses to another, the girl's father privately told the suitor that he could hang his hammock over the girl's hammock when they reached their destination. That change of hammock position was as close as the Barí came to a marriage ceremony. It was not so much a wedding as a wedding announcement, a sign to the rest of the local group that the bride had been turned over to the groom. If the groom was already living in the bride's hearth group, she might hang her hammock under his.

Parental consent was crucial. There were quite a few life histories in which the girl's parents refused permission. In all but one the boy eventually went off to seek a wife elsewhere. The only elopement without parental consent that we know of produced a child, one of our elderly informants, but failed after about a year. The woman returned to her parents and later married a man they approved of, with whom she had many additional children. Our elderly informant's vigorous, almost shrill insistence that his father was not the same man as the father of his siblings led us to suspect that the original man was the love of his mother's life and that she had made that plain to her only child by him.

The second common route to marriage was instigation by the parents of the bride. When a girl was involved in an affair with a boy of whom her parents approved, one of her parents—usually her mother—might suggest marriage. Often, this push was all it took for the boy to hang his hammock above the girl's, again usually after a migration from one long-house to another.

Although marriage required permission from the bride's parents (or her brother if they were dead), it did not always require that the new husband move into his father-in-law's hearth group. Postmarital residence was contingent and negotiable (see below). Nevertheless, over half of all marriages followed the uxorilocal rule, and some informants stated that uxorilocality was always required when both the bride's parents were alive and in good health. After the couple had a child or two, they usually established their own hearth group.

Most women became pregnant within a few months of marrying.[2] Barí ideas about pregnancy were not uniform. All informants agreed that a man placed a substance that would grow into a fetus in a woman's womb. Some said that if two men had intercourse with a woman at about the same time, then the fetus was composed of a mixture of the substances of the two men. Others said only the first man to have sex with her contributed the basic substance of the fetus. Informants agreed that once a fetus was present it had to be anointed with repeated baths of semen in order to develop properly (some people said at least once a night for the first three months of pregnancy). Several informants likened this anointing with semen to the way Barí fathers rubbed their daughters with their saliva during puberty rites and the way that people spit sanctified tobacco on those who were sick in order to transfer their strength and health to someone in a vulnerable state.

An insufficient rate of intercourse would result in a pregnancy that lasted too long and produced a sickly, rickety child with a small head. A woman's husband might provide all the semen necessary, but in just under one quarter of all pregnancies the woman also took a lover. One reason women gave for taking a lover was to avoid tiring their husbands excessively.

Another reason for taking a lover—less frequently mentioned but potentially just as decisive for pregnant women—was that the lover, here as everywhere else in the world, gave presents to his mistress. Among the Barí, these presents were fish and game, attractive gifts for a woman eating for two. The lover also had an obligation to provide subsequent gifts of fish and game to the child whose partial father the Barí believed him to be.

The frequency of taking lovers might or might not be related to the fact that the profile of Barí pregnancy outcomes was rather poor. The Barí were somewhat unusual among tribal peoples in that memories of miscarriages and stillbirths were not suppressed. That women were able to include these events in the reproductive histories they gave for their deceased mothers and sisters suggested that these matters were openly discussed among closely related women.

Our sample of 114 postreproductive women for whom we collected complete reproductive histories indicated that over 10% of remembered pregnancies ended in a spontaneous miscarriage, a stillbirth, or a perinatal death (i.e., death within a week of birth). Of the 916 pregnancies remembered by these women, 95 ended in one of these fatal ways.

When a woman neared the end of her pregnancy, she usually prepared a place in the forest just beyond the house-surrounding field in a location corresponding to the placement of her hammock inside the longhouse. She cleared a spot where she put a mat, preferably one woven by her mother. When her labor pains became intense, she went to the prepared place, ideally accompanied by her mother, at least one other woman who was okdyibara to her, and a sister or two. (The sisters might help with preparations, but as sagdodyira they were not allowed to see the woman's genitals and thus could not catch the baby.) If the expecting mother had daughters, one or more of them might come too. The husband was also allowed to be there, although we believe this was somewhat unusual.

Barí women gave birth squatting over the mat and holding on to a small tree trunk or an overhead branch. The husband, if present, might support his wife from behind. If the baby was slow to emerge, one of the accompanying okdyibara women stroked and pushed on the woman's belly from the front. If this procedure failed to speed the birth, an attending woman (or sometimes her husband if he was there) knelt behind the mother, wrapped her arms around her, and pressed on her belly. Another woman, an okdyibara kneeling in front of the mother, caught the baby as it emerged.

One of the okdyibara women, often the mother of the woman who has just given birth, cut the umbilical cord with a knife if the baby was a girl or with an anhinga's serrated beak if it was a boy. The mother then lay on her back, and the baby was placed on her breast.

When the placenta was expelled one of the birth attendants buried it in the leaf litter at the base of a nearby tree. For the rest of the life of the child, he or she had a spirit twin who lived in that tree. At the end of life they went together to the land of the *basungchingba* (spirits of the dead).

Some informants have told us that especially when the woman's husband was not present for the birth, the mother told the birth attendants, "The father of this baby is . . . ," naming the man or men with whom she had had intercourse around the beginning of and during her pregnancy. The okdyibara birth attendant then returned to the longhouse and told the man or men who were named, "You have a son [or daughter]."

Other informants stated that the birth attendant knew who the fathers were, but the mother did not name them just after the moment of birth and the attendant did not make an announcement in the longhouse. This information was simply common knowledge among those concerned.

What we have just described is the fullest, most elaborate form of birthing practiced by the Barí. Often, especially for higher parities, when a woman was experienced in giving birth she was accompanied only by her mother or a single sister. There were a number of cases of women giving birth alone, and one of our informants told us proudly that her mother had instructed her that since she, the mother, had given birth to her children unassisted her daughter had to do the same. This woman had had all her children without any assistance. When we asked her if she had been afraid, especially the first time, she said simply that she had a strong heart.

After resting for a while, the new mother returned to the longhouse with her baby. There she might rest on her mat for some time, but eventually she took to her hammock with her baby. Neither she nor the baby was washed until the following day.

For about four months after giving birth, a woman did no work: she did not go the garden to harvest or weed and was not allowed even to come near it; nor did she cook. Her husband harvested, and her sister or daughter cooked for her. She spent most of her time in her hammock, recuperating and nursing her baby. (She preferentially ate the teats and udders of game animals at this time, and the rumps of birds, which exude a white fluid, so that she would make plenty of milk.) If she had no sister or daughter, her husband cooked. After this vacation she returned to her usual routine.

Barí children were exclusively breast-fed for about half a year. Then weaning foods, bananas and manioc masticated by the mother, were introduced. Children were more or less completely weaned by the time the mother's next child was born, usually when they were around the age of three (see below).

Child care was mainly the work of women; new mothers carried their babies almost constantly, and they nursed on demand. Husbands were tender and indulgent with infants, but they spent much less time carrying them than did their wives. However, little girls as young as four or five helped their mothers with their younger siblings, carrying them around and watching over them. They appeared to lighten a mother's workload substantially. As discussed below, a woman whose first live-born child was a girl had, on average, one more pregnancy during her reproductive life than a woman who had a boy. Little boys were essentially exempt from child and infant care.

A woman's childbearing period was typically twenty to twenty-five years, from her mid-teens until her late thirties or early forties. On average she experienced about eight pregnancies during that time and gave birth to about seven live-born children.

Because uxorilocality was the most common form of postmarital residence among the Barí, a women not only raised her own children, and had a major voice in the marriages of her daughters, but also typically assisted her daughters in childbirth and played an important part in raising her grandchildren. We have even (very occasionally) seen a grandmother nursing her grandchild. Thus a woman looked after her reproductive interests even after she herself had ceased to reproduce.

Marital Histories

The following sketches of the events and decisions surrounding marriages, extracted from our life history field notes, illustrate the variety of marriage practices among the Barí.

Akaando: As a pubescent girl, Akaando was living in a hearth group with her parents, her mother's mother, her siblings, and her older sister's husband. The father of her sister's husband, who lived in the same longhouse, asked her if she wanted to have sex with him; she said yes. Shortly thereafter she had her first period and went through her puberty ritual. After that she was wooed by the son of her sister's husband by his first wife, who also lived in the same longhouse. The boy talked first to her and after getting her consent, talked to her parents, who agreed to accept him as a son-in-law. He moved to her hearth group and hung his hammock over hers. They had twelve children.

Daarikbí: She had sex for the first time with a visitor who came from another local group to sing; he was staying with her hearth group. She does not remember his name. Shortly after, she had her first period and her puberty ritual. About three years later she married a boy from her own hearth group with whom she had been having an affair. He was her stepfather's sister's son; thus this match was in effect a MBD-FZS marriage. She told him she was going to hang her hammock under his, and he said yes. She also talked to her mother and father, and they agreed. They stayed in the same hearth group and had nine children.

Akariká: As a young man, Akariká fell in love with a girl in his own longhouse and made love to her at night. When she got pregnant her mother told him to marry her, apparently with her father's approval. He brought his hammock from his hearth group to theirs and hung it above her hammock.

About four years later, after his first wife died, along with the two children she had borne him, her mother took the hammock of her next older sister and hung it next to his first wife's. This sister was in love with another man, who had asked for her hand, but her mother had told him no. The sister did not like her new husband at first, but her mother and father had turned her over, and she did not rebel.

Less than a year later her mother (again apparently with the consent of her father) hung the hammock of another of her daughters under his, even though he had not thought about marrying this woman. This third wife bore him one child and then left him for another man. The second wife remained with him and bore him nine children.

Baashká: When he was about twenty Baashká wanted to get married, but almost all the girls in his local group were already promised to other men. He went to the longhouse of a local group from another territory, probably with other bachelors from his local group, to look for a wife. He sang with all the men in that longhouse. He stayed with one hearth group and indicated an interest in the daughter of an older couple living in another hearth group. The girl's mother asked him if he were willing to stay. He said no, but apparently a tentative compromise was reached. He returned to his local group, and sometime later his prospective wife's family (all but one grown brother) followed him.

They joined his local group, establishing their own hearth within it. They still did not hand over their daughter. When the local group moved to another of its longhouses, he was allowed to visit his intended and eventually to marry her. He joined her hearth group. She bore him five children and died when the youngest was about three. At about the same time he married his wife's younger sister, who bore him ten children. His third marriage was to the younger sister of his first two wives, who bore him three children.

Baashká also had one daughter with a widow who already had four children; she lived at a separate hearth in the same longhouse. He did not marry her, but he brought her fish and game.

By the time his mother- and father-in-law died (within a month of each other) all his children were grown, leaving him alone with his wives. One of his brothers-in-law had married one of his daughters (a MB-ZD marriage, a good match among the Barí), and they had their own hearth group in the same longhouse.

Asharí: His future first wife lived in the same longhouse. She asked him to marry her, and he asked her mother and father if they wanted him as a son-in-law. They accepted him, and he joined her hearth group, where she hung her hammock below his. They ate with her hearth group until they had their first child, then established their own hearth. She died of snakebite around 1960, after bearing him three children, two of whom are still alive. He married his second wife shortly after the death of the first; she lived in the same longhouse with her mother, sister, brother, and five-year-old son by a man who had not married her. Her father was dead. She asked him to marry her, and then her mother repeated the request, and he did. His new wife's family joined his hearth group. She bore him eleven children.

Arukbishí (female) and *Arorokba* (male): About three years after Arukbishí's first menstruation she married. There was a man in the longhouse, Araktadou, who wanted to marry her. He had spoken to her but not to her mother. She did not want to marry that man but wanted to marry Arorokba. Her mother was also opposed to the marriage with Araktadou but agreed to a marriage with Arorokba, who was about eighteen. It was her mother who spoke to Arorokba and asked him to marry her daughter. He was already in love with her and agreed. It was also her mother who took her daughter's hammock and hung it under his, in his hearth group. We do not know if the bride's father was alive at this time.

Aboraaba: His first wife was from the same longhouse. Her mother caught them together and said that they could marry if they wanted to. (Her father was still alive but very old.) Shortly after, the local group migrated to a different longhouse, and when they arrived he hung his hammock over his new wife's hammock and ate with her, her father, her mother, her mother's two co-wives, and his wife's three sisters. These three sisters were all married to the same man, who also belonged to this hearth group. Three or four years later his first wife died; she had borne him one daughter, whom he gave to his wife's mother to raise. (His wife's mother had left her elderly husband for another man by this time, but he still had his other two wives.)

A year or two year later, the mother of a young woman asked him to marry her daughter. (The mother was a widow who had remarried, and the daughter was the child of the deceased husband.) He accepted and joined their hearth group. About three years later this wife died childless in the postcontact epidemics. The rest of his matrimonial history belongs to a study of culture change.

Okachiá: About three years after her first menstruation and her puberty ritual, she and her family were visiting (possibly with her whole local group) in the longhouse of another local group. There she had sex for the first time, with a man from that group. Okachiá's father suggested that he marry her. They married and established their own hearth in another of the longhouses of his local group. Her family of origin also established itself in this longhouse, at a separate hearth.

Her new husband died about a month after they married, and she rejoined her parents' hearth group. About five years later her father suggested to a young man who had come visiting from another territorial group that he marry his daughter. They married and established their own hearth. She had one child by this young man, and then he died of snakebite, about three years after they married. She returned to her parents' hearth. About a year later she married the paternal half brother of her first husband. They established their own hearth, and she bore him seven children before he died in the pericontact epidemics. The rest of her marital history belongs to a study of culture change.

Akaachidou (male) and *Okbaibai* (female): Most of the girls in Akaachidou's local group did not like him; they said he was ugly. He asked for the hand of a little girl named Okbaibai in the longhouse he lived in, and her mother promised her to him but said he had to wait until she grew up. This girl's father was dead, but her mother had remarried, and her stepfather, who had raised her, was still alive. When the girl was grown, he moved his hammock to her family's hearth group. They had nine children, six of whom are still alive.

Abacachara: About five years after her first menstruation, a family related to hers but from another territorial group came to visit and to sing in her longhouse. One of the members of this party was a young man who had come along because his father had told him there were a lot of girls in her local group. This father was the brother of her mother's father.

He sang with her father and her older brother, and he began an affair with her. Her father said to him, "You are together. You should get married and treat her well." When her local group moved to the next longhouse in their cycle, her father (he was *nyatobaye*) "turned her over" to her lover, and he joined her hearth group. (The *nyatobaye* of a longhouse is the man who suggested it be built and directed its construction.) She bore him nine children. Eventually he also married her younger sister, who bore him five children; she died a couple of weeks after giving birth to the last child.

Sakoksó: He was living in his parents' hearth group and having an affair with a girl in the same longhouse. His parents spoke to hers. Then the girl told him that if he did not bring his hammock to her hearth group he could find another girlfriend. He moved in with her, and she got pregnant right away. She died pregnant with their sixth child.

Ashiroó: A young man in her longhouse, full grown but unmarried, asked her if she wanted to have sex with him. She said yes. A few months later she had her first period and her puberty ritual. (The puberty ritual was minimal in her case, possibly because her period came when her hearth group was visiting in the longhouse of another local group.) A while later she married another boy in her own longhouse. (They were probably having an affair.) His mother asked her mother if the two could marry. Her mother asked her if she wanted to marry him, and she said yes. Her father was still alive, but she did not mention his role in this agreement. The boy hung his hammock over hers, in her hearth group, but the next day the local group migrated to another of their longhouses, and there she joined her new husband's hearth group. They had ten children. He also married her sister.

Asaami: He wanted to marry, but his father told him he was too young. He joined a group of men and women going to visit and sing at another territorial group because he was looking for a girl to marry despite his father's reservations. On the way they stopped at a longhouse belonging to another local group of his own territorial group. There he did not sing but met a girl living with her mother and siblings whose father was dead. He went on with his companions and sang with many men at the longhouse of the other group, then returned to the longhouse where he had met the girl and married her, not returning to his local group.

However, shortly thereafter his wife's family and his family of origin moved to yet another longhouse, Burubungda, which belonged jointly to his group and to another group. (They built it together as a refuge from criollo attacks.) There he and his wife established their own hearth group. Her nine pregnancies produced five children who are still living.

Korokonda: He was attracted to a girl in his local group. Her father, worried by signs of encroaching criollos, took her and the rest of his hearth group to visit another local group of the same territorial group until the danger passed. Korokonda, whose father was dead, followed them with *his* hearth group, his mother and siblings. One of his intended's brothers noticed them together and said, "Marry my sister."

Apparently her parents were in agreement, because they let their daughter join Korokonda's hearth group. Her parents ate apart, but he gave them half his fish and game. Not long thereafter both hearth groups returned to their original local group.

Aburubú: He lived in a hearth group with his mother, his brother, and his brother's wife. In the same house was a girl of eight or ten who was the only girl in a large set of brothers. Her mother said to him, "Raise this girl. When she is big, she will be your wife." It was the mother who said this to him even though the girl's father was still alive. He took her into his hearth and eventually married her. She had borne him two daughters when she and the surviving daughter were murdered by Indian killers.

Barikoksá (male) and *Arukaani* (female): When he was about eighteen, Barikoksá told his parents he was going off to sing. He went to the longhouse of another local group, where he stayed five months in the hearth group of the nyatobaye, singing with all the men in the house and then staying on. He courted a girl named Arukaani in another hearth group who was expected to marry someone else, but after he appeared on the scene he was the first choice of the nyatobaye (who was the girl's FZH) and of the girl's mother. Her father was reluctant to approve this change in marriage plans but eventually came around. Immediately after her father turned her over, Barikoksá and his new wife returned for a visit to his local group, and his father insisted he make good his absence by helping to weed the fields. After three days of fast work, he and his new wife returned to live in her hearth group. They had thirteen children.

Arokchiká (male) and *Ashirai* (female): Their hearth groups of origin belonged to the same local group. Ashirai was living with both her parents; Arokchiká was living with his mother and stepfather. They were already having an affair. Her mother asked him what he thought of her daughter, whether he wanted to marry her, and he replied, "You yourself

are saying this to me, and I agree. I am going to marry your daughter."
Her mother liked him because he was a good hunter. Her father also spoke
to him and gave his consent. Her father was his mother's paternal half
brother, so this was going to be an MBD-FZS marriage.

The mother then told her daughter that she had chosen Arokchiká as
her husband. When their local group moved to the next longhouse on
their round, she openly got into her new husband's hammock. A little
later she hung her hammock next to his. Although she had moved into his
hearth group, he sent fish and game to her father from time to time. They
lived with his family until their second child was born, then established
their own hearth. They had seven children.

Achidakdá: She was in her early or mid-teens but had not yet had her
first period and was still a virgin. There was a widower in her longhouse
who had four daughters, the oldest about twelve. He caught her in the
clear space around the house when everyone else was inside and raped
her. She screamed, but he covered her mouth. While he was raping her,
he said he was going to marry her. When she went back into the house,
her mother asked her why she was crying, but she said nothing. She had
her first period shortly after. The widower spoke to her father, and they
agreed to have her marry him. She agreed to marry him about a month
later. He took her hammock and other belongings to his hearth and hung
her hammock under his, and she began cooking for him and his daughters. She eventually bore him six children. When we interviewed her it
was clear that the memory of the rape was still painful to recall.

Obikará (female) and *Asokarí* (male): Obikará's father was dead, and
she lived with her mother and siblings in Karibaigdakaira. Her brother
Korokonda fished and hunted for the hearth group. Asokarí, who lived in
Ishdabakbaikaig, came to visit her longhouse along with his brother-in-
law Aichugdakira. Asokarí, who was considerably older than she was, told
her he was unmarried and took her virginity. He then hung his hammock
over hers, indicating a marriage. However, when Aichugdakira left Karibaigdakaira to return to Ishdabakbaikaig he told Obikará that Asokarí was
married to his two sisters there and had five children by them.

Asokarí stayed in Karibaigdakaira after Aichugdakira left, but when
Obikará's mother found out he already had two wives, she took her daughter, along with the rest of her family, to Ihchidayosá. Asokarí followed
them, and there in Ihchidayosá he again hung his hammock over hers.
Her mother did not object. Asokarí fished and hunted for their hearth.

When Asokarí's previous two wives heard he had moved in with Obikará and her family, they were angry and sent word for him to return. He did not. Then their brother Atairi handed over the two wives to Ashimaká, one of Asokarí's brothers. The parties to this new marriage accepted the change, but ever after whenever the two former wives ran into Obikará, they said, "There goes the husband thief." Obikará bore Asokarí eleven children.

Demographic Matters

Demographic data speak to many important issues in human evolutionary ecology. After all, evolution itself is the result of demographic processes. Unfortunately, our information about the Barí was not sufficient to address many of these issues because we did not have the temporal control needed (e.g., most important, reliable precontact birth dates). Limited to the databases we describe below, we were able to trace the growth of the Barí population over the past few decades and to provide a few basic demographic parameters. Using these parameters and the databases used to generate them, we were able to address such questions as the following:

1. Effects of contact on reproduction. Not surprisingly, we found that the trauma of contact and introduced disease caused a major decrease in reproduction.
2. Sex ratio of the Barí population. The human sex ratio (number of males/number of females) has been a focus of anthropological interest for a long time, largely because considerable attention has been directed by theoretical biologists to the topic of sex ratios in general (Sieff 1990). For decades anthropologists working with the peoples of South America, in both the lowlands and the highlands, had reported a higher sex ratio at birth than had been found in other regions. Early data were summarized over a generation ago by Bolton (1980) and Millard and Berlin (1983.) There was debate as to whether this repeated finding was a result of female infanticide, underreporting of female infants, or an actual surplus of male births. Our Barí materials largely supported the reality of a live-birth sex ratio bias (although there were some problems) and suggested that the discrepancy was not a matter of infanticide or underreporting. In exploring this issue, we found an unanticipated connection between sex ratio and partible paternity, reported in the next section.

Various factors related to differential reproductive success, for example:

1. Effect of environmental richness of reproduction. It had been widely found in ecological studies that animals tended to have higher reproductive success in places where and times when resource abundance per individual was elevated. This correlation had been noted in red deer (Albion, Clutton-Brock, and Guinness 1987), Soay sheep (Crawley et al. 2004), red squirrels (Wauters and Lens 1995), and bank voles (Koivula et al. 2003), among other mammals. Our Barí data appeared to provide a human example of the phenomenon.

2. Effect of the sex of the firstborn child on total reproductive success. It had been found in at least one subsistence-level tribal society (Turke 1988) that women whose firstborn children were girls had more children than those who had a boy first. The suggested explanation was that an initial girl could help her mother with subsequent child care and thus lighten her load to the point of actually sustaining the mother's reproductive health for a longer time than what was achieved by women who had boys first. This finding has not been replicated since, however (cf. Hames and Draper 2004). Our Barí data indicated that while more pregnancies did indeed occur with girl-first mothers, they did not result in more children eventually raised to adulthood.

3. Reproductive success of superior hunters and fishermen. It had been proposed that men who were particularly good hunters (and perhaps particularly good fishermen, in societies where fishing was the major source of protein) were especially attractive as husbands and therefore tended to have more—and younger—wives than less accomplished men and in parallel fashion to have more children as well. Ethnographic data from a number of cases were assembled and analyzed by Smith (2004), who found support for the proposal. Although Smith dealt only with hunters and gatherers, our Barí material also supported this proposition and offered details as to its mechanisms.

4. Reproductive consequences of sororal versus nonsororal polygyny. The literature on human evolutionary ecology implied (although we never found an explicit statement of this prediction in a simple declarative sentence) that co-wives who were sisters ought be more concerned with the welfare of each others' children than unrelated co-wives and thus that polygynous men who married sisters ought to have a higher fraction of their ever-born children survive to adult-

hood than polygynous men whose wives were unrelated. We found little or no support for this proposition.

5. Consequences of the fundamental asymmetry in male and female reproductive constraints for male and female reproductive strategies. In almost all known human societies, men have higher variance in their reproductive success than do women (for caveats, see Brown, Laland, and Borgerhoff and Mulder 2009). It could hardly be otherwise. A woman can produce a fairly limited number of offspring no matter how many men she mates with (in our sample, the maximum number of pregnancies was fourteen). A man can fertilize an indefinitely large number of women—especially in a society, such as that of the Barí, in which polygyny is permitted. In general, in a polygynous society because some men have multiple wives, others have none. On the other hand, almost all women are married. Thus, although the *average* male reproductive success must be approximately equal to the average female reproductive success (assuming roughly equal numbers of men and women), the variance for men is considerably higher than that for women. How do men and women respond to this difference in their reproductive opportunities? Our attempt to answer to this last question bridges the gap between this section and the last section, where we deal with partible paternity.

We examine these questions in order below, after dealing with basic demographic rates and other population parameters.

The Data and the Population

THE DATA

There have been four complete censuses of the Venezuelan Barí. The first two were conducted by R. Lizarralde—in October 1982–February 1983 (OCEI 1985; Lizarralde and Lizarralde 1991) and in September 1992 (OCEI 1992), each as part of the Venezuelan National Indian Census. The third was carried out by the Barí themselves during the Venezuelan National Census of November 2001, but the information was incorporated into the report on the general Native American population of Venezuela in a way that makes it problematic to extract the Barí data alone. The fourth, a count associated with the (still-unachieved) legal titling of Barí lands, was begun by R. Lizarralde in November 2004 with a count of the Barí living in the mountainous part of their reserve and finished in July 2006 by personnel from the Venezuelan Ministry of the Environment, working with the off-reserve lowland Barí. There are obvious problems of comparison between the two parts of this last census, which is still unpublished.

In addition, 110 reproductive histories were obtained from a sample of 55 male and 55 female Venezuelan Barí in 1988–1989 by Zaldívar, Lizarralde, and Beckerman (1991). A medical census of 526 individuals, about one-third of the then-living Venezuelan Barí, was taken in 1992 by a team led by Rebecca Holmes (Holmes 1993). An extensively cross-checked database of the reproductive histories of 114 postreproductive women was compiled by Lizarralde and Beckerman from interviews in the late 1980s and early to mid-1990s and data from Lizarralde's censuses and field notes dating to the early 1960s.

On the other side of the border, an unpublished census of the Colombian Barí was taken by the anthropologist Orlando Jaramillo in 1985, but due to difficulty of access (the area was already under the control of the ELN and the FARC), it contained less information than the Venezuelan censuses.

THE POPULATION

Lizarralde estimated that at the time of his peaceful contact in July 1960 there were about 1,200 Barí, total, in Venezuela and Colombia. These people were decimated by the postcontact epidemics that reached this virgin soil population in 1962, again in 1964, 1965, and, with most devastating effect, 1966. Lizarralde and Beckerman (1982) estimated that at its low point in the second half of 1966, the total Barí population was no more than 850 and may have been 10 to 15% smaller.

According to the Venezuelan National Indian Censuses, the Venezuelan Barí population rose from 1,071 in 1983 to 1,520 in 1992, showing an average annual growth rate of around 4%. This rate is remarkably high, but it occurred in a population that had been devastated by measles epidemics between 1962 and 1966. Measles is considerably deadlier to adults without previous exposure than it is to children. The children who survived the epidemics were in their early reproductive years in the early 1980s, while the older people who had died in the measles epidemics were of course not counted in the 1983 census, which for this reason recorded a population with a high proportion of reproductive age people.

The 2004 and 2006 censuses enumerated 2,137 people, if the parts from the two different years are simply added together. This sum would imply an annual growth rate of around 2.5% between 1992 and 2006.

However, if the 2004 component had grown at the 2.5% annual growth rate between 2004 and 2006, there would have been 2,172 Barí in 2006 (a minor change; the average annual growth rate would still have been around 2.5%). Assuming that this growth rate maintained itself, there are now (2012) about 2,500 Barí in Venezuela.

The only reliable census of the Colombian Barí of which we are aware, the Jaramillo census of 1985, recorded 488 people in that country (Jaramillo pers. com.). Assuming that the Colombian population followed the growth trends of the Venezuelan population (4% growth until 1992, 2.5% growth thereafter), and assuming negligible migration, there are now 1,025 to 1,050 Barí in Colombia. The total Barí population is thus in the range of 3,525 to 3,550.

SOME BASIC DEMOGRAPHIC PARAMETERS

OVERALL FERTILITY   The 114 postreproductive women in our sample of women whose complete reproductive histories were known reported a mean of 8.04 ± 3.02 pregnancies (mean ± standard deviation), with a modal number of 10 pregnancies and a median of 8.5. Their mean number of live-born children was 7.16 ± 2.80; both the mode and the median number of live-borns was 8. Children were counted as live-born if they survived for a week after birth. (We chose this definition of liveborn because the Barí, who have a high rate of cleft lip/cleft palate [Ballew, Beckerman, and Lizarralde 1993], sometimes produce infants who cannot nurse and are thus inherently nonviable even though they live for a few days.) The postreproductive women whose reproductive histories provided these data were themselves born between about 1900 and the late 1950s.

It is important to note that the numbers given above are derived from the reproductive histories of postreproductive women, not from instantaneous birthrates. None of them are equivalent to the total fertility rate (TFR) used by demographers.

BIRTH INTERVALS   To explore the effects of contact on reproduction, we looked for a change in birth interval. We estimated interbirth intervals for two different sets of women. One set consisted of 28 women who were first observed and recorded by Lizarralde as young children during the three years just after contact. They included all the girls who lived to reproduce who were estimated to have been eight years old or younger on the date Lizarralde first observed them, on the grounds that the age of a child in that age span can be accurately estimated. Thus the birth years of these women were reasonably well established. Their children's birth years, all postcontact, were also known from mission records and Lizarralde's notes. We assumed that all children's births occurred at midyear. For 179 birth intervals closed at both ends, the mean interbirth interval was 32 ± 14 months (mean ± standard deviation).

We also extracted from our 114 life history interviews a database of 41 married women, nonoverlapping with the 28 women noted above, composed of those women whose reproductive years spanned the date of peaceful contact. That is, they began reproduction before 1960 and continued to bear children after that year. The years of birth of their precontact children were reliably estimated in the main, because Lizarralde met the great majority of these children in the years just after contact, when it was possible to estimate their ages with acceptable accuracy. These women's postcontact children's birth years were also reliably known from Lizarralde's censuses and mission records. Thus although the birth dates for these women were fuzzy, the years of their children's birth were acceptable.

These 41 women were of course all born before the 28 women whose birth years are reliably estimated, and their postcontact reproductive histories thus represented the childbearing experience of a somewhat older cohort of women. For 337 birth intervals closed at both ends, with all births assumed to occur at midyear, these 41 reproductive histories revealed an average interbirth interval of 35 ± 27 months.

Disaggregating this database allowed the exploration of the effects of contact. When Beckerman began work with the Colombian Barí in 1970, they were concerned that women did not seem to be having children. Lizarralde heard the same complaint at the Colombian mission of Catalaura, on the Venezuelan border, in 1966. It was an impression shared by both Protestant and Catholic missionaries to the Colombian Barí, as well as other observers. Most non-Barí attributed the notably small number of pregnant women at that time to the shock of contact, epidemic mortality, and radical change in the conditions of life.

The implication here was that in precontact times maternal age at first birth may have been younger, and interbirth interval shorter, than around the time of the trauma of contact, disease, and missionization. Although we had no reliable information on maternal age at first birth in this data set, the data were adequate to explore changes in interbirth intervals.

The effect of contact could be seen by partitioning the interbirth interval data into three subsets: intervals whose closing years ran up to but not after the contact year of 1960; intervals whose opening years occurred after 1960; and intervals that spanned 1960 (i.e., the opening year was 1960 or earlier and the closing year was later). This exercise yielded a mean interbirth interval of 31 ± 12 months for the 116 precontact birth intervals and a mean interbirth interval of 34 ± 32 months for the 181 postcontact intervals—an unimpressive disparity in the means, although a notable difference in the standard deviations. More interestingly, this analysis also revealed a mean interbirth interval of 51 ± 30 months for the 41 interbirth intervals that spanned the year of first contact. The Barí were correct in their assessment of an immediately postcontact period of lowered fertility. Possibly this episode of lowered fertility lingered for many years among some women while others returned more quickly to normal fertility, thus giving rise to the larger standard deviation in the postcontact birth intervals. If this interpretation is correct, it suggests that the lowered fertility just after 1960 may not have been simply a matter of the physiological effects of the epidemics per se but may also have reflected a component of psychological trauma.

REPRODUCTIVE LIFE SPAN It was possible to use the databases compiled for the examination of the effect of contact on reproduction to generate estimates for a few other demographic parameters. We estimated reproductive life span from our sample of forty-one women whose childbearing spanned first contact; they provided the most reliable data for this purpose. These women, whose childbearing spans ranged from 7 to 31 years in length, had a mean reproductive period of 23.7 ± 6.3 years; the median was 25 years.

We estimated mother's age at first birth from our sample of 28 women whose birth years were reliably estimated. They showed a mean age of 17.8 ± 3.3 years at first birth. The range of age at first birth was large: 14 to 28 years. Since all these women began childbearing after first contact, there were obvious problems with these figures. All these women were little girls when first observed in postcontact fieldwork; their sexual maturation, their initiation of sexual activity, their marriages, and all their pregnancies took place after the shock of contact—and after the devastating epidemics of the 1960s.

Mother's mean age at last birth was a more difficult issue than mean age at first birth. We were able to obtain information about which we are reasonably confident on the year of last birth only for a subsample of twenty-two of the reliably aged 28 women. The range of ages at last birth was large, 22 to 45 years old, and the younger extreme was not due only to the early deaths of a few of these women. (In fact, the woman who had her last child at 22 had only a single child and is still alive—and a grandmother). The mean age at last birth for this small subsample was 34.5 ± 6.3 years. The median age was 35.5, and the mode was 32. These figures are of course subject to all the cautions mentioned in the previous paragraph—and still more.

SEX RATIO

The sex ratio within the Barí population is an issue of interest. It has long been remarked that South American Indian populations tend to display a male-biased sex ratio, considerably above the worldwide average at birth of about 105 males to 100 females (Bolton 1980; Millard and Berlin 1983).

According to the 1982–1983 census, of the 1,071 Barí then living in Venezuela, 558 were male and 513 female (sex ratio 109:100); the median age was 14, and the proportion under 20 was 63% (Lizarralde and Lizarralde 1991).

The age and sex structure of the Venezuelan Barí population at the time of the 1982–1983 census (Table 6.1) was unexceptional for lowland South American Indian populations, given the small numbers of people in each age group, except for the striking absence of women in the 20 to 24 age range. This lack was almost certainly related to events surrounding the pericontact epidemics that staggered the Barí in the early to mid-1960s. In those years "Barí adults and missionaries pointed out that 'many' baby girls were taken by non-Indians . . . allegedly to rescue them from the peri-contact epidemics, and as a future source of free domestic labor" (Lizarralde and Lizarralde 1991: 459). The abduction of little girls and female infants figured repeatedly in our life history interviews; boys were occasionally also taken, but the preference was for girls who could be brought up as domestic servants.

This practice of the abduction of female children is well known among anthropologists who work in the South American lowlands, although it is seldom mentioned in publications. Most of these children die of neglect and Old World diseases, not only in the Barí case, but generally in South America.

R. Lizarralde, who conducted the 1982 Barí census (and the 1992 census as well), knew the specifics of many of these Barí abductions from his previous fieldwork and was able to track down and interview most of the surviving girls. The majority of the absent females in the 20- to 24-year-old age group in the 1982 census were not missing or passing as

Table 6.1. Age and sex structure of the Venezuelan Barí population according to the October 1982 census

Age Range	Total	Male	Female
0–4	200	100	100
5–9	199	110	89
10–14	175	84	91
15–19	105	48	57
20–24	67	44	23
25–29	74	42	32
30–34	70	38	32
35–39	60	24	36
40–44	49	28	21
45–49	27	13	14
50–54	18	11	7
55–59	17	10	7
60–64	4	1	3
65–69	5	4	1
70–74	0	0	0
75–79	0	0	0
80+	1	1	0
Total	1,071	558	513

Note: 1982 census taken by R. Lizarralde for the Venezuelan Indian Census. The ages assigned to people born after peaceful contact in 1960 can be presumed to be accurate to within a year; they were calculated from Lizarralde's notes from his frequent field trips after 1960, each of which involved taking a census of each settlement he visited and noting all births since his last visit. Ages assigned to people born between about 1945 and 1960, who were children or early adolescents when Lizarralde first saw them in the early 1960s, are likely to be accurate to within two years. Ages of people born before about 1945 were assigned by Lizarralde on the basis of the ages of their children and their recollections of known events that had occurred in their childhood.

criollos. They were dead. Nevertheless, as discussed below, the sex ratio of the Barí population was high even after discounting for the kidnapped girls.

According to the September 1992 census, there were at that date 1,520 Barí in Venezuela—800 males and 720 females (sex ratio 111:100; OCEI 1992). The proportion under 20 was 59%. The age and sex structure at that time (Table 6.2) revealed a population that had aged with respect to that of a decade earlier.

Lizarralde took a census of the on-reserve Barí in the Sierra de Perijá in 2004. He counted 731 males and 674 females (sex ratio 108:100.) This census was completed by a count of the off-reserve Barí in the lowlands taken in 2006 by the Ministry of the Environment, whose workers counted 383 males and 349 females (sex ratio 110:100).

In addition to these complete censuses, there are other sex ratio data available. A medical census taken by the Holmes team around the same time as the 1992 Venezuelan National Indian Census (Holmes 1993: 26–44) counted 526 individuals living in and around two large Barí settlements, Samaidodyi and Campo Rosario. The sex ratio for these people was 110:100 (Holmes 1993: 35–36).

The data from the 114 reproductive histories compiled by Lizarralde

Table 6.2. Age and sex structure of the Venezuelan Barí population as recorded for the September 1992 Venezuelan Indian Census

Age Range	Total	Male	Female
0–4	296	151	145
5–9	216	111	105
10–14	194	105	89
15–19	192	108	84
20–29	272	132	140
30–39	147	80	67
40–54	141	79	62
55+	62	34	28
Totals	1520	800	720

Note: Compiled by R. Lizarralde for the September 1992 Venezuelan Indian Census. Age cohorts according to those used in the official publication (OCEI 1992: I:394). Age estimate reliability as described in Table 6.1.

and Beckerman for our partible paternity research conformed roughly to the postcontact censuses reported above. The sample of 916 remembered pregnancies of these postreproductive women was made up of 485 males, 420 females, and 11 births/spontaneous abortions for which sex was undetermined or unremembered. The overall sex ratio at birth here, 115:100, was typical of lowland South American peoples. Evidence that this high sex ratio was not simply a result of the postcontact abduction of little girls and female infants during the epidemics was provided by partitioning the 916 pregnancies into two parts, one containing all births and miscarriages taking place before the end of 1961 (i.e., all the precontact conceptions) and the other containing all births and miscarriages from 1962 on.

Of the 916 remembered pregnancies, 446 ended by birth or spontaneous abortion before the end of 1961. The products of these 446 pregnancies were 240 males and 204 females, plus 2 fetuses whose sexes were not remembered, for a sex ratio of 118:100.

The 470 pregnancies that ended after 1961 produced 245 males, 216 females, and 9 fetuses of unknown or unremembered sex, for a sex ratio of 113:100.

The difference in sex ratio between the precontact and postcontact periods may reflect a tendency for the patrilineal Barí to remember boys more vividly than girls years after the death of a young child. It may also reflect higher male-biased fetal wastage and perinatal death after contact as a result of disease and (perhaps) nutritional stresses.

Among the 916 remembered pregnancies in this sample were 95 that produced stillbirths or infants who died in under a week. These nonviable births were made up of 51 males, 33 females, and 11 fetuses whose sexes were not remembered. The excess of males among the nonviable pregnancies is consistent with the generally higher mortality of males from the moment of conception on, especially in societies without modern medical care (cf. Waldron 1983).

Counting all children who survived for a week or more as viable live births, we found a live-birth sex ratio of 433:388, or 112:100 in this sample.

This database also showed that of the 560 offspring of all birth dates recorded as reaching the age of 15, 294 were male and 266 were female — sex ratio 110:100. There were an additional 10 individuals whose survival to the age of 15 was questionable. (The rest of the 916 pregnancies were composed of deaths, including miscarriages and stillbirths, that occurred before age 15 plus living people who were under 15 when we closed our database in 1996.)

These postepidemic censuses can be compared with data Lizarralde re-

**Table 6.3. Age and sex structure of a sample
of the pre-epidemic Barí population of 1961**

Age Range	Total	Male	Female
0–4	34	17	17
5–9	29	13	16
10–14	12	6	6
15–19	23	11	12
20–29	28	15	13
30–39	13	6	7
40–54	5	3	2
55+	2	2	0
Totals	146	73	73

Note: Age cohorts conform to those used by OCEI
for the 1992 Indian Census. Age estimate reliability is
greatest for the youngest members of the population.

corded in the earliest years of contact, before Old World diseases found
the Barí. In April and May 1961 he visited the longhouses of Ohbadyá
and Karibaigdakayra and took a census in each; ages were of course only
estimated, but for children there is no reason to believe they were not ac-
ceptably accurate.

Ohbadyá had its full complement of residents at that date, but most of
the inhabitants of Karibaigdakaira (probably the largest, most populous
longhouse the Barí ever occupied) had gone to live at another longhouse,
Otaká. Lizarralde reached Otaká in April 1963 and again took a census.
These three longhouses were the only ones he was able to census before
they were struck by the epidemics.

By adjusting the Otaká census ages to what they were in May 1961
and eliminating people born after that date, it is possible to add the 1963
Otaká data to those from Ohbadyá and Karibaigdakayra in 1961 and
arrive at an approximation of the Barí population before the epidemics
(Table 6.3).

The Barí were probably a young population. Of the 146 people in the
sample, which comprised two of the three local groups of a single territorial group, 67% were estimated to be under the age of twenty. Also in
this sample, there were 73 males and 73 females (sex ratio 100:100), and at
first inspection we had to entertain the possibility that something close
to a balanced sex ratio may have been characteristic of the Barí in pre-

contact times. Arguing against this possibility were the data from all the postcontact censuses plus (and more directly relevant) the analysis above of the precontact births culled from our 114-woman reproductive history database.

But even more important was what we knew about the immediately prior history of Karibaigdakaira and Ohbadyá. As mentioned in chapter 3, these people were the victims of mass murder in 1960, just after Lizarralde's first contact. Three heavily armed men who arrived in a helicopter invited them to drink a sweet red liquid. As described to us by survivors, the Barí, jubilant at the prospect of peace, were laughing and jostling each other at Karibaigdakaira to get to the men handing out the poisoned drink. One man told us that he wanted to try it but could not get through the crowd. It is more than likely that boys and younger men, the most boisterous of the residents, were disproportionately successful in pushing their way to the front. We are convinced that the Karibaigdakaira figures represent a population that had selectively lost males the year before it was censused.

On the other hand, an additional piece of evidence to the effect that the overall sex ratio of the precontact Barí may have been essentially balanced was presented in a study by Zaldívar, Lizarralde, and Beckerman (1991) that examined the reproductive histories of 110 postreproductive people — 55 men and 55 women. All had been born 45±5 years before their reproductive histories were recorded in 1988, and most of them had spent the first few years of their reproductive lives before contact. Some of them (16 men and 8 women) had died before they reached 45, and their reproductive histories were truncated by death rather than menopause. Men were considered to be postreproductive if both they and their youngest wives were over 45.

The people in this sample had produced 569 remembered pregnancies and 545 live-born children. Zaldívar and colleagues tracked the sex ratio of their remembered children at birth and at one year, five years, and fifteen years. They reported, "The sex ratios of the offspring are not significantly different from one at any of the stages measured, starting at birth and ending at 15 years of age" (1991: 480).

However, there were questions about this sample. Only 32 women were interviewed about their own reproductive histories. In the other cases making up the 110 reproductive histories, the information came from interviews with others, about half of them men, with gaps in many cases supplemented by mission records and Lizarralde's records. Although there was good reason to believe that Barí women remembered and discussed the miscarriages and infant deaths that befell their mothers, sisters, and daughters as well as themselves, there was less certainty that men remembered these events accurately. Nor was it certain that these events, especially when they occurred in outlying settlements, were reported to the nuns who kept the mission records.

This point was underlined by another comparison. As mentioned above, in our sample of 114 reproductive histories, the overwhelming majority of them collected from the mothers themselves, about 10% of remembered pregnancies resulted in a miscarriage, stillbirth, or perinatal death. In the Zaldívar et al. (1991) sample, only about 4% of pregnancies ended in one of these outcomes. If the majority of early deaths were male (as suggested by the figures for stillbirth and perinatal death presented above) and if these early deaths tended to be unmentioned by male informants, then the live-birth sex ratio of the offspring of the people included in the Zaldívar et al. (1991) sample might have been closer to the typical pattern of an excess of males at birth.

The Zaldívar et al. (1991) sample had the only demographic data that showed an essentially balanced sex ratio, once the Ohbadyá-Karibaigdaira-Otaká figures were considered in their historical context.

DIFFERENTIAL REPRODUCTIVE SUCCESS

We were very interested in features, ecological or otherwise, that might have contributed to differences in reproductive success. One obvious candidate was region of residence.

REGIONAL SUCCESS   Many Venezuelan Barí indicated that the intermontane valley in Territory 3 (see Map 1.1) was the most bountiful environment they knew—with ample good soil, outstanding fishable rivers rich in bocachico, and abundant game. It was also a safe place to live, far from the frontiers of criollo invasion. Contrariwise, it was Territory 1 that experienced the worst effects of that invasion—attacks, dispossession, and general abuse. Although we did not have weight-for-height or skin-fold measurements or other such biometric data to evaluate the physiological impacts of the natural abundance of Territory 3, or the abuses that occurred in Territory 1, we did explore our database of those 114 Venezuelan Barí women whose childbearing histories were known for indications of territorial differences in their reproductive performance.

When the women were separated by their territories of origin (which,

Table 6.4. Mean lifetime number of pregnancies per woman for women raised in the four Venezuelan territories

Territory	Number of Women	Mean Number of Pregnancies	Standard Deviation
1	27	6.70	3.01
2	13	8.00	2.58
3	26	9.85	2.82
4	47	7.81	2.89

Note: From the sample of 114 women whose reproductive histories are complete. The total number of women noted here sums to 113 because one woman's territory was not recorded.

the Barí being normatively uxorilocal, were generally the same as their territories of adult residence) we saw that women in Territories 1 and 3 appeared to stray from the population mean in opposite ways with respect to lifetime number of pregnancies (Table 6.4). These deviations were in the expected directions, and one-tailed t-tests revealed that Territory 1 women were significantly less fruitful than the average for all women (p = .006) and Territory 3 women were significantly more so (p = .0003).

A more conservative approach to this issue of territorial variation would not prejudge the direction in which any territory's women would deviate from the overall mean number of lifetime pregnancies but would simply ask if any particular territory or territories were significantly different in either direction. The probability value for a two-tailed t-test is simply double that of a one-tailed t-test. Thus, even if we had not had prior knowledge of the direction in which women in Territories 1 and 3 were expected to differ from the mean, we would still have discovered that they were significantly different from the overall mean for pregnancies per woman.

As far as these data take us, there was a reproductive advantage to living in Territory 3, as predicted. In the absence of biometric data, we cannot definitively attribute this advantage to better nutrition (lack of predation by non-Barí may also have had a role), but that hypothesis remains promising. It is consistent with the evidence presented in chapter 4, on production, that suggests the Barí were food maximizers in their hunting and fishing activities. Both the foraging and the demographic evidence are consistent with a situation in which individuals, although clearly not undernourished, could improve their reproductive success by obtaining additional animal fat and protein.

SEX OF FIRST LIVE-BORN CHILD   We next looked at the effect on reproductive success of the sex of the first live-born child. It had been suggested in the literature on tribal demography (Turke 1988) that because of the employment of little girls in child care (a robust trait among the Barí), women whose first child was a girl had higher lifetime reproductive success as a result of this assistance.

In our sample of 114 women with complete reproductive histories, 56 had a girl as their first live-born, 57 had a boy as their first live-born, and one had no live-born children (three pregnancies, all ending in stillbirths). Those whose first live-born was female had a mean of 8.63 ± 2.98 remembered pregnancies over the course of their entire reproductive lives, while those whose first live-born was male had 7.54 ± 2.94 total pregnancies, a significant difference; $p = 0.028$, one-tailed t-test. Similar but weaker results obtained when the women's reproductive success was limited to live-born children and not total number of pregnancies. Female-first mothers had a mean of 7.66 ± 2.55 live-borns over their reproductive years, while male-first mothers had 6.78 ± 2.74, again a significant difference; $p = .042$, one-tailed t-test.

The 57 women who had a boy as their first live-born child produced 277 children known to have survived to age 15, for a mean of 4.96 ± 2.32 children per woman. The 56 women who had a girl for their first live-born child produced 283 children who reached 15, for a mean of 5.05 ± 1.78 children per woman. A one-tailed t-test confirmed the obvious: There was no significant difference; having a girl as her first live-born child did not confer on a woman any advantage in the number of children she raised to maturity.

One possible explanation of this result is that the number of children a Barí woman and her husband were able to raise successfully to adulthood was on average less than the number the woman was able to give birth to. Although having a little girl to help with infant and child care increased the number of pregnancies (and live births) the woman was able to achieve, the girl's help was irrelevant to such critical juvenile survivorship issues as nutrition and care when sick, which still fell to the mother and her husband.

Another possibility, different from but compatible with this suggestion, arises from studies (e.g., Ibrahim et al. 1994) that have suggested that high parity children may be inherently more fragile than their earlier-born siblings. If this tendency existed among the Barí, it might have operated in tandem with the irrelevance of the firstborn girl in nutritional and sick-care issues to truncate the distribution of children surviving to 15.

Another possible explanation is that the mother's helpers were, after all, children themselves. Stories about little girls dropping the babies they were caring for are not rare. It is possible that being cared for by a young sister actually raised the accidental death rate for infants.

Yet another possible explanation is that the lack of significant effect of firstborn girls on their mothers' ultimate reproductive success may have been a historical anomaly driven by the tremendous mortality of the postcontact epidemics. Many of the children in this sample perished in the epidemics, and it may be that this catastrophic mortality masked the benefits of a firstborn girl.

MALE QUALITY Our next exploration dealt with differences among individual men. As discussed below, polygynous men had elevated reproductive success. Was there any personal or social characteristic that distinguished men with multiple wives from men who married only once? Multiple informants confirmed what an elderly woman told us in the 1980s: "In the old days, the girls always fell in love with the best hunters." Further questioning indicated that good fishermen were also attractive, although perhaps somewhat less so than good hunters.

Perhaps more important, there was consensus that the mothers of marriageable girls also thought highly of good hunters and fishermen. For the uxorilocal Barí, having a Nimrod join the family was an attractive prospect for an aging woman anticipating the decline of her own husband's foraging abilities. We suspect it is in this light that one should interpret the marriage histories above in which a man's mother-in-law turned over her daughters one by one to the husband of the eldest—an old woman's strategy for keeping her son-in-law in her hearth group.

Both authors had made casual enquiries about good hunters and fishermen over the years. To explore further, we obtained, partly by our own additional questions but mainly through interviews carried out by Nubia Coromoto Korombara in 2009, a list of men named by elderly informants as the best hunters and the best fishermen in the last longhouses in which these informants had lived in traditional times. A total of fifteen longhouses were represented, and a large number of men were named, some of whom we had in our records and some of whom were new to us—at least under the names by which they were reported to Korombara.

Because some men named themselves as the best and some women named their husbands or fathers as the best and because we suspected that further special pleadings may have entered into an unknown number of additional reports, we decided to restrict our list of mighty hunters and fishermen to those men who were named best in the longhouse by at least two separate informants, neither of whom was the hunter or fisherman himself and whose marital histories we knew or could uncover. It turned out that these limitations produced eight names each for hunters and fishermen—a smaller sample than we would have liked but one that had the virtue of being the best approach we could make to assuring that the chosen men met the essential criteria.

The eight hunters who met this test averaged 2.75 ± 1.67 wives per man. Polygyny was curiously distributed among them. Three men were monogamous, one man had two wives, three men had four wives each, and one man had five wives. The eight fishermen meeting the same test averaged 2.13 ± 1.13 wives per man. They had a somewhat less peculiar distribution of numbers of wives. Three men were monogamous, two men had two wives each, two men had three wives each, and one man had four wives.

The rough similarity in polygyny rate was not surprising: five men appeared on both lists. This occurrence was not surprising either. To hunt and fish the Barí way was essentially a test of athleticism. It was only to be expected that the men with the fastest reflexes, the greatest endurance, and the sharpest eyesight would excel at both activities.

The most appropriate database we had to compare to these expert hunters and fishers was our sample of 130 husbands (discussed below), all of whose wives were already identified. We extracted from these 130 the five men who also appeared on our list of eight mighty hunters, leaving a pool of 125 less remarkable hunters. (Three great hunters were not in the sample of 130.) These 125 ordinary men averaged 1.53 ± 0.80 wives per man. A one-tailed t-test showed a significant difference (p = .04) between the 125 run-of-the-mill men and the eight great hunters in mean lifetime number of wives acquired. Informants had been right: marriageable girls and their mothers looked favorably on good hunters.

We repeated this exercise with the sample of eight famous fishermen, redoing the pool of ordinary men to reflect the extraction of good fishermen rather than good hunters. There were 126 men in this pool, and they averaged $1.56 + 0.87$ wives per man. The fishermen averaged 2.13 ± 1.13 wives per man. The difference between the two groups was not significant at the $p < 0.05$ level, although given the small sample size, we think it is important not to assert that this result closes the book on this matter.

To explore the subject further, we looked at the reproduction of the renowned hunters and fishermen. This project was problematic because we did not have complete information on the reproductive history of two of the hunters. (For two of the men who had four wives we were lacking reproductive data for one wife each.) Nor did we have it for all the fishermen. (For one man with three wives and one man with four wives, we were missing data for one wife each.) Nevertheless, we were able to come up with a *minimum* figure for the reproduction of the famous hunters and fishermen, assuming that the wives for whom we had no data had no pregnancies at all.

The parallel minimum number of pregnancies reported for all the wives of all the 130 men in our database averaged 8.16 ± 4.91 pregnancies per man. We removed from this list of 130 the men who also appeared on the lists of mighty hunters and fishermen, reducing the former list to 123 men and its mean number of pregnancies per man to 7.78 ± 4.70. This new list of ordinary men was what we compared to the acclaimed hunters and fishermen.

The mighty hunters averaged a minimum number of 12.5 ± 6.57 pregnancies per hunter, whereas the mighty fishermen showed a considerably smaller mean of a minimum of 9.13 ± 5.87 pregnancies per fisherman. A pair of one-tailed t-tests showed that by this measure, as in the case of numbers of wives, the hunters were significantly different from ordinary men ($p = .04$) in the numbers of pregnancies achieved by their wives, while the fishermen were not. Again, it is important to remember that sample sizes were small.

We concluded that strength of the preference for good hunters as husbands and sons-in-law, and their consequent elevated reproductive success, and the weakness of a parallel preference for good fishermen, responded to the difference in variance of returns for these activities that we discussed in Chapter 4. Hunting was inherently riskier and more variable than fishing. Further, during good fishing times, hunting was also possible, but during bad fishing times, hunting was the only way of obtaining enough meat. Thus marriageable women, and their mothers, focused their matrimonial intentions on expert hunters; they were the men who could get them through the potentially lean times.

POLYGYNY   The context and consequences of the sex of ego for ego's reproductive strategy were an obvious extension of the previous investigation.

The 1991 Zaldívar et al. study focused on one highly significant difference in reproductive success between men and women. (The reproductive success of a man was assumed for purposes of this study to include all the children born to all women married to a man, without discounting for possible nonpaternity.) Although the mean number of live births among the men (7.32) was statistically indistinguishable from that among the women (7.71,) the variance of the distribution for men (19.93) was more than twice that for women (8.73). Zaldívar et al. (1991: 485–486) reported similar results for children surviving to the age of five: the mean number of surviving offspring for men (5.40) was not statistically different from that of women (5.73), but the variance for men (13.66) was one and a half times that of women (8.91).

The reason, of course, was polygyny. Restricting the sample to the 39 men and 47 women who survived to around 45 years of age,[3] the authors found that the women who had been married only once had 8.04 ± 2.95 live births and those who had been married more than once— sequentially, because the Barí do not practice polyandry—had 8.67 ± 2.01 live births. The difference by marital status for the two classes of women was statistically indistinguishable. The pattern was the same for their children surviving to age five.

However, for men the mean number of live births for those who had been married only once was 6.93 ± 2.65, not significantly different from that of women, while that for men who had had more than one wife was 13.00 ± 3.85. The differences in reproductive success between polygynously married men and monogamously married men, and between polygynously married men and all women, were highly significant (Zaldívar, Lizarralde, and Beckerman 1991).

We revisited this issue with our reproductive history database. Among these 114 postreproductive women, 75 had had only one husband, 33 had had two husbands, 5 had had three husbands, and 1 had had four husbands—a total of 160 marriages. There were seven women who had at one time or another gotten pregnant out of wedlock. Five of these women had experienced a single pregnancy each, after contact, seduced by Colombian laborers around the missions, and had the rest of their children with Barí husbands. The sixth had her first four pregnancies while single (three of them before contact), then married and had five more pregnancies. The seventh woman had five pregnancies while married, then had eight more as a widow. None of the eight pregnancies of her widowhood, which spanned the date of first contact, produced a surviving child.

When we examined the effect of single versus plural marriages on the reproductive success of these women, we found that the 75 women who reported only one husband experienced a mean of 7.52 ± 3.02 pregnancies, while the 39 who reported plural husbands recalled 9.07 ± 2.78 pregnancies. The difference was significant ($p = .007$, two-tailed t-test) and probably reflected at least two systematic differences in the two groups of women. The former group contained a few women who died young; the latter did not. In addition, the former group also contained some women who experienced substantial periods of solitary widowhood, whereas the latter was weighted with those who remarried shortly after losing their husbands.

These 114 women were married to at least 135 different men at one time or another in their marital histories (we say "at least" because it is possible we may have missed some marriages that produced no offspring). We were able to identify and trace the additional wives of 130 of these 135 men. These 130 known husbands, in turn, were married not only to the 114 women for whom we have complete reproductive histories but also to at least another 54 women who were not included in the database of the 114 because they were not yet postreproductive at the time we closed the database, because it had not been possible to obtain information on whether each of their children had one or more secondary fathers or for some other reason having to do with the absence of complete data on their reproductive careers. In later investigations of these 54 women, we were able to obtain histories of their reproduction *while married to the 130 husbands of the 114 women in the partible paternity database* for 50 of them.

We examined the reproductive success of the husbands from two perspectives. First, we looked at the numbers of pregnancies attributed to these 130 men *only by the 114 women in the partible paternity reproductive history database*. Second, we looked at the total numbers of pregnancies attributed to these husbands by *all* their wives, the 114 plus the additional 50 wives not in the initial database for whom we had reproductive data. (This examination covered only 126 of the 130 known husbands, because reproductive data were not available for four of these men's wives.)

These 130 husbands averaged 6.90 ± 4.19 pregnancies per man with their 114 wives. When we divided the husbands into those who had only one wife among the 114 women and those who had more than one among these same women, we found that the 107 men who had only one wife fathered a mean of 6.04 ± 3.50 pregnancies, while the 23 who had two or more wives fathered a mean of 11.17 ± 4.95 pregnancies. These figures corresponded to the Zaldívar et al. (1991) findings.

When we looked at the total fatherhood of the husbands of the 114 women in the reproductive history database, it was necessary to take into account the wives and children of these men who were omitted from that database, for the reasons mentioned above.

These 130 men were married a total of 212 times. (Some of them were married to more than one of the 114 women in the reproductive history database, either simultaneously or sequentially, and some of the women were married to more than one of these men, always sequentially—hence the discrepancies among the total number of husbands, the total number of wives, and the total number of marriages.) As mentioned above, we were able to acquire reproductive data for all the women who were married to 126 of these 130 men.

These 126 husbands averaged 8.10 ± 4.60 pregnancies per man with all their wives. When we divided these 126 husbands into those who had been married only once (73) and those who had had two or more wives (53), we found that the singly married men had fathered an average of 6.05 ± 3.29 pregnancies, while the multiply married men had fathered an average of 10.92 ± 4.69 pregnancies. Again, these figures corresponded to the Zaldívar et al. (1991) findings.

In the cases explored just above, 53 of 126, or 42%, of married men had had more than one wife. However, plural marriage was highly variable in time and space. In 1963–1965, Lizarralde checked three local groups from three different territorial groups in Venezuela (total population around 180) and found that 73% of the married men were currently polygynous. In contrast, in 1971–1972 Beckerman collected data from five local groups (total population about 175, mostly from different territories) in Colombia and found that only 18% of the 39 married men in those groups were currently polygynous. (It is important to note that both these surveys dealt with postcontact and postepidemic local groups.) In the case of the 126 men, men married to more than one wife included both serial monogamists and polygynists. However, there is little doubt that polygyny contributed the lion's share of the reproductive advantage a multiply married man had over one who married only once.

How did polygynously married men acquire plural wives? One route to polygyny, illustrated in several of the marriage histories sketched above, was to marry sisters. Of the 53 polygynous husbands discussed just above, we able to determine the kinship status of the wives of 47, along with the reproductive histories of the wives in question. Twenty-two of these 47 polygynous men were married to two or more sisters (including half sisters); the remaining 25 were married to women who were not related or at least not as closely related as sisters. An interesting question arose. One might expect that sisters would be more liable to look out for each others' children, to share child care, and to help each other in general than unrelated co-wives. Thus a polygynous man might favor his own reproductive success by marrying sisters rather than unrelated women.

Separating the men whose plural wives were sisters from those whose wives were not primary kin, we found that the former group averaged 12.18 ± 4.26 pregnancies by all their wives, while the latter averaged 10.52 ± 4.67 pregnancies. The difference was not significant at the $p < 0.05$ level. A similarly insignificant difference appeared when we measured reproductive success by live-born children rather than all pregnancies. Nor were we able to find a significant reproductive advantage to marrying sisters when we repeated the exercise using only the children who survived to age 15.[4]

Thus, although about half the polygynously married men in this sample acquired their multiple wives by marrying sisters, we found no reproductive advantage to this variety of polygyny as compared with marriage to unrelated women. As far as these data took us, it was multiple wives per se, not a particular kin configuration of multiple wives, that led men to augmented reproductive success.

Overall in this investigation we found evidence that some Barí men, particularly those with good hunting skills, were able to take advantage of the practice of polygyny to further their reproductive success. There was no surprise here. In the vast majority of societies, men with exceptional abilities, exceptional kin connections, or exceptional wealth achieve an exceptional number of matings, whether these matings take place within marriage or outside it. For men, the winning fitness strategy—the default strategy, in a sense—is to focus on quantity: the man with the largest number of children born usually comes out on top in the individual fitness scuffle. Even if many of those children die, a man can make up the loss by impregnating even more women.

For a woman, whose total fertility is limited by the duration of pregnancy and the period of partial sterility brought on by nursing, the winning strategy is to ensure the survival and success of the much more limited total number of children that she can produce. This observation brings us to the last section of this chapter, the institution of partible paternity.

Partible Paternity Examined Further

We discussed the ideas about conception and fetal development that underlie Barí reproductive practices in the section on reproduction in the life cycle. Here we deal with the biological effects of those ideas. The overall shape of the biodemographic consequences of partible paternity

> is known from life history interviews with post-reproductive Barí that reveal that most women, both in precontact times and currently, took one or more lovers during at least one of their pregnancies. These lovers were believed to contribute to the development of the fetus and were considered secondary fathers of the eventual child. Women's husbands were usually aware of the lovers, and there is no evidence that the husbands objected. This last feature accords with considerable evidence in our notes attesting to a Barí woman's complete control over her sexual activity, once she had completed her puberty seclusion. Although she needed her parents' assent to marry, an unmarried post-pubertal girl might have sex with any okdyibara she wanted; and as a married woman, she apparently retained this authority over her own sexual behavior. Our life history interviews contain a number of incidents in which women volunteered that they had objected to adultery on the part of their husbands, but none in which men reported that they had objected to adultery on the part of their wives.
>
> In the great majority of cases, the married woman stated that she took a lover only after she was pregnant. However, further inquiry revealed that the indication of pregnancy used by these women was simply a missed period. In this population, where hard physical labor was the norm, the diet was low in fat, and prolonged nursing of the most recent infant was universal, a missed period was far from infallible as an indicator of pregnancy. Only genetic fingerprinting can be conclusive on this point, but some women who believed themselves to be pregnant may have been made pregnant by the lovers they took, after reaching the conclusion that they were already with child. (Beckerman et al. 2002: 32)

The life history interviews we conducted between 1988 and 1996 were intended to explore the reproductive results of this ideology of partible paternity and its accompanying practices of licensed lovers for married women and multiple fathers for their children. In particular, we searched for advantages that might accrue to a woman and her children as a result of having multiple fathers for a single pregnancy.

When we closed the database, we had the reproductive histories of 114 postreproductive women and their 916 remembered pregnancies (details in Beckerman et al. 2002). To recapitulate the previous section, the number of pregnancies per woman varied from 2 to 14, with a mean of 8.04 and a mode of 10. Of the 114 women, 77 (67.5%) had had at least one pregnancy involving a lover; of the 916 pregnancies, 214 (23.4%) involved at least one secondary father. A statistical analysis of the database was reported by Bai (1999) and summarized by Beckerman et al. (2002).

Several noteworthy conclusions emerged from the analysis; we discuss them below. But to clear the way for this discussion, it is helpful to note at the outset that it quickly became clear that although pregnancies involving a single secondary father were indeed advantaged in several ways with respect to pregnancies with only a single father, pregnancies in which two or more secondary fathers were involved mainly showed a disadvantage. On examination, it turned out that the 25 pregnancies involving two or more secondary fathers (the product of 12 women) were overweighted with unmarried women supporting themselves by something akin to prostitution. Having *multiple* secondary fathers for a single pregnancy, then, was both rare and in many if not most cases an index of distress on the part of the mother. For these reasons, the comparison below of the results of having secondary fathers versus having only a single father is limited to this dichotomy: Cases in which a pregnancy had only one secondary father and those in which there was no secondary father at all.

In exploring the question of whether it was advantageous to have a secondary father, we first looked into survival to age fifteen. (Fifteen was the approximate age at which Barí girls began to marry and at which Barí boys became independent enough to visit other local groups, sometimes staying for months to check out the girls.) There were 841 pregnancies in our database that took place 15+ years before we closed the database in 1996. As noted above, 25 of these pregnancies are disregarded here because they had more than one secondary father; we deal with the remaining 816.

Of these 816 pregnancies,[5] 639 had no secondary father and 177 had a single secondary father; 64% of the former group (409 of 639) survived to age fifteen, compared to 85% of the latter (150 of 177). A simple chi-square test demonstrated that the difference was robust ($p < .0001$, one-tail).

The next question, of course, was how and why a pregnancy with a secondary father was more likely to produce an offspring who survived to fifteen. We first asked if it was a matter of a prenatal benefit or a benefit to the child that was received after birth. We separated the deaths that occurred before fifteen into two categories: those that produced offspring who were dead at birth and those that produced offspring who survived birth but died before fifteen. Dead at birth was defined as a miscarriage, a stillbirth, or a perinatal ($<$ 1 week) death. We added this last item because the Barí, with their high rate of cleft lip and cleft palate (Ballew, Beckerman, and Lizarralde 1993), sometimes gave birth to nonviable infants whose mouths were so deformed they could not nurse, even though they lived for a few days.

We looked at the odds ratios in these two categories (Beckerman et al. 2002). To make the odds ratio metric clear, consider the calculation two paragraphs above. In that example of 816 pregnancies, the odds of dying before the age of fifteen with a single secondary father were $27:150 =$ 0.18, whereas the odds of dying before fifteen without any secondary father were $230:408 = 0.56$. The odds ratio, then, was $0.18/0.56 = 0.32$.

When we looked at those dead at birth who had one secondary father versus those who had none, we found an odds ratio of 0.18, p = .001. Then when we looked at children who died after birth but before fifteen, again comparing those who had one secondary father and those who had none, we found an odds ratio of 0.37, p = .0014.

The interpretation was simple. A single secondary father provided both prenatal and postnatal benefits, but the prenatal advantage was more pronounced, about twice as big as the postnatal benefit. It was also more difficult to specify.

In our report we asserted that the "advantage was presumably related to extra provisioning with fish and game that the secondary father provided to the mother during the pregnancy" (Beckerman et al. 2002: 38). Additional possibilities existed, however.

One of them was that men offering themselves as secondary fathers were more attracted to younger, healthier women, whose pregnancies were more likely to have successful outcomes. To the extent that this explanation was the case, the presence of the secondary father would have been an effect of a positive outlook for a pregnancy, not a cause.

A third possibility was related to the small size of the Barí population and the two known bottlenecks it experienced in the last two and a half centuries. Inbreeding depression may have been a problem in Barí reproduction. If it was, then it might have been the case that some women were married to men so genetically similar that their prospects of producing a viable pregnancy were seriously compromised. These women might have improved their fertility by becoming pregnant by other men, the secondary fathers. If this explanation was correct, the improved fetal survival of pregnancies with a single secondary father was a matter of heterozygosity and not support provided by the secondary father during pregnancy. But none of these three explanations necessarily excluded either of the others, and we do not currently foresee an opportunity to untangle this problem.

The improved survival of secondary-father children after birth was a more tractable problem. The advantage here was almost certainly related to improved nutrition, a result of the animal food gifts the secondary father made to the child's mother when the child was very small and later to the child directly: "Several informants volunteered that when a child with a secondary father reached the age at which it could understand such things, the child's mother pointed out the secondary father to the child, saying, 'That man is also your father. He will give you fish. He will give you meat'" (Beckerman et al. 2002: 33).

In addition to nutritional support, one cannot ignore the possible advantage of having an additional pair of eyes looking after a child exposed to the various dangers of living in a tropical rainforest. Nevertheless, we are persuaded that this benefit, if it existed, was of minor importance compared to nutritional supplementation.

A puzzle that cropped up in our first report on Barí partible paternity (Beckerman et al. 1998) was resolved in the 2002 work. Looking for possible extended benefits of secondary fathers, we had separated the offspring of our 114 mothers into three groups: those who had a secondary father; those who had no secondary father but had at least one sibling who did have a secondary father; and those who came from sibling sets in which no one had a secondary father. Our expectation was that children with secondary fathers would have the best survivorship, followed by those single-father children with siblings who had secondary fathers, and that children from sibling sets with no secondary fathers would bring up the rear in survivorship.

We made this prediction on the basis of our observations that the typical Barí mother at times handed out between-meal snacks to her young children. As we wrote, "Surely any fish or game given to her to prepare by a secondary father of one of her children could have found its way to all of them" (Beckerman et al. 2002: 39).

Our prediction was wrong. It turned out that children with secondary fathers did have the best survivorship, but they were followed by children from sibling sets in which no one had a secondary father. Children who did not have secondary fathers but whose siblings did had the poorest survivorship.

A likely explanation of this unexpected result was that the children of the last group, the single-father siblings of children with secondary fathers, was inherently overweighted with children who had died. Exploration of the data revealed that a woman was about twice as likely to take a secondary father during one of her pregnancies if she had already lost a child from a previous pregnancy.

We tentatively concluded that "women who might have been reluctant to take a secondary father for any of their children (women on the way to producing . . . [a sibling set with no secondary fathers]) became more likely to produce . . . [children with secondary fathers] after they had already experienced poor survivorship among their previous children, thus creating a set of . . . [children whose siblings had secondary fathers even though they did not] only after the survivorship of the siblings in this set was already compromised" (Beckerman et al. 2002: 40).

M. Lizarralde investigated the way Barí women may have thought about this issue. Later Nubia Coromoto Korombara interviewed additional women on the topic. When a child fell sick, the most effective traditional cure was believed to be for men to spit powdered tobacco on the patient, in addition to reciting incantations. Any man could perform this rite, but those most motivated to do so (and perhaps thus most effective) were of course close kin.[6] Further, not all men knew all the incantations. "It is easy to imagine a bereaved Barí mother thinking to herself that if only she had provided a secondary father for her dead child, she might have saved him, and vowing to provide that benefit for her next child" (Beckerman et al. 2002: 40).

In further explorations of the possible consequences of partible paternity, we asked whether there were biological benefits to having a secondary father beyond improved juvenile survivorship. Recalling the Barí preference for cross cousin marriages, we noted that a man with a secondary father had not only two fathers but also (unless his primary and secondary fathers were brothers) two sets of father's sisters. Thus he had, potentially, a double set of patrilateral cross cousins. We investigated the possibility that men with secondary fathers had greater marital success than men with only a single father.

From our sample of 916 remembered pregnancies, each of which had been identified as having a secondary father or not, we extracted the males who lived past fifteen and compared those who had a secondary father with those who did not, in terms of the numbers of wives these men acquired. There was no significant difference between the two categories.

Then we limited the sample to those men who had been born at least eighteen years before pacification (i.e., 1942 or earlier) on the grounds that the missionaries have opposed polygyny in the postcontact years, and this influence might have obscured a traditional pattern. We also limited this sample to men who had survived at least until age eighteen. Again, there was no difference in marital success between men with a secondary father and those without.

We were not able, because of our lack of reliable precontact birth dates, to explore the questions of whether men with secondary fathers married younger than those without or whether their wives tended to be younger and have longer reproductive lives ahead of them as a result of their patri-lateral kin connections.

We did find something unanticipated that connected secondary father-hood, territory, and pre- and postcontact reproduction with sex ratio. These connections are still under active investigation (Beckerman and Parker in prep.); we present preliminary findings here.

When we extracted the live births alone from our database of 916 re-membered pregnancies and removed cases that had two or more sec-ondary fathers, we were left with 813 live births—637 with no secondary father and 176 with a single secondary father. The overall sex ratio was 114, essentially the same as for the whole sample of 916 pregnancies mentioned above. But for those with no secondary father the sex ratio was 109 while for those with a single secondary father it was 131. This disparity did not reach significance at the $p < .05$ level with any simple statistical test, but it certainly attracted our attention.

There was a further aspect of this sex ratio finding that compounded its mystery. When we divided the live births into those that took place up through 1960 and those that happened in 1961 or later (i.e., those that had been conceived after contact) a peculiar bifurcation took place. For the 381 births that occurred up through 1960, the sex ratio was essentially the same for those with and without a secondary father—120 for those without any secondary father and 121 for those with a single secondary father. But for births taking place in 1961 and later, the sex ratio was 101 for children without a secondary father and 143 for children with one. Ap-parently, contact had had a notable effect on the interaction of secondary fatherhood and live birth sex ratio, but what it was, was not immediately clear.

To make the matter even more curious, it turned out that Territory 3 (which we had already established was the richest territory, with a sig-nificantly elevated number of pregnancies per reproductive period) also showed an elevated percentage of secondary fatherhood and the highest live birth sex ratio of any of the territories.

In addition to the sex ratio connections reported above, other questions concerning partible paternity among the Barí remained unanswered. The major one: Given that there was a clear advantage to providing a secondary father for a child, why did not all Barí children have secondary fathers?

As noted above, only about 23% of Barí children had one or more secondary fathers, and one-third of Barí women never took a secondary father for any of their children. Barí women we asked about the process of acquiring a lover were unanimous that women did not seek out men. In fact, they considered the prospect of a woman making sexual advances to a man hilarious. (One old woman separated herself from a group of women who were laughing their heads off after Beckerman asked what a woman did to find a man, put her hand on his arm, and said [freely translated from the Barí-aa], "I don't know how it is with your people, Steve, but around here, it's the boys who chase the girls.")

The most common answer to our question to a woman, "Why does this child not have a secondary father?" was "Nobody offered." That said, we remained skeptical that there is any culture in which women do not have a way of signaling to a man that a gallant proposal will not fall on deaf ears. Furthermore, sometimes women rejected men who wanted to become their lovers. In fact, one-third of women rejected all potential lovers and had only their husbands as fathers for their children. Those of these faithful women whom we asked why they had never taken a lover answered only that they did not want one, that they didn't go in for that kind of thing.

This blanket refusal was investigated further by M. Lizarralde. He reported that although he was unsatisfied with his current understanding of the issue, there was evidence that some men were believed to have a special ability to understand animals, an ability that made them superior hunters. It was also believed that this ability could be lost if their wives had sex with other men.

Further inquiry by Nubia Coromoto Korombara revealed a more elaborate set of ideas. As we now understand the matter, it had to do with a man's ability to visit the land of the basungchingba, the spirits of the dead, by soul travel. (Only men could travel there.) In the land of the basungchingba, a man could understand the speech of animals and talk to them. This ability made him a superior hunter.

A certain social restraint was necessary for soul travel to the land of the basungchingba. It included being reserved, not talking too much, and sexual moderation. A man had to confine his sexual activity to his wife or wives, and his wives had to reserve themselves for him alone. An elderly informant, interviewed in 2007, was eloquent about the importance of chastity. He used to be chaste, he said, having sex only with his wife, and only after marriage. But eventually he had an affair and now had a child with another woman. He could not communicate with the basungchingba anymore. Hence he had not had sex with his wife for two years, trying to regain his chastity and his ability to communicate with the basungchingba.

A younger female informant reported that men who had been secondary fathers could in time acquire (or regain) the ability to travel to the land of the basungchingba if they stopped having sex with other women and limited their attentions to their wives. This statement accorded with the behavior of the elderly male informant reported above.

However, we remained unclear about the role of a man's wife in this situation of loss of chastity. Informants appeared to agree that a woman's husband's ability to visit the basungchingba came to an end if she had an affair. It was not clear whether a woman could regain her chastity by later abstaining from sex with other men, and thus restore her husband's soul-traveling powers, or if the impediment to her husband's ability to visit the basungchingba was permanent.

Notes

1. The fact that one's own mother is an okdyibara is now suppressed among the Barí, in response to what the Barí have learned about how non-Barí believe the classification works. The nuns who teach at the mission schools believe that okdyibara simply means "marriageable" or "available for sex." Mission-educated Barí have been taught as much, and all Barí know that the non-Barí with whom they have regular contact understand the classification that way; they are concerned that non-Barí not believe that they practice incest. When Beckerman interviewed people at an isolated longhouse in 1972 he asked a man several times whether his mother was sagdodyira or okdyibara and was answered with an increasingly exasperated, "She's my *mother*." Eventually, in response to the ethnographer's obtuse insistence on an answer to the question as asked, he giggled, "Okdyibara."

In the early 1980s Beckerman interviewed a man in his late twenties in the company of his mission-raised teenaged wife. When asked whether his mother was his okdyibara or sagdodyira, he replied in excellent Spanish, "I wouldn't know how to answer that question, Steve, because she's my mother." His wife looked up indignantly and insisted, "Sagdodyira!"

In 1989 Lizarralde and Beckerman interviewed an elderly couple about their genealogies, in the company of their grown daughter. They asked, in Barí-aa, whether the husband's mother was his okdyibara or his sagdodyira. He hesitated, and the daughter interjected nervously, still in Barí-aa, "Sagdodyira, tell them she's sagdodyira."

The classification of one's own mother as okdyibara does not, of course, mean that the Barí ever practiced mother-son incest. It simply means that they had a ranked set of rules regarding marriage and sexual activity. The first rule proscribed any sexual activity with any primary relative; the second rule allowed such activity with anyone classified as okdyibara who was not covered by the first rule. The change in what younger informants believe and what almost all informants now say is a lesson in how quickly people can change their descriptions of their own culture, and indeed their beliefs about their own culture, in response to the fear of scorn from outsiders.

2. We know of very few cases of children born before a woman's first marriage, but some did occur.

3. Of the 55 women, 53 had at least two live-born children and 2 never had a child. Eight of these women died before approximately age 45; all 8 had only one husband. Of the 47 women who survived to the presumed age of menopause, 26 had only one husband and 21 had more than one, sequentially. Of the 55 men, 16 died before the presumed age of 45; all 16 had only one wife. Of the 39 who survived past 45, 28 had only one wife and 11 had multiple wives. In this sample, all 11 had at least some period in their adult lives when they had simultaneous multiple wives.

4. The sample for this last test was smaller than the previous two (because of the difficulty of obtaining survivorship information for the children of those of the wives of the polygynously married men who were not in the original partible paternity database), and the difference between numbers of offspring of sister co-wives and nonsister co-wives was barely significant at the 0.1 level. We do not want to make too much of this weak tendency, but it is possible that a larger sample might be consistent with the proposition that sister co-wives tend to look out for each others' children more than nonsister co-wives and thus enjoy higher survivorship among their offspring.

5. This figure of 816 pregnancies is a bit larger than the sample we analyzed in Beckerman et al. 2002; for that earlier analysis we eliminated pregnancies for several reasons, such as unknown places of birth, in addition to having been born less than fifteen years before we closed the database. For the current analysis only births taking place less than fifteen years before the database was closed were eliminated.

6. This description differs from that in Beckerman et al. 2002. We got several points about traditional curing wrong in that volume.

CHAPTER 7

Conclusions

Perspectives

After our examination of the ecology of the Barí, concentrating on their practices in production, protection, and reproduction, there remained the task of putting these matters in wider perspective. Several points of views might have been appropriate. The most obvious was ethnographic comparison. Two possibilities presented themselves in this connection. We might have compared Barí ecological strategies with those of the other speakers of languages in the Chibchan family, a linguistic category that includes the Barí and is found from Central America (where it may have had its origin around the Panama–Costa Rica border [Costenla-Umaña 1995]) down into Colombia and western Venezuela. This tack would have been based on the familiar anthropological assumption that people who speak related languages share other aspects of their culture, due to descent from a common ancestor. Implicit in such an exercise was the idea of diversification, "descent with modification" from a mother culture, resulting in a suite of distinct daughter cultures whose differences spoke to specific adaptations to differing natural and cultural environments as well as different historical trajectories.

More broadly, we might have compared the Barí with all the other lowland neotropical horticulturalist peoples whose ecology had been adequately studied, irrespective of their linguistic and cultural affiliations. This second tack did not imply an assumption of diversification but rather implicitly invoked convergence as its main underlying process, as initially different cultures became similar enough to make comparison profitable when they adapted to similar environments in similar ways.

In addition to these two sorts of basic ethnographic comparison, another useful perspective from which we might view the Barí material was with respect to enduring questions in the cultural anthropology and culture history of lowland South America. Old and conspicuous among these topics was the question of why the ethnographically known peoples of the neotropical rain forest exhibited such small and widely dispersed populations. The literature revolving around this issue went back over half a century and rested on a fundamental distinction between riverine peoples and interfluvial peoples. The Barí were interesting in this connection because they were both riverine and interfluvial, switching between these environments over the course of a seasonal round. The Barí material might offer insight into the question of why the neotropical peoples we see today live in much smaller settlements and at much smaller population densities than are known both historically and presently among paleo-tropical peoples in ecologically similar regions in Africa and Asia.

A final perspective from which to view the Barí material related to its relevance to the ecology of human societies in general. Human ecology has been criticized as reducing culture to "digestion writ large," and one of the themes of this book, with its tripartite division of the central text into chapters on production, protection, and reproduction, was to insist that there was more to human ecology than subsistence.

Ethnographic Comparison

In this final chapter we take up these three perspectives in the order mentioned above, beginning here with the matter of simple ethnographic comparison. It will be recalled that two types of comparison suggested themselves—resemblance and contrast with other daughters of a Chibchan or proto-Chibchan mother culture and resemblance and contrast with other lowland neotropical forest cultures irrespective of cultural descent—the former implying divergence and the latter convergence.

The first of these possibilities we reluctantly but rapidly rejected. The current consensus of linguistic (Costenla-Umaña 1981, 1991, 1995, 2008), genetic (Torroni et al. 1994; Keyeux et al. 2002; Melton 2004; Melton et al. 2007), and archaeological (Cooke and Ranere 1992; Hoopes and Fonseca 2003; Cooke 2005) research coincided on a general scenario for the history of the Chibchan-speaking peoples. The ancestral Chibchan language arose in Central America, possibly in western Panama/southwestern Costa Rica, not much less than 10,000 years BP. By 7000 BP at the latest, the language and the people who spoke it had begun to spread out both northwest and southeast and to diversify their material culture and their language, probably in response to climate change and the arrival of maize and manioc (the former first domesticated in Mexico, the latter in Amazonia) as subsistence crops. By 5000 B.P. there were ancestral subfamilies of Chibchan that had themselves begun to diversify into distinct languages. Of about twenty-five Chibchan languages known to be in existence in 1492 (there were probably many more, now lost) only about fifteen survive, and several of those have only a few living speakers. Four surviving subfamilies are recognized (Costenla-Umaña 1991, 1995, 2008): Pech (spoken in Honduras), Votic (Nicaragua and Costa Rica), Isthmic (Costa Rica and Panama), and Magdalenic (northern South America, i.e., northern Colombia and northwestern Venezuela).

The Barí language is usually classified in the Magdalenic subfamily of Chibchan. The other major surviving tribal peoples in the Magdalenic subfamily are the inhabitants of the Sierra Nevada de Santa Marta (the Kogi, Ijka, and Arsario) to the northwest of the Barí and the U'wa (Tunebo) to the southwest. Farther south, the densely populated and now admixed and Spanish-speaking people who inhabited the Sábana de Bogotá at the time of the Spanish conquest, and whose aboriginal language was known from missionary documents, also spoke a Magdalenic Chibchan.

Analyses of blood groups, serum protein systems, mitochondrial DNA, and Y chromosome markers have demonstrated "the relatively isolated development of these [Chibchan] groups and their low genetic variability" (Segura W. W. and Barrantes 2009: 357). In particular, "the majority of Chibchan populations are characterized by low haplotype diversity values, relative to most other South American groups. In addition they all have extremely low M values, suggesting that there is low maternal gene flow between groups in the region" (Melton et al. 2007: 767). These findings suggested to Melton (2004; cf. Melton et al. 2007) that Chibchan speakers had already migrated to northern South America by about 5000 B.P. and that they had little to do biologically with earlier or later migrants. Their societies developed in situ and with little admixture. Melton concluded that "while there are biological similarities between the Chibchan speakers from the Sierra Nevada de Santa Marta and the Panamanian isthmus, they diverged in the distant past" (2004: ii). In accord with Melton's genetic findings, Costenla-Umaña's (1981, 1991, 1995, 2008) classification of the Chibchan languages seconded the point that the Central American Chibchans were not closely related to the Barí. This remote association was one reason to be wary of the usefulness of comparisons of the Barí with other Chibchan speakers: Barí relations with the Chibchan mother culture—and thus with the other contemporary Chibchan speakers—were lost in time and did not speak clearly to the question of diversification. But there were larger reasons to question the utility of this tack in comparative contextualization.

More persuasive was that there was not a great deal known about the aboriginal practices of the other Chibchan-speaking peoples in subsistence, defense, and reproductive activities, and much of what was known and appeared at first sight to be appropriate for comparison turned out to pertain to peoples whose ecological relations were post-Columbian adaptations. The Central American Chibchan speakers, some of whom do remain in forested lowland areas similar to those in the Barí homeland, were not only distant relatives; they were also highly reduced populations with long histories of contact with Europeans. New crops and domestic animals, as well as new tools and agricultural methods and new weapons and loss of game habitat, had obscured their original subsistence patterns. Forced pacification and new diseases, in addition to modern medicine, not to mention a long and tragic history of interaction with the armed forces of modern states, had changed or eradicated their traditional means of defending themselves against the dangers of life. Enforced Western ideas about marriage and sexual behavior had obscured their aboriginal reproductive ecology.

Further, most Chibchan speakers in South America did not and do not inhabit tropical forests. Those closest to the Barí in both geographical proximity and (arguably) language were the Tunebo (or U'wa, as they called themselves) of Colombia. They were known to share some interesting features with the Barí, such as a semisedentary residence pattern involving seasonal migration, but they were fundamentally mountain slope people, not lowlanders. Also, like the Central American Chibchan peoples, they exhibited ecological relations that had been highly modified by contact with European-derived peoples (Osborn 1982: 4–5). Further, the literature on the Tunebo was limited, and aside from a few genetic studies most of it dealt with their language (Headland 1973; Headland and Headland 1976), their social anthropology and mythology (Osborn 1982, 1985), and (in newspaper articles, web postings, and other ephemera) their recent and ongoing struggle to defend their lands from oil companies.

In sum, although a comparison of the Barí with the other Chibchan-speaking peoples was an initially obvious way to put our findings in a wider context, on examination that project turned out to be unpromising for lack of significant comparability and unfeasible for lack of appropriate data. We mention one or another Chibchan-speaking group in the text that follows, when there are relevant data, but we concentrate our efforts below on comparisons with other, non-Chibchan, lowland South American peoples who inhabit neotropical rain forests similar to those in which the Barí live, maintain their aboriginal subsistence systems largely intact, and have not yet (at least as of the time they were described in the literature) been much subjected to the domination of the modern state and its agents—in other words, to people who maintained much of their traditional way of life when their ethnographers visited them.

Production

We begin the comparison with production, asking how the subsistence practices of the Barí compared with those of other traditional lowland neotropical peoples. In keeping with the organization of our earlier chapter on this subject, we explore agriculture, fishing, and hunting, then both fishing and hunting, in that order.

Agriculture

Comparative figures for lowland South American swidden agriculture compiled over twenty years ago (Beckerman 1987) revealed the Barí to be unexceptional as slash-and-burn manioc cultivators in most ways. They were near the middle of the pack in such matters as the size of their fields, the durations of the cropping and fallow periods of those fields, the labor they invested in the various stages of swidden cultivation, and the returns they got from agriculture, both per unit land and per unit labor (Table 7.1). They were somewhat unusual in the small numbers of cultivars they grew and in the large amount of land they kept under crop at any one time, the latter a consequence of their semisedentary residence pattern. The pattern of zoning their crops in concentric rings was a minority practice but one well known in Amazonia (Beckerman 1983a; Stocks 1983a; Beckerman 1984).

The Barí were also unusual in the amount of time some of their fields remained under crop, but this feature, too, was a consequence of their semisedentary residence pattern. As mentioned in chapter 4, Barí manioc could take care of itself after an initial weeding. Until the closed canopy was broken by harvesting, their cultivars of *Manihot* could shade out competitors and keep growing indefinitely. The same was true for bananas and plantains. Fields that were harvested occasionally and replanted immedi-

Table 7.1. Gross parameters of lowland neotropical manioc swidden cultivators

People	Mean Field Size (ha)	Years under Crop	Labor (mnhr/yr)	Productivity (104 kg/ha/yr)
Barí	0.4	3–15	800–1,000	25
Shuar	0.6	3–5		
Aguaruana	0.5	2–4		37
Huambisa	0.25	2–4		20
Achuara	0.37	2–15	3,000–4,000	17
Candoshi	0.5		1,000	
Ye'kuana	1.6		589	6.8–25.0
Kuikuru	0.65	2–5	900	7.5–21.0
Cubeo	0.4	3–5		
Siona-Secoya	0.6		600	20.0
Machiguenga	0.49	3–5	2,600	13.0
Campa	0.7			
Cocamilla	1.0	1–3	1,113	
Mekranoti	3		1,641	29

Note: The list is confined to peoples whose staple crop is manioc.
Sources: Barí, this book; Shuar, Harner 1973; Aguaruna, Boster 1980, pers. com.; Huambisa, Boster 1980, pers. com.; Achuara, Descola 1994; Candoshi, Stocks 1983a; Ye'kuana, Hames 1983; Kuikuru, Carneiro 1983; Cubeo, Goldman 1963; Siona-Secoya, Vickers 1983, 1989; Machiguenga, Johnson 1983; Campa, Denevan 1971; Cocamilla, Stocks 1983a; Mekranoti, Gross et al. 1979 and Flowers et al. 1982.

ately, especially if they were located on good alluvial soil or were fertilized by ash, cooking scraps, and human waste, could maintain themselves for a long time. Thus some Barí fields that were lightly harvested during the migration cycle lasted for over a decade.

Descola (1994: 312) demonstrated that the Achuara Jívaro kept considerably more manioc under crop than they consumed. Johnson (1983) reported a similar finding for the Machiguenga a decade earlier, as did Carneiro (1983) for the Kuikuru. The same was true for the Barí, and probably for the same reasons: food security and (among the Achuar and Barí at least) the prestige that accrued from being able to host a substantial number of visitors for a substantial period of time and the biological benefits that followed such prestige.

The small number of cultivars recorded for the Barí was an interesting mystery. Many neotropical rain forest manioc cultivators whose food crop inventories had been carefully studied were known to cultivate around fifty different species (Salick 1989; Balée 1994; Descola 1994). The traditional Barí cultivated only around twenty-five (M. Lizarralde 1997: 42.) The Bribri and Cabecar, distant Chibchan-speaking relatives of the Barí in the rain forests of Costa Rica, had forty-nine domesticated food crop species (Ramos García-Serrano and Del Monte 2004; cf. Zaldívar et al. 2002).

Among the manioc staple peoples, even those with relatively restricted inventories of food crop *species* typically had over twenty different *varieties* of manioc (Chernela 1987; Elias et al. 2004; Arroyo-Kalin 2012). Some had more than one hundred (Boster 1984; Chernela 1987). The Barí had only four, and two of those may postdate 1960. Why the anomaly?

It may be that the Barí lost many of their crops as a consequence of their persecution by and flight from Old World peoples over the past five centuries, including their period of mission captivity. A variant of this possibility was that they more or less deliberately gave up some demanding crops, such as maize, when the extermination of their indigenous neighbors provided them with abundant land and plentiful fish and game. Maize and beans eaten together are a satisfactory protein source, but if fish and game are abundant it is a lot more fun to spend your time fishing and hunting than clearing brush and pulling weeds. Alternatively, the Barí might never have had the large number of cultivars common among many other lowland neotropical peoples—in which case one might ask how long they had been in the tropical forest.

The back story for this last possibility might run as follows. The Barí may have descended directly and recently (say, within the last thousand years) from the montane peoples in and around the Sierra Nevada de Santa Marta or the Sábana de Bogotá. While those peoples were ultimately derived from the lowland Central American Chibchan mother culture, they had been in the mountains long enough to have lost many of their original lowland cultigens and to have developed a different, high-altitude crop inventory. Thus the Barí, after they left the mountains for the lowlands, brought with them only a reduced inventory of cultivars suitable for both high and low altitudes. They had not had time to develop or obtain others by the time of Old World contact.

Archaeological data that bear on these alternative explanations for the curiously small Barí crop inventory may one day emerge. However, there is no useful current evidence for evaluating the possibilities.

Fishing

As was the case with cultivation, Barí fishing had a few features that were sufficiently unusual as to be worthy of note but nothing strikingly anomalous. The Barí were not known to use nets or fish traps, which were common among other neotropical peoples; nor did they make canoes, although they must have known about them in historical times from their contacts with the lacustrine peoples to the east. Yearly average Barí fishing returns per man-hour were somewhat low in comparison to those of a number of other lowland rain forest peoples (Table 7.2), but a substantial part of the calculated difference was probably a result of the exclusively aboriginal practices to which we restricted our productivity data. (Many of the published data for other neotropical lowlanders included post-Columbian fishing techniques (steel hooks, nylon nets, even dynamite), which tended to be more productive than strictly aboriginal methods.)

There was another feature that contributed to the low hourly returns of Barí fishing in our reckoning: women were counted as full participants in the most common kind of fishing, the double-weir expedition. In calculating returns per hour, women, who built one of the pair of weirs, guzzled for Loricarids and crabs, cleaned the fish the men speared, and carried the fish home, were counted as full members of the trips. Ideally, it would have been better to discount the sometimes substantial amount of time that women spent sitting on the bank and chatting during the latter part of these double-weir expeditions, after the Loricarids were gathered and when the spearing became desultory. However, we did not collect those data, and therefore the denominator for the hourly rate calculation for fishing simply comprised the total number of women plus men who took part, multiplied by the full duration of the fishing trip. Among a number of other peoples noted in Table 7.2, only men were counted as participants in fishing, and it was not always clear whether women went along and what their contribution was.

In fishing, the Barí (like most people, and indeed most living organisms) appeared to be rate maximizers, behaving so as to make the return per unit time of their foraging effort as high as possible. There are two ways to accomplish this goal—to strive to get the largest amount of food possible in a relatively inflexible amount of time (food maximizers) or to strive to spend the smallest amount of time possible in acquiring a relatively fixed amount of food (time minimizers). We mentioned in chapter 4 that the finding that the Barí fished more in the dry season, when hourly returns for fishing were higher, suggested that with respect to protein ac-

Table 7.2. Return rates for neotropical lowland fishing

Language Family	People	Yearly Mean (g/mnhr)	Monthly Maximum (g/mnhr)	Monthly Minimum (g/mnhr)
Chibchan	Barí	350	578	150
Tukanoan	Siona-Secoya	675–1,000[a]		
	Makuna	300–555[a]		
	Tukano	570		
Arawakan	San Carlos	620	1,100	150
Tupian	Cocamilla	2,120	5,590	620
	Wayampi	540	1,220	270
Ge	Mekranoti	200		
	Bororo	680		
	Xavante	400		
	Kanela	50		
Panoan	Shipibo	140	2475	524
Yanomaman	Yanomamo	80–170[a]		
Unclassified	Pumé	405	1060	100

[a]Depending on location.
Note: In order to achieve a sufficient number of cases, this list includes some forest and grassland as well as rainforest peoples; it also includes some swidden peoples whose staple crop is not manioc. Because rivers often travel through different life zones, allowing fish to pass habitually from one to another, and because rivers are bordered by ribbons of evergreen forest even in grasslands, we believe the eclectic cases assembled here are usefully comparable.
Sources: Barí, this book; Siona-Secoya, Vickers 1989; Makuna, Arhem 1976; Tukano, Chernela 1989; San Carlos Arawakans, Clark and Uhl 1987; Cocamilla, Stocks 1983b; Mekranoti, Werner et al. 1979; Bororo, Werner et al. 1979; Xavante, Werner et al. 1979; Kanela, Werner et al. 1979; Shipibo, Bergman 1980; Yanomamo, Lizot 1977; Pumé, Gragson 1989.

quisition they were food maximizers rather than time minimizers. It was also mentioned that this finding contrasted with Stocks's (1983b) research among the Cocamilla of Peru, who fished less when fishing was most productive, leading their ethnographer to conclude that the Cocamilla were time minimizers.

We were persuaded that both conclusions were likely correct. Food maximizing and time minimizing are two ends of a continuum of marginal returns trade-offs between time and energy (Winterhalder 1983). The underlying question is when it is in the best interests of the actor to spend more time in activities other than the food quest and when it is best to obtain more food. The answer to this question varies with the condition of the actor and the characteristics of the actor's environment. Hence in this case our evaluation of the discrepant results was based on the raw numbers behind two cases. As shown in Table 7.2, the *minimum* monthly return rate for fishing for the Cocamilla (kg/hr) was higher than the *maximum* return rate for the Barí. The yearly *average* fishing return rate for the Cocamilla was six times that of the Barí. The Cocamilla could afford to be time minimizers because they lived in a much more bountiful and reliable fishing environment; their protein needs were easily covered, indeed saturated, and they quickly turned to other activities when fishing returns rose. The Barí, on the other hand, while they were hardly protein deprived, felt they could benefit from additional animal flesh in their diet. When fishing returns rose they took advantage of the situation to eat royally during the dry season. We believe it was the failure to construct the food maximizer versus time minimizer question around the marginal trade-off tipping point that led to the inconsistent results in Hames's (1989) ambitious attempt to discover whether Amazonians as a whole were food maximizers or time minimizers with respect to animal protein acquisition.

Hunting

Barí hunting, like their fishing, was not particularly unusual for rain forest lowlanders. They hunted only with bow and arrow (there is no evidence they ever used the spears and blowguns common in some parts of Amazonia) and took the usual suite of neotropical animals. There were few game taboos apart from the proscription of felids, raptors, most snakes, and scavengers, all very common prohibitions in South America. They did add sloths and rats to this list of animals not to be consumed.

Hunting returns were conspicuously low in comparison to those recorded for most other peoples in similar environments (Table 7.3). However, much of the scantiness of the Barí return rate was attributable to our exclusion from our calculations of all game taken with firearms. Most (but not all) of the comparable return rates in Table 7.3 included animals killed with shotguns. A prominent exception were the Waorani. Yost and Kelley (1983) presented separate figures for game taken with shotguns and game taken with traditional methods (spears and blowguns); their figure for hourly returns taken by traditional methods alone (presented in Table 7.3) was over an order of magnitude higher than that which the Barí achieved and an illustration of the game riches of the Waorani homeland.

Table 7.3. Return rates for neotropical lowland hunting

Language Family	People	Yearly Mean (g/mnhr)
Chibchan	Barí	135
Tukanoan	Siona-Secoya	3,200
Cariban	Ye'kuana	1,600
	Bakairi	240
Tupian	Cocamilla	470
	Wayampi	1,680
	Aché	660
Ge	Mekranoti	690
Panoan	Shipibo	1,600
Yanomaman	Yanomamo	450
Unclassified	Waorani	2,070
	Makú	1,520

Note: This list includes only evergreen neotropical forest peoples, in order to maintain as much consistency as possible in the faunal assemblage being hunted.
Sources: Barí, this book; Siona-Secoya, Vickers 1988; Ye'kuana, Hames 1979; Bakairi, Picchi 1982; Cocamilla, Stocks 1983b; Wayampi, Ouhoud-Renoux 1998; Aché, Hill and Hawkes 1983; Mekranoti, Werner et al. 1979; Shipibo, Bergman 1980; Yanomamo, Hames 1979; Waorani, Yost and Kelley 1983; Makú, Milton 1984.

Fishing and Hunting

We were quickly persuaded, when looking at the seasonal distribution of hunting and fishing effort with respect to productivity, that fishing drove hunting among the Barí. That is, when fishing was good, hunting became a conspicuously less important activity. Hunting rose above fishing in the proportion of animal protein it supplied only during the rainy season when fishing returns were low to zero. The amount of time dedicated to each activity followed this pattern, once we took into account the inherently lower return rate of hunting. However (and this fact puzzled us), there was no month in which hunting was completely abandoned. Even in February, the height of the dry season, when people might fish for several hours every other day, hunting never dropped out of the male activity schedule.

Both these findings, that fishing drove hunting and that even so hunting never completely disappeared, were common among neotropical peoples who had access to riverine resources. (Extreme interfluvial peoples, who avoid any watercourse larger than a small stream, of course obtain almost all their animal protein from hunting.)

Why keep hunting when fishing was bountiful? We considered several possible explanations for this apparent deviation from the optimal allocation of foraging time. In hunting, there was always the possibility of a jackpot kill—a tapir, a herd of peccaries—that was too attractive to pass up. Hunting by its nature involved reconnaissance, which was a useful tradition to maintain among people who were until recently subjected to murderous raids. Game animals were more appreciated and brought higher status than fish. It was important to maintain one's hunting skills against the season when they were important. Hunting was more fun than fishing. We were never able to reject any of these possibilities, but we did not investigate them systematically either.

The only possibility we were able to reject was the suggestion (Beckerman 1983b) that hunting trips also served as scouting trips to appraise the state of the rivers and thus to increase the yield of fishing trips by directing them to the most abundantly stocked fishing spots. Further inquiry on this topic met with universal denial that such was the case.

Again with respect to fishing and hunting taken together, it will be recalled that the average Barí man spent 125 ± 20 hours per month in the sum of these activities (Beckerman 1983b) and that this figure was remarkably inelastic with respect to month (i.e., season) and location (riverine or interfluvial). Descola (1994: 289–294) found something similar among the Achuara Jívaro: the average married man spent 120 ± 30 total hours per month in the sum of fishing and hunting, irrespective of his location (riverine or interfluvial) or the number of wives he had to provide for (range $= 1$–4). Both figures represented not the mean plus or minus one standard deviation but the mean plus or minus the entire range of variation.

The inelasticity of Barí foraging time restricted the implications of our tentative conclusion that the Barí were food maximizers. Given the amount of free time remaining to them after all subsistence activities were accounted for, it was clear that the Barí could have devoted a great deal more effort to fishing and hunting had they wanted to. That they did not do so argued that they simply were not hungry enough to feel the need.

Food maximizers they might have been, but they were hardly famished. In maximizing, they simply took advantage of the boom times during the drier part of the year to eat abundantly. There were sometimes lean periods at the height of the rainy season, but even then there was no evidence that men had to strain and toil to keep their families fed.

Protection

The two most important threats the Barí had to confront were disease and war.

Disease

As noted in chapter 5, the Barí, like the generality of the currently surviving peoples of the South American rain forest, were somewhat shielded from the effects of contagious diseases by their small and dispersed settlements. Infection traveled with difficulty from one isolated longhouse to another. In both the 1780s and 1790s and again in the 1960s, when the worst epidemics struck them, it was primarily the abnormal concentration of multiple local groups of Barí at mission settlements and other Western outposts that led to devastation.

There was nothing unusual about this pattern, which had been repeated innumerable times in the five hundred years of the Old World colonization of the New. In the lowland neotropics the densely settled aboriginal peoples were essentially wiped out within a century or two of Old World contact. The great majority of people who were concentrated at mission stations also died. The sparsely distributed people—some of them at least—survived. The story of the Barí was no different from those of hundreds of other tribal groups of the neotropics who survived by being isolated and widely dispersed.

Apart from dispersion, there was another aspect of Barí behavior that shielded them considerably from contagion: they were bellicose. With the exception of the period of pacification between 1772 and 1818 and of the current, post-1960 pacification, they were always at war with the rest of the world. This situation protected them from diseases transmitted by direct contact and probably helped, because of the wide berth their neighbors usually gave them, even with those diseases carried by non-human vectors such as mosquitoes. In one of the unintentional ironies of history, the existence of human antagonists protected them from microscopic enemies. Again, there was nothing unique here; it was the story of the Yanomamo, the Waorani, the Shuar, the Achuar, the Huambisa, and the Aguaruna as well.

There was yet another feature of the Barí response to disease, also mentioned in chapter 5, which was somewhat unusual and probably also had a protective effect. Many historical accounts of epidemics among peoples of the neotropical forest mentioned that as people fell sick they began to flee, as if the disease were a predator that could be escaped. The typical Barí response to getting sick was to climb into a hammock and withdraw from social relations. The effect of this perhaps unusual cultural response—sick people acted as if they were embarrassed, even ashamed, and stayed put—was probably to diminish the transmission of infection from one longhouse to another among the local groups that maintained a traditional settlement pattern.

Warfare

Infectious disease became a major problem for the Barí—and all the other native inhabitants of the New World—only after 1492. Warfare was a much older challenge. As discussed in chapter 3, the weight of the evidence suggested that the Barí had been prey to larger, denser populations for centuries before contact, and the state of affairs was only aggravated when the Europeans arrived. One of the ways they dealt with an environment of chronic raiding and the ever-present threat of massacre and slavery was their semisedentary residence pattern.

We have described Barí migrations from one longhouse to another largely as subsistence choices, partly because greater abundance of food resources at the destination site was the single most common explanation we received when we asked why people had moved from A to B and partly because our own measurements generally confirmed this interpretation. However, there were other times when informants explicitly mentioned avoidance of raiding as the major motive for a particular migration. Also, we were not able to ignore the inherent difficulty of raiding people who did not stay in one place, no matter what their immediate reasons for moving might have been.

The origin of semisedentism, a trait the Barí shared with the Tunebo and the Kogi, was unknowable, but whatever the initial source of their long-standing program of migrating around several different, widely separated longhouses over the course of a year, there could be little doubt that it served them well as a defensive military strategy. They were hard to find, and when they were located and attacked they had ready-made places to regroup and carry on. About a quarter of longhouse locations were chosen with the primary motive of providing a place to run to, or a place so remote that it would never be found. It was not clear how many other locations were selected with defensive purposes as a secondary consideration.

In post-Columbian times, the reasons for raids on the Barí were clear. Slavery was an early motive for the European invaders, soon followed by revenge, as punitive expeditions were mounted in response to Barí raids for iron tools and other booty. A somewhat later motive was simply the extermination of the Barí by those coveting their land or the oil underneath it.

Pre-Columbian motives were less well documented. The evidence for slaving by the lacustrine people around Lake Maracaibo was mentioned in chapter 3. We presumed that the capture of women was an at least occasional component of raids, here as virtually everywhere else in the tribal world. We also entertained seriously the evidence that revenge itself was sufficient motive for an endless exchange of hostilities, without any material reward of goods, slaves, or women (Beckerman 2008). Once different peoples become enemies they often enter a cycle of blood revenge, with each hostile encounter providing the motive for the next. (We return to this point below.)

What we did know was that in many if not most places in the pre-Columbian lowland neotropics, warfare was chronic and was habitually characterized by recurrent hostilities between large, densely settled polities (often but not always centered along major rivers) and smaller groupings of interfluvial peoples with more widely dispersed populations (cf. Lathrap 1968, 1970; Santos-Granero 2009). There was abundant evidence of the killing of men and the capture of women and children.

These considerations led us to conclude that whatever the origins of Barí semisedentism, the main reason for its perpetuation was to be sought more in protection than in production. In other words, we found little evidence that subsistence constraints alone kept the Barí on the move (although once multiple longhouses had been built, the immediate effect of moving from one to another was often a higher input/output ratio in local food production). Rather, we became persuaded that the avoidance of enemies was at least as important a consideration as the optimization of the diet in the preservation of an unusual and laborious system of residence and territorial occupation.

We were reinforced in this conclusion by the evidence of the Waorani of Ecuador (Yost 1981a, 1981b; Beckerman et al. 2009) who were also low-land manioc cultivators, also at war with the rest of the world (and in their case with each other as well), also blessed with generally abundant food supplies, and also practitioners of a semisedentary residence pattern. The biodiversity hot spot where the Waorani lived was so well provided with game and so underpopulated with people, that as far as we were aware no one had ever suggested any motive for Waorani semisedentism except for military considerations.

That the Chibchan-speaking Kogi and Tunebo also manifested a semi-sedentary settlement pattern, like that of the Barí, provided evidence that the Barí practice was pre-Columbian. These former peoples were not raided in the near past, however, and their semisedentary migrations in the present day had to be ascribed to nondefensive motives. However, the Barí, who maintained semisedentism in the face of ongoing raiding that only ended after 1960, were in effect preserving an aboriginal means of defense. The identities of their enemies had changed, but the threat had not gone away, or greatly changed its shape, and their defensive strategy remained remarkably effective for a long time. Ultimately, of course, it was no match for the progressive destruction of the rain forest that had sheltered them for so long, or for modern firearms and aircraft.

Reproduction

We take up the issues addressed in chapter 6 in the order in which they were addressed there.

Population Growth

The remarkably high overall rate of population growth (approximately 4% per annum) found between the Venezuelan Barí census of 1983 and that of 1992 could probably be attributed largely to the effects of the epidemics that preceded the earlier of them. The 1983 population was still enriched with people of reproductive age because older individuals had been disproportionately killed by the epidemics of 1962–1966.

Following a more speculative track, if our estimate of a maximum of 850 Barí in Colombia and Venezuela combined in 1966 was roughly correct and if Jaramillo's count of 488 Barí in Colombia in 1985 was reasonably accurate, then the average growth rate of the total Barí population between the mid-1960s and the mid-1980s was not much under 4% per annum. Of course, the yearly growth rate must have fluctuated widely. Just after the epidemics, for instance, there was every reason to believe that the double traumas of massive imposed culture change and massive disease mortality must have reduced the reproductive rate to very low levels, as noted just below. Nevertheless, despite a slow start on recovery, the total Barí population was in the vicinity of 1,650 souls in 1985 if the Jaramillo count was correct.

The message of this rudimentary exercise was that the Barí were able to increase their population substantially during the 1970s and early 1980s, when subsistence practices, for most of the population, were still largely aboriginal and their territory was shrinking rapidly (Lizarralde and Beckerman 1982). Their immediate postcontact history, like the productivity figures for their agriculture, fishing, and hunting, showed nothing to indicate that their population was limited by scarcity of subsistence resources.

Effects of Trauma

That the shock of contact and the ensuing dislocations, abuses, and epidemics had a negative effect on Barí birthrates came as no surprise. The evidence of the magnitude of the effect—the raising of the mean interbirth interval from thirty-one to fifty-one months—gave evidence of the severity of the trauma. What was perhaps surprising was the speed with which the population recovered from the known assaults.

Sex Ratio

We devoted a good deal of space to exploring sex ratios within the Barí population, because the peculiarly high sex ratio found among many lowland neotropical peoples remained an anomaly with important evolutionary implications (Sieff 1990) but no generally accepted explanation and because it had been invoked to explain lowland South American village fissioning and warfare, among other things (Divale and Harris 1976). Much of the discussion revolved around the live birth sex ratio. Chagnon et al. (1979) reported a live birth sex ratio of 129 among the Yanomami; and Early and Peters (2000) later reported a live-birth sex ratio of 126 for the precontact phase of their sample of Mucajaí Yanomami (the weighted average of all their phases was 116). Among foraging peoples, Hurtado and Hill (1987) found a live-birth sex ratio of 117 for the Cuiva of Venezuela, and Hill and Kaplan (1988) found a figure of 116 for the Aché of Paraguay.

The Barí manifested a similar live birth sex bias in a conspicuous way, and the usual rationalization for brushing off this phenomenon — "It must be female infanticide" — was unpersuasive in their case. As discussed above in chapter 6 and below in the section on partible paternity, we also found an interaction of the presence or absence of a secondary father, precontact versus postcontact birth date, territory of birth, and the live birth sex ratio that was striking — and as yet unexplained. Work on this matter is ongoing (Beckerman and Parker in prep.).

Differential reproductive success was one of the areas we explored in various ways; reproduction is one of the major engines of evolution, so differences therein are expected to have important consequences. We looked at factors that might have led to significant differences in number of pregnancies per woman, number of wives per man, the survivorship of children, and so forth.

Environmental richness was one of the most obvious factors that might have an impact on reproductive success, and we were able to demonstrate that women from Territory 3, acknowledged by the Barí to be the most bountiful of the Venezuelan territories, had on average almost two more pregnancies over their reproductive lives than the weighted average of pregnancies per woman in all territories combined. We were not able to discover any similar finding among other lowland South American peoples.

The sex of the firstborn child had been offered as an influence on a woman's lifetime reproductive success (Turke 1988). Our Barí data revealed an advantage of about one pregnancy per reproductive life span to a woman who had a girl as her first child but no increase in the number of children she eventually raised to maturity. Again, we were not aware of parallel results in the literature.

The issue of whether better hunters had more wives and/or more children than less talented men had been raised in the human evolutionary ecology literature and recently explored by Smith (2004) in a comparative article dealing with hunting and gathering peoples. We were not able to find comparative information from horticultural peoples but were not surprised that skilled Barí hunters appeared to achieve an advantage parallel to what was seen among hunters and gatherers. The evidence was that they acquired significantly more wives and probably had significantly more children. Skilled fishermen were somewhat less advantaged than hunters in these areas, and although their reproductive benefits did not rise to statistical significance at the $p < .05$ level, we suspected that a larger sample would have shown that fishermen, too, gained reproductive benefits from their foraging talents.

We investigated sororal versus nonsororal polygyny to see if sister wives took better care of each other's children than unrelated women married to the same man and found no significant difference, although again there might be a sample size caution attached to this result. As far as we were able to determine, this issue had not been previously explored among horticulturalists of the lowland neotropics.

We also explored the inherently different reproductive strategies of men and women and verified that among the Barí, as among practically every other people in the world, the variance in reproductive success was far greater for men than for women. Among the Barí, the difference between male and female variance was widened by the frequency of polygyny.

Finally we explored partible paternity among the Barí. Since our first publications on this topic (Beckerman et al. 1998; Beckerman et al. 2002; Beckerman and Valentine 2002; Beckerman and Lizarralde 2003), a comprehensive review by Walker, Flinn, and Hill (2010) had demonstrated that partible paternity was widespread and probably quite ancient in lowland South America. Although much work remained (and still remains) to be done on native theories of conception and fetal development, it appeared that the Barí were somewhat unusual in that they generally held that only one act of intercourse was sufficient to create a pregnancy. Subsequent coitus was to speed the development of the fetus and make it strong and healthy. Many other peoples apparently held that multiple sex acts were necessary even to begin a pregnancy.

South American Culture History

In William Vickers's (1989) thoughtful and data-rich ecological study of the Siona-Secoya of Ecuador, he posed a long-standing question in lowland South American ethnology: Why were the tropical forest societies characteristically of such low population density and their settlements so dispersed and transitory? He pointed to two unifactorial explanations offered for this set of features, descriptive of the Barí as well as the Siona-Secoya—and indeed of most other peoples of Amazonia and the Amazon fringe. He pointed out that some of the suggestions went back as far as Liebig's 1840 "law of the minimum," the observation, first made with respect to crop plants, that growth was limited by the abundance of the nutrient that was scarcest in relation to the nutritional needs of the plant (the "limiting factor"). Increasing other nutrients already present in abundance did not increase crop yield; only augmenting the limiting factor escalated growth. This principle was later extended to the reproduction as well as growth of many biological populations, including *Homo sapiens*, although sometimes in terms more metaphorical than rigorous.

It was employed by Betty Meggers (1954), who argued that the poverty of rain forest soils limited agricultural productivity and hence human population growth and thereby prevented the emergence of large political units in Amazonia. Robert Carneiro (1961) published evidence that called into question the agricultural limitations of Amazonian soils when planted in manioc, the most common Amazonian staple. Meggers (1971) was unconvinced, but most other Amazonian anthropologists were.

A second limiting factor argument was presented by Daniel Gross (1975), following earlier suggestions by Lathrap (1968) and Carneiro (1970). Gross suggested that it was animal protein rather than agricultural land that limited human population growth in the Amazon. This argument was persuasive to Roosevelt (1980, 1991), although there were objections to this unifactorial position as well (e.g., Beckerman 1980b). Carneiro (1995) wrote a detailed account of who published what, and when, on this topic.

Vickers's response to the debate was to point out, following a classic text in ecology (Odum 1971), that Liebig's law of the minimum was only applicable under steady state conditions, in which the rate of input of matter and energy was equal to their rate of output—in the current case, the rate of influx of the food was in equilibrium with the rate of production of biomass plus respiration and egestion in the population that was limited. And Vickers saw clearly that this equilibrium was at best transitory among the Amazonian peoples, because the rate of input, whether of agricultural products or wild game, varied widely in time and space.

Vickers's argument, inspired by meticulous fieldwork with the Siona-Secoya, applied a fortiori to the semisedentary Barí. Vickers's rejection of the protein limitation hypothesis was taken up by Philippe Descola (1994), who demonstrated its weakness in accounting for settlement size and distribution among the Achuara Jívaro of Ecuador, as well as the allocation of labor in and returns from their protein procurement activities.

Our appreciation of the evidence, based on our measurements of Barí subsistence productivity in horticulture, fishing, and hunting and even more on our data concerning reproduction, was that Vickers and Descola were quite correct. Those populations were not limited by either lack of horticultural land or by meager protein supplies. In fact, protein resources may have been generally underexploited in the lowland neotropics (Beckerman 1979).

Our larger interpretation of the facts and figures for the lowland rain forest overall followed the work of Lathrap (1968, 1970) and was bolstered by archaeological studies by Roosevelt (1999a, 1999b) and Heckenberger, Petersen, and Neves (1999). That is, in late pre-Columbian times, peoples in most major riverine regions did not live in small, sparse settlements; they inhabited substantial communities—large towns, in effect—that were often closely packed. Where there was empty land between stretches of communities, it was warfare, rather than nutrition, that excluded potential inhabitants. It was similarly warfare that kept the upstream and interfluvial peoples in small, widely spaced, and temporary settlements.

Our view of the importance of warfare in the pre-Columbian tropics was not supported only by measurements of subsistence practices or the research of a few ecologically oriented anthropologists. It was also based on considerable historical documentation. In fact, it was nicely articulated by the (nonecological) ethnographer and ethnohistorian Fernando Santos-Granero (2009), who in a study of New World raiding and slaving between the Tropic of Cancer and the Tropic of Capricorn discussed five peoples ranging from the Calusa of southern Florida to the Guaicurú of Paraguay. He included two tropical forest manioc horticulturalists, the Tukano of the Vaupés River in Colombia and Brazil and the Conibo of the Ucayali River in eastern Peru. His understanding of the state of affairs regarding these peoples was based on a reading of early documents, not current ecological relations. He described the situation as follows:

> Relationships with . . . less powerful peoples were characterized by permanent raiding, pillaging, and the taking of captives, generally children and young women. . . . The same societies that had been victimized by hegemonic peoples sometimes in turn victimized their weaker neighbors. . . . The only economic trait that seems to be common to these capturing societies is that all of them occupied what can be considered the richest environments from the point of view of their particular lifestyles. . . . Tukano, Conibo, and Guaicurú lived along the largest rivers in their respective areas, in areas of fertile soils and rich aquatic resources, from which they attacked the peoples living in the less fertile headwaters and interfluves. . . . In these asymmetrical power relationships, weaker

peoples were constantly harassed and placed in a position of actual and ideological subordination. . . . [T]hey were considered to be prey and were hunted as actual forest animals. (Santos-Granero 2009: 42–43)

After 1492, Old World diseases reversed the direction of adversity in this situation. The demographic catastrophe that followed, and indeed in some cases preceded, the first wave of Spanish and Portuguese colonization simply wiped the large riverine populations from the face of the earth. However, contagious diseases moved with considerably more difficulty among the small, sparse settlements of the interfluvial peoples. The last were now first. What had begun as an adaptation to chronic raiding turned out to be a preadaptation to infectious disease. The peoples who survived, and whom we see today, are mainly the descendants of the dispersed interfluvial peoples, in some cases augmented by refugee remnants of the ravaged riverine peoples. Their populations have been battered by measles and malaria, plague and tuberculosis, cholera and smallpox for the past five hundred years and continue to be assaulted by these deadliest of enemies.

Our response to the question of the small size and sparsity of contemporary neotropical populations was ecological but not focused primarily on subsistence ecology. The literature on the ecology of predation influenced our thinking, as did concepts from disease ecology. These strands came together in a scenario informed mainly by what we found for the Barí.

There were indeed more and less favored locations in the lowland neotropics. Prominent among the advantages of the better places were areas of abundant, fertile várzea soils and rich riverine resources, particularly fish and turtles. Peoples who inhabited these favored localities tended to have more children and higher survivorship in pre-Columbian times than their upstream and interfluvial neighbors, largely because of better nutrition. This disparity did *not* mean that the peoples of the smaller rivers and the interfluves were malnourished. Indeed, as shown by the evidence presented here and in the work of Descola (1994) and Yost and Kelley (1983), who provide data that are probably representative of other Amazonian peoples who maintained traditional subsistence when studied, the people who lived away from major rivers had perfectly adequate diets. The difference, we concluded, was a matter of adequacy versus abundance, as reflected in reproductive success.

As an estimate of the demographic consequences of adequacy versus abundance, we looked to the Barí reproductive figures in Table 6.4. The mean number of pregnancies per woman in our database of 114 post-reproductive women was 8, but women from the especially well favored Territory 3 had an average of 9.85 pregnancies. This difference might roughly mirror the reproductive spread between the major riverine and the upland peoples. It did not in any way imply that the upstream and interfluvial peoples were dying out from low natural fertility.

On the contrary, the evidence of Barí demographic history and the pre- and postcontact reproductive histories of the women we interviewed showed that they reproduced at far above replacement when not reeling from disease and massacre. We were persuaded that the Barí case was instructive for the aboriginal lowland neotropics in general. Of course, disease was not a major issue before 1492. Homicide and slavery, however, certainly were.

Our appraisal of the pre-Columbian situation gave full attention to the way in which upstream and interfluvial peoples were under regular assault from their more populous mainstream neighbors. These assaults, not malnutrition or disease, were the initial reason for the small, sparse settlements of the former.

There were two ways in which chronic warfare curtailed the growth of large populations and large, permanent settlements away from the major rivers. First, small, widely dispersed settlements were in and of themselves a defensive strategy (Beckerman 1991b). They raised the required exertion and lowered the rewards for expeditions aimed at taking captives. Settlement geography would have been highly dispersed even if overall population had been considerably higher than it was.

However, overall population was not of the scale seen along the major rivers because, second, raiding for women and children braked the population growth of the losers. Populations that were not limited by scarce resources were nonetheless constantly trimmed by homicide and slaving. Preferred captives all over the tribal world are young women and girls on the brink of puberty. Fertile females are of course the limiting factor in the reproduction of any population. Extracting even a modest fraction of them can have major demographic effects. In Amazonia, children were also habitually taken to be used as slaves and servants; of course, many of these children were female.

A characteristic of Amazonia, as Santos-Granero (2009: 226–227) stressed, was that considerable proportions of the large riverine societies were composed of war captives. He estimated that 10% of the Conibo population and 8% of the Tukano population was made up of captive slaves. The Tukano also had living with them whole groups of interfluvial

Makú who had been extracted from the deep forest and reduced to collective servitude, bringing the "war captives and attached servants" to 28% of the Tukano population.

Overall in Amazonia, we saw a situation in which the flow of migration, violently coerced, was from the slower-growing populations toward the more rapidly reproducing societies. And that outmigration, combined with considerable warfare mortality visited on adult men and old people of both sexes, was the other reason for the absence of large villages and large populations in the Amazonian hinterlands. The upriver and interfluvial communities constantly lost members, reproductively crucial members especially, to larger, stronger societies.

After the arrival of men and diseases from the Old World, the major riverine societies rapidly shrank and then almost entirely disappeared. Many upriver peoples survived. The postures of settlement and residence they had adopted to protect themselves from the mainstream indigenous warriors now served to protect them both from the Spanish and Portuguese slavers and missionaries and, more important, from the diseases brought by those invaders. To a small extent, in a few remote places, they still do. For the Barí, these postures had served for nearly five hundred years.

Human Ecology Writ Large

We quoted above the statement, made by an eminent anthropologist, that human ecologists tended to regard culture as "digestion writ large." While we certainly agree that among the aspects of humanity that can be productively studied there are vastly more things, events, processes, and ideas than can be covered under the rubric of ecology, we wanted this book to demonstrate that ecological relations are not confined to the getting and consuming of food. Ecology deals with competition, predation, distribution, abundance, disease, mobility, mating, reproduction, demography, and so forth, as well as food. The argument we put forward above to explain the small, dispersed nature of neotropical settlements and the low overall population density of the nonriverine peoples of the neotropics used subsistence data mainly to show that subsistence alone could not account for the phenomenon. Our explanation appealed mainly to intraspecific competition (for mates and for revenge) and differential rates of fertility, mortality, and migration as the major actors.

The general points we wanted to emerge from this book were, first, that all sorts of relationships between people and their environments were worthy of study; second, that quantitative data concerning these relationships were rewardingly explanatory; third, that the environment included not only plants and nonhuman animals but (very importantly) human beings as well; fourth, that relationships between people and their environments were not limited to eating but also minimally included fighting, avoiding, and mating as inevitably important components of ecological relations. The extent to which younger anthropologists are persuaded of the utility of this approach will be the measure of the success of this book.

APPENDIX

Additional Data on Barí Horticulture

Area under Cultivation per Longhouse

Unfortunately, we cannot give precise, extensively sampled figures for the amount of land an individual or a longhouse actually has in active production at any one time. On the ground, it is often impossible to measure or pace off the axes of mature subsidiary fields because trails are not maintained through them (as they are in active house-surrounding fields). Aerial photographs from precontact times are not of direct use in answering this question because it is generally impossible to distinguish among actively productive fields, fields recently planted but not yet in production, and early fallow fields in this black-and-white imagery.

Compounding the problem, in early fieldwork we were often uncertain whether we had visited all the subsidiary fields associated with some longhouses. An estimate of the range of the area in active production per individual and per longhouse can nevertheless be derived from the following observations.

Lizarralde visited the traditional longhouse of Ohbadyá, population 44, in 1961. The house-surrounding field encompassed 0.4 ha. These people also made use of four subsidiary fields associated with a recently abandoned longhouse of theirs, Bariduá. These fields had areas of 1.4, 0.7, 0.6, and 0.6 ha. Thus the total area in active production associated with this longhouse provided its inhabitants with the produce of 0.08 ha/person of cultivated land.

A full-sized traditional longhouse (Antraikaira) with a population of 50 had a house-surrounding field of 0.70 ha or a bit less (as assessed by pacing trails through the field) and a nearby subsidiary field of 0.65 ha, as measured on an aerial photograph. Beckerman was told when he visited Antraikaira in 1972 that the house-surrounding field and the single nearby subsidiary field were the only ones in production at this longhouse. This sum of actively productive land works out to 0.027 ha/person, barely above the minimal figure calculated as needed to produce a year's supply of manioc.

These people planted a new subsidiary manioc field of about 1.5 ha during Beckerman's stay at Antraikaira, bringing the per capita land under crop at this house to 0.06 ha. This local group also had two other longhouses in their migration cycle, each with its own fields, and had recently abandoned a fourth.

A small but traditional longhouse (Ashtakakaira) with nine inhabitants had a measured 0.39 ha in active production in the house-surrounding field in 1970 (Beckerman 1983a: 94). This area is equivalent to 0.04 ha/person. These people also had within 200 m of their longhouse an abandoned temporary house, where they had lived while building Ashtakakaira, whose tiny associated manioc field (about 160 m²) they harvested and weeded.

About an hour and a half away was the former longhouse of these nine people, with its house-surrounding field of about 0.36 ha. This overgrown house-surrounding field was clearly at the edge of abandonment. No one weeded it, and it was harvested only occasionally, and then merely for minor crops such as sweet potatoes. Nevertheless, it still contained considerable manioc that could have been harvested if need had arisen. Including it in the active field inventory brings the productive area up to 0.090 ha/person. These people were experimenting with sedentary life and possessed no other longhouses at this time.

Another full-sized traditional longhouse (Culebritaskaira, population 55 when visited in 1972) had a house-surrounding field of over 2.3 ha, various private subsidiary fields, and a communal subsidiary field, also in active production, whose roughly paced axes generated an area of about 0.8 ha. These people had recently planted an additional 0.3 ha with manioc in the center of a new field that was not yet producing. They intended to grow *Musa* on the remaining 0.6 ha of the land they had cleared for this new field. The people at Culebritascaira must have had well over 0.06 ha/person in active production, even without counting the new field. This group at that time had only one other longhouse in its migration cycle.

It is easier to produce figures for total land under crop—that is, the sum of newly planted fields, fields in active production, and fields in early fallow—because these data can be obtained from aerial photographs.

In 1960 a local group comprising 103 people had five longhouses in its migratory cycle: Otaká, with a total of 3.9 ha of fields (house-surrounding field plus subsidiary fields) associated with it, had 0.04 ha/person. Ishtrondakaira, with 5.3 ha of associated fields, had 0.05 ha/person. Tanakani, with 7.5 ha of associated fields, had 0.07 ha/person. The large longhouse of Karibaigdakaira, built to accommodate several local groups (who would perhaps come from other territories) with a total of 5.5 ha of fields associated with it, had 0.05 ha/person; and Shiboibadá, which was not photographed and whose field area is unknown, presumably had something in the range of the other four longhouses. Thus these people had comfortably over 0.2 ha/person of land under crop in their full assembly of longhouses.

In sum, for an individual longhouse, total land under crop, the sum of land planted but not yet producing, land in active production, and land in early fallow but still bearing harvestable cultivars ran roughly between 0.05 and 0.1 ha/person for the longhouses represented in these data. Longhouse land in active production (regularly harvested land currently under mature crop) was about half that figure, ranging from 0.025 to 0.05 ha/person or a little more. Total land under crop at all longhouses belonging to a local group (for the one local group for which we have the necessary data) was around 0.25 ha/person.

Size of Individual Fields

HOUSE-SURROUNDING FIELDS

The size of house-surrounding fields can be measured for eighty-eight such fields visible on aerial photographs from numerous series flown over Venezuelan (and adjacent parts of Colombian) Motilonia at various dates between 1936 and 1964 (R. Lizarralde 1968).

In this sample the sizes of house-surrounding fields range from 0.15 to 2.1 ha. The mean area of these house-surrounding fields is 0.7 ha (SD = 0.43). The modal size is 0.6 ha.

To obtain a more accurate figure for the amount of land actually in crop in a house-surrounding field, one should subtract the area of the uncultivated land in its center occupied by the longhouse itself and the bare ring of soil that encircles it. This figure ranges (for a full-sized longhouse with ~50 inhabitants) from 300 m^2 to 900 m^2 (0.03–0.09 ha), suggesting that the 0.7 ha mean for a house-surrounding field developed above ought to be reduced by 5% to 15% for purposes of dealing with the amount of land dedicated to food production.

It is of interest that some of the house-surrounding fields examined in the aerial photographic record changed size over the years. Between 1954 and 1958, for instance, the residents of Nankatdukaya enlarged their house-surrounding field from 0.4 to 1.0 ha. The inhabitants of Barikoksanda increased the size of theirs from 0.6 to 1.1 ha between 1937 and 1943. We suspect that the mean size of the house-surrounding field of a brand-new longhouse may be somewhat smaller than the 0.7 ha found for houses of all ages—perhaps in the neighborhood of 0.4 or 0.5 ha.

Shortly after peaceful contact, substantially larger house-surrounding fields— up to 6.8 ha—began appearing in a handful of places.

We tentatively attribute the late appearance of a few large house-surrounding fields to increased sedentism brought about by accelerated territory loss and peaceful contact. Even before peaceful contact in 1960, settlement density of occupied land under 600 m (the maximum elevation at which longhouses were ordinarily established) in Colombian Motilonia rose from about 0.9 longhouse per 100 km^2 in 1937–1939 to over 1.5 longhouses/100 km^2 in 1958–1960 (Beckerman 1976). In Venezuela in 1947 the figure was 1.1 longhouses/100 km^2 (the maximum elevation for a longhouse reached as high as 800 m). This increase suggests that Barí may have been running out of acceptable alternative settlement locations and may have been forced to make more intensive use of the ones they already had. Increased access to iron tools, beginning with air-dropped gifts of axes and machetes (as well as cooking pots, knives, cloth, etc.) in 1948–1950, in the "peace bombs" dropped by Capuchin missionaries in Venezuela, may also have been important in allowing people to be more efficient in cutting their fields.

In on-the-ground appraisals from the ethnographic present, the house-surrounding fields of traditional longhouses visited early on by Lizarralde had areas of 0.4 ha (Ohbadyá, 1961), 1.15 ha (Karibaigdakaira, 1961), and 0.8 ha (Otaká, 1963). Two traditional longhouses that Beckerman visited in 1970–1972 had house-surrounding fields that measured roughly 0.7 and 2.3 ha. Most of these houses had populations of around fifty. Karibaigdakaira had been planned and built to accommodate at least twice that number, and Otaká had eighty-one inhabitants in May 1961. Two smaller longhouses (population only ±10) both had house-surrounding fields of around 0.4 ha. The house-surrounding field of a traditional-style longhouse (population ±30) constructed at a mission station was over 3.0 ha (Beckerman 1983a). In this last case the missionary had requested the inhabitants to plant sufficient manioc to feed numerous visitors from other local groups.

In Venezuela in 1966 Lizarralde visited the traditional longhouse Shidakayra, population forty-five, which was surrounded on all sides by cattle ranches. It had a single, house-surrounding field of 6.0 ha, of which about 4.0 ha were planted in manioc and the rest, the outer ring, was in bananas and plantains. A semitraditional longhouse, Kirongda, population sixty-one, that Lizarralde visited in 1965 also had a single, house-surrounding field of 2.8 ha, nearly all in manioc. Another semitraditional longhouse, Angbarikayra, population thirty, that he visited in 1966 likewise had a only a single, house-surrounding field measuring 4.0 ha. The inhabitants enlarged it the following year to a total of 6.8 ha.

The figures mentioned above indicate that in pre- and pericontact times, for local groups with multiple longhouses and a semisedentary residence pattern, the mean and mode of the size of the house-surrounding field was close to 0.7 ha. When and where contact imposed sedentarism, and available land was expropriated by ranchers, the mean size of the house-surrounding field increased several-fold within less than five years.

SUBSIDIARY FIELDS

In addition to the omnipresent house-surrounding field, traditional longhouses acquire subsidiary fields at various distances. It is common practice when a longhouse reaches the end of its useful life to build its replacement within 100 to 200 m of the original, whose subsidiary fields remain in use. However, when the first longhouse is built in a new area, it typically begins life with only its house-surrounding field and acquires subsidiary fields as the years pass.

Aerial photographs taken in Colombian Motilonia in 1937 and 1939 show a size range from 0.2 ha to 3.8 ha, with a mean area around 1.0 ha, mode about 0.6 ha (n = 36). Photographs taken in 1958 and 1961 reveal fields (n = 43) ranging in size from 0.2 ha to 5.8 ha. Modal field size is a little over 1.0 ha, but mean size is 1.6 ha, due to half a dozen giant fields between 3.6 and 5.3 ha in extension. Again, sedentarization, peaceful relations, and relatively abundant iron tools are probably responsible.

Three newly planted subsidiary fields Beckerman paced in 1970–1972, belonging to the two full-sized traditional longhouses referred to above, were roughly 0.8, 0.9, and 2.2 ha in extent, again illustrating the variability of these fields.

In Venezuela, Lizarralde (1968) measured the fields associated with eighty views of longhouses and their associated gardens in aerial photographs taken from 1936 to 1964. The average number of subsidiary fields per longhouse was 5.66 ± 2.45 (mean ± standard deviation). The mean total area of the subsidiary fields associated with a longhouse was 4.65 ± 3.11 ha.

The House-Field Complex

Lizarralde (1968) also measured the total amount of area under crop for his longitudinal sample of eighty views of longhouses and their associated fields. The mean area of all the fields (house-surrounding field plus subsidiary fields) associated with a longhouse was 5.36 ± 3.24 ha. As above, this figure refers to newly planted but as yet unproductive fields and early fallow fields as well as gardens in active production, since it is not possible to distinguish these phases of field life in the aerial photography.

The House-Field Complex over Time

Lizarralde (1968) was able to plot the developmental history of two Venezuelan longhouse sites and their associated fields over decades, using aerial photographs taken in various oil company overflights. One of these sites, located in the valley of Kainkokbarí Creek, a little over 3.0 km north of the río Antray (known as the río Intermedio in Spanish), held a longhouse named Barikoksanda at the time of first contact; its predecessor longhouses in the same locale probably bore the same name. The record illustrates the way longhouses were rebuilt and relocated, as well as the development of their associated fields and field complexes.

In 1937 the longhouse in this site was about 25 m long. Associated with it were two subsidiary fields (1.2 and 2.8 ha in area) on terra firme (upland colluvial) soils and four subsidiary fields (0.9, 0.7, 0.5, and 0.3 ha in extent) on alluvial soils along Kainkokbarí Creek.

By 1943 this longhouse had been abandoned and another, about 50 m long, had been constructed 300 m from the original. This larger house had two subsidiary fields on terra firme soils. One of them, 4.1 ha in extent, was an enlargement of the 2.8 ha field photographed in 1937; the other, 3.2 ha in area, was new. This longhouse also had six contiguous alluvial fields along Kainkokbarí Creek, about one km from the house. These fields covered 2.4, 1.8, 1.1, 0.8, 0.5, and 0.2 ha.

In 1947 a new longhouse had been constructed on the same spot as the 1943 house. This one was smaller, however—only about 30 m long. The 4.1 ha terra firme field was still there, as were five of the six contiguous alluvial fields from 1943. They now measured 2.1, 1.4, 1.0, 0.8, and 0.2 ha. A new alluvial soil field, 3.0 ha in extent, had been constructed inside a bend of the río Antray.

In 1949 the longhouse remained in the same place. The 4.1 ha terra firme field of 1947 was now somewhat smaller, 3.5 ha, as the forest had been allowed to reclaim part of it. The five alluvial soil fields of two years previous were still visible, although the forest had encroached on the larger ones and the smallest had been enlarged. In the order given in the previous paragraph, their areas were now 1.7, 1.0, 0.9, 0.8, and 0.6 ha. The 3.0 ha alluvial field that was new in 1947 was still present, and another, 4.0 ha in extent, had been established inside the same bend of the río Antray, contiguous to the former.

By 1954 a new longhouse had been built, 140 m from the location of the houses seen in the 1943–1949 imagery. The 3.5 ha upland field noted in 1949 was still there. All the alluvial soil fields along Kainkokbarí Creek had been abandoned.

In the same bend of the río Antray mentioned above, the two previously noted alluvial soil fields now measured 4.0 and 2.6 ha. Upriver from these two fields, some 300 m along the Antray, a large new alluvial soil field, 2.8 ha in extent, had been made.

By 1958 the longhouse seen in 1954 had been abandoned and a new longhouse had been built, located 1 km from the previous one. The 3.5 ha upland field was still there. There were also three alluvial soil fields associated with this house— two small ones (0.4 and 0.2 ha) about one km away along Kainkokbarí Creek and the previously mentioned 4.0 ha field inside a bend of the río Antray.

A flight in 1961 revealed that the longhouse was gone, as well as all its alluvial fields, leaving only the 3.5 ha terra firme field still visible.

The second case (R. Lizarralde 1968) concerns a site whose last longhouse was named Wairikayra, which may have been the name of the previous longhouses in this site as well. The location is just south of the río Wairi, which discharges into the río Dagda not far from this site.

A flight in 1937 photographed a longhouse about 25 m long with a 3.3 ha terra firme field 700 m from the house and three alluvial fields (0.5, 0.3, and 0.2 ha) along the río Wairi.

Ten years later a flight revealed that the original longhouse had been abandoned and a new one of the same size constructed 700 m away, at the edge of the now-abandoned large terra firme field noted in 1937. The three alluvial fields of 1937 had also been abandoned, and five new alluvial fields (1.1, 0.9, 0.6, 0.4, and 0.2 ha in area) had been made along the Río Wairi.

In 1949 the new longhouse was still there, accompanied by a large 2.3 ha terra firme field next to it, as well as another 0.8 ha terra firme field. The five alluvial fields noted in 1947 had changed size somewhat, their areas now being 1.3, 1.0, 0.5, 0.5, and 0.15 ha, in the order given in the previous paragraph. There were also two new alluvial soil fields (0.5 and 0.2 ha) on a large island in the Dagda just above the mouth of the Wairi.

The same longhouse was recorded in photographs taken in 1954. It had two terra firme fields in its vicinity, one 140 m away and the other 800 m. They measured 1.9 and 1.1 ha, respectively. There was a third terra firme field 2.4 km distant from the house, only 0.3 ha in area. The five alluvial fields along the río Wairi now measured 1.0, 0.9, 0.5, 0.5, and 0.25 ha. The alluvial fields on the island encompassed 0.4 and 0.2 ha.

Four years later the same longhouse had only alluvial soil subsidiary fields associated with it. There were eight, all of them along the río Wairi. They measured 2.0, 1.9, 1.3, 1.2, 1.0, 0.8, 0.4, and 0.3 ha in extent.

By 1961 the longhouse noted in the years 1947–1958 had been abandoned, leaving a 0.8 ha terra firme field on its site. The replacement longhouse has been constructed about 400 m away. It had a particularly large (2.1 ha) house-surrounding field, as well as another terra firme field of 1.0 ha close by. There were now nine alluvial soil fields along the río Wairi, with areas of 1.7, 1.4, 1.3, 1.2, 1.0, 1.0, 0.9, 0.8, and 0.6 ha.

Bibliography

Documents

Archivo General de las Indias (AGI)
 1637 Escribanía, Legajo 1188

Archivo Histórico Nacional de Colombia (AHNC)
 1773 Caciques e Indios, tomo 62, folios 290–291

Archivo General de Venezuela
 1876 Miyares 1799

Publications

Acevedo Latorre, Eduardo, ed.
 1969 *Atlas de Colombia*. 2nd ed. Bogotá: Instituto Geográfico "Agustín Codazzi."

AID (U.S. Agency for International Development)
 1968 *Venezuela: National Inventory of Resources*. AID/EARI Atlas No. 8, Engineer Agency for Resource Inventories, Department of the Army. Washington, DC: Department of the Army.

Aguado, Fray Pedro de
 1987 *Recopilación historial de Venezuela*. Biblioteca de la Academia Nacional de la Historia, Serie: Fuentes para la Historia Colonial de Venezuela, vols. 62 and 63. Caracas: Italgráfica.

Albion, S. D., T. H. Clutton-Brock, and F. E. Guinness
 1987 Early development and population dynamics in red deer. II. Density independent effects and cohort variation. *Journal of Animal Ecology* 56(1): 69–81.

Alcácer, Fray Antonio de
 1962 *El indio motilón y su historia*. Centro Capuchino de Historia y Antropología. Ediciones "Paz y Bien," vol. 13. Bogotá: Editorial Iqueima.

1965 *En la sierra de los Motilones: Sudores sangre y paz.* Centro Capuchino de Historia y Antropología, Ediciones "Paz y Bien," vol. 20. Valencia: Domenech.

Álvarez Bernal, Fernando
1983 *Atlas climatológico de Venezuela.* Caracas: Universidad Central de Venezuela.

Arellano Moreno, Antonio
1960 *Orígenes de la economía venezolana.* Madrid: Editorial Edime.

Arellano Moreno, Antonio, ed.
1964 *Relaciones geográficas de Venezuela.* Biblioteca de la Academia Nacional de la Historia. Serie: Fuentes para la Historia Colonial de Venezuela, vol. 70. Caracas: Italgráfica.

Arhem, Kai
1976 Fishing and hunting among the Makuna: Economy, ideology, and ecological adaptation in the northwest Amazon. *Gotesborgs Etnografiske Museum Arstryek* 27–44. Reprinted in *El Dorado* 2, no. 2 (1977): 37–54.

Arnold, Ralph, George MacReady, and Thomas Barrington
1960 *The First Big Oil Hunt: Venezuela, 1911–1916.* New York: Vantage Press.

Arroyo-Kalin, Manuel
2012 Slash-burn-and-churn: Landscape history and crop cultivation in pre-Columbian Amazonia. *Quaternary International* 249: 4–18.

Bai, Jie
1999 Methods for correlated binary responses with application in anthropology. MA thesis, Pennsylvania State University.

Balée, William
1994 *Footprints of the Forest: Ka'apor Ethnobotany: The Historical Ecology of Plant Utilization by an Amazonian People.* New York: Columbia University Press.

Balick, Michael
1986 *Systematics and Economic Botany of the* Oenocarpus-Jessenia *(Palmae) Complex.* Advances in Economic Botany, vol. 3. New York: New York Botanical Garden.

Ballew, Carol, Stephen Beckerman, and Roberto Lizarralde
1993 High prevalence of cleft lip among the Barí Indians of western Venezuela. *Cleft Palate-Craniofacial Journal* 30(4): 411–413.

Baltasar de Lodares, Fray
1930 *Los franciscanos capuchinos en Venezuela.* Vol. 2. Caracas: Gutenberg.

Beckerman, Stephen
1975 The cultural energetics of the Barí (Motilones Bravos) of northern Colombia. PhD dissertation, University of New Mexico.
1976 Los Barí: Sus reacciones frente a la contracción de sus tierras. In *Tierra, tradición y poder en Colombia,* ed. Nina Friedemann, 65–83. Biblioteca Básica Colombiana. Bogotá: Instituto Colombiano de Cultura.

1977   The use of palms by the Barí Indians of the Maracaibo Basin. *Principes— Journal of the Palm Society* 21(4): 143–154.

1978   Datos etnohistóricos acerca de los Barí (Motilones). *Montalbán* 8: 255–327.

1979   The abundance of protein in Amazonia: A reply to Gross. *American Anthropologist* 81(3): 533–560.

1980a   Fishing and hunting by the Barí of Colombia. *Working Papers on South American Indians* 2: 67–109.

1980b   More on Amazon cultural ecology. *Current Anthropology* 21: 540–541.

1983a   Barí swidden gardens: Crop segregation patterns. *Human Ecology* 11(1): 85–101.

1983b   Carpe diem: An optimal foraging approach to Barí fishing and hunting. In *Adaptive Responses of Native Amazonians*, ed. Ray Hames and William T. Vickers, 269–299. New York: Academic Press.

1983c   Optimal foraging group size for a human population: The case of Barí fishing. *American Zoologist* 23:283–290.

1984   A note on ringed fields. *Human Ecology* 12(2): 203–206.

1987   Swidden in Amazonia and the Amazon rim. In *Comparative Farming Systems*, ed. Billie Turner and Stephen Brush, 55–94. New York: Guilford Press.

1991a   Barí spear fishing: Advantages to group formation? *Human Ecology* 19(4): 529–554.

1991b   The equations of war. *Current Anthropology* 32(5): 636–640.

1994   Homage to San Sebastian; or why do the Barí have so many different kinds of arrows? *Boletín del Museo Arqueológico de Quibor* 3: 37–47.

2008   Revenge: An overview. In *Revenge in the Cultures of Lowland South America*, ed. Stephen Beckerman and Paul Valentine, 1–9. Gainesville: University Press of Florida.

Beckerman, S., P. Erickson, J. Yost, J. Regalado, L. Jaramillo, C. Sparks, M. Iriomenga, and K. Long

2009   Life histories, blood revenge, and reproductive success among the Waorani of Ecuador. *Proceedings of the National Academy of Science* 106(20): 8134–8139.

Beckerman, Stephen, and Roberto Lizarralde

1995   State-tribal warfare and male-biased casualties among the Barí. *Current Anthropology* 36(3): 497–500.

2003   Paternidad compartida entre los Barí. In *Caminos cruzados: Ensayos de antropología social, etnoecología y etnoeducación*, ed. Catherine Alès and Jean Chiappino, 255–271. Mérida, Venezuela: Universidad de Los Andes, GRIAL.

Beckerman, Stephen, Roberto Lizarralde, Carol Ballew, Sissel Schroeder, C. Fingleton, A. Garrison, and Helen Smith

1998   The Barí partible paternity project: Preliminary results. *Current Anthropology* 39(1): 164–167.

Beckerman, Stephen, Roberto Lizarralde, Manuel Lizarralde, Jie Bai, Carol Ballew, Sissel Schroeder, Dina Dajani, Lisa Walkup, Maysiung Hsiung, Nikole Rawlins, and Michelle Palermo
2002 The Barí partible paternity project, phase one. In *Cultures of Multiple Fathers: The Theory and Practice of Partible Paternity in Lowland South America*, ed. Stephen Beckerman and Paul Valentine, 27–41. Gainesville: University Press of Florida.

Beckerman, Stephen, and Paul Valentine, eds.
2002 *Cultures of Multiple Fathers: The Theory and Practice of Partible Paternity in Lowland South America*. Gainesville: University Press of Florida.

Behrens, Clifford A., Michael G. Baksh, and Michel Mothes
1994 A regional analysis of Barí land use intensification and its impact on landscape heterogeneity. *Human Ecology* 22(3): 279–316.

Bergman, Roland
1980 *Amazon Economics: The Simplicity of Shipibo Indian Wealth*. Dellplain Latin American Studies 6. Syracuse, NY: Syracuse University Department of Geography.

Bolton, Ralph
1980 High-altitude sex ratios: How high? *Medical Anthropology* 6: 107–143.

Boster, James
1980 How the exceptions prove the rule: Analysis of informant disagreement in Aguaruna manioc identification. PhD dissertation, University of California, Berkeley.
1984 Classification, cultivation and selection of Aguaruna cultivars of *Manihot esculenta* (Euphorbiacae). In *Ethnobotany in the Neotropics*, ed. G. T. Prance and J. A. Kallunki, 34–47. Advances in Economic Botany 1. New York: New York Botanical Garden.

Breton, A. C.
1921 The Aruac Indians of Venezuela. *Man* 21: 9–12.

Brown, Gillian, Kevin Laland, and Monique Borgerhoff Mulder
2009 Bateman's principles and human sex roles. *Trends in Ecology and Evolution* 24(6–14): 297–304.

Buenaventura de Carrocera, Padre
1973 Los indios motilones en el segundo centenario de su primer contacto pacífico (1772–1972). Madrid: Raycar, S. A., Impresores. Reprinted from *Misionalia Hispánica* 89: 191–224.

Carneiro, Robert
1961 Slash-and-burn cultivation among the Kuikuru and its implications for cultural development in the Amazon Basin. In *The Evolution of Horticultural Systems in Native South America: Causes and Consequences*, ed. Johannes Wilbert, 47–67. Antropológica, suppl. 2. Caracas: Sociedad de Ciencias Naturales La Salle.
1970 Hunting and hunting magic among the Amahuaca of the Peruvian Montaña. *Ethnology* 9(4): 331–341.
1983 The cultivation of manioc among the Kuikuru of the upper Xingú. In

Adaptive Responses of Native Amazonians, ed. Ray Hames and William T. Vickers, 65–111. New York: Academic Press.

1995 History of ecological interpretations of Amazonia: Does Roosevelt have it right? In *Indigenous Peoples and the Future of Amazonia*, ed. Leslie Sponsel, 45–70. Tucson: University of Arizona Press.

Cassler, Clark L., Elsa González B., Margarita Romera, Jesús Toledo, and José Brito
1990 Inventario de la ictiofauna del río Palmar y afluentes, Estado Zúlia, Venezuela. *Boletín del Centro de Investigaciones Biológicas* (24)1: 1–50.

Cesáreo de Armellada, Padre
1962 Entrada a los Motilones el año 1728. *Venezuela Misionera* 283: 296–299.
1964a Pueblos motilones en el siglo XVIII. *Venezuela Misionera* 297: 10–12.
1964b Los pueblos motilones en el siglo XIX. *Venezuela Misionera* 298: 40–42.

Chagnon, Napoleon, Mark Flinn, and Thomas Melançon
1979 Sex-ratio variation among the Yanomamo Indians. In *Evolutionary Biology and Human Social Behavior: An Anthropological Perspective*, ed. Napoleon Chagnon and William Irons, 290–320. North Scituate, MA: Duxbury Press.

Chernela, Janet
1987 Os cultivares de mandioca na área do Uaupés (Tukâno). In *Suma etnológica brasileira*, vol. 1: *Etnobiologia*, ed. Darcy Ribeiro, 151–158. Petrópolis: Editora Vozes.
1989 Managing rivers of hunger: The Tukano of Brazil. In *Resource Management in Amazonia: Indigenous and Folk Strategies*, ed. Darrell Posey and William Balée, 238–248. Advances in Economic Botany 7. New York: New York Botanical Garden.

Clark, Kathleen, and Christopher Uhl
1987 Farming, fishing and fire in the history of the upper Río Negro region of Venezuela. *Human Ecology* 15(1): 1–26.

Coley, Phyllis D.
1982 Rates of herbivory of different tropical forest trees. In *The Ecology of a Tropical Forest: Seasonal Rhythms and Long-Term Changes*, ed. Egbert G. Leigh Jr., A. Stanley Rand, and Donald M. Windsor, 123–132. Washington, DC: Smithsonian Institution Press.

Conklin, Harold
1961 The study of shifting cultivation. *Current Anthropology* 2: 27–67.

Cooke, Richard
2005 Prehistory of Native Americans on the Central American land bridge: Colonization, dispersal, and divergence. *Journal of Archaeological Research* 13(2): 129–187.

Cooke, Richard, and A. J. Ranere
1992 The origin of wealth and hierarchy in the central region of Panama (12,000–2,000 YBP), with observations on its relevance to the history and phylogeny of Chibchan speaking polities in Panama and elsewhere.

In *Wealth and Hierarchy in the Intermediate Area*, ed. F. Lange, 243–315. Washington, DC: Dumbarton Oaks.

COPLANARH (Comisión del Plan Nacional de Aprovechamiento de los Recursos Hidraúlicos)
1975   *Atlas: Inventario nacional de tierras. Región Lago de Maracaibo*. Caracas: Ministerio de Agricultura y Cría, Centro Nacional de Investigaciones Agropecuarias.

Costenla-Umaña, Adolfo
1981   Comparative Chibchan phonology. PhD dissertation, University of Pennsylvania.
1991   *Las lenguas del área intermedia: Introducción a su estudio areal*. San José: Editorial de la Universidad de Costa Rica.
1995   Sobre el estudio diacrónico de las lenguas chibchenses y su contribución al conocimiento del pasado de sus hablantes. *Boletín del Museo de Oro* (Bogotá) 38–39: 13–55.
2008   Estado actual de la subclasificación de las lenguas chibchenses y de la reconstrucción fonológica y gramatical del protochibchense. *Lingüística Chibcha* (San José, Costa Rica) 27: 117–135.

Crawley, M. J., S. D. Albon, D. R. Bazely, J. M. Milner, J. G. Pilkington, and A. L. Tuke
2004   Vegetation and sheep population dynamics. In *Soay Sheep: Dynamics and Selection in an Island Population*, ed. T. Clutton-Brock and J. Pemberton, 89–112. Cambridge: Cambridge University Press.

Cunill Grau, Pedro
1987   *Geografía de poblamiento venezolano en el siglo XIX*. Vols. 1 and 2. Caracas: Ediciones de la Presidencia de la Republica.

Dahl, George
1963   El "bocachico" y su ambiente. In *El "bocachico": Contribución al estudio de su biología y de su ambiente*, ed. George Dahl, Federico Medem, and Alonso Ramos Henao, 93–100. Departamento de Pesca de la Corporación Autónoma de los Valles del Magdalena y del Sinú—CVM. Bogotá: Talleres Gráficos del Banco de la República.
1971   *Los peces del norte de Colombia*. Bogotá: Ministerio de Agricultura y Cría, INDERENA.

Dávila, Vicente
1949   *Encomiendas*. Vol. 5. Caracas: Imprenta Nacional.

de Espinosa, V., and C. Gimenez B.
1974   Estudio sobre la biología y pesca del bocachico (*Prochilodus reticulatus*) (Valenciennes) en el Lago de Maracaibo. Ministerio de Agricultura y Cría, Oficina Nacional de Pesca. Informe Técnico 63. Caracas.

de Lozada, Mirza, and Mercedes de Mellior
1984   *Isolíneas de escurrimientos superficiales medios anuales para la región occidental de la cuenca del Lago de Maracaibo*. MARNR (PT) Serie Informes Técnicos DGSPOA/IT/93. Caracas: MARNR.

de Oviedo, Basilio Vicente
1970   Cualidades y riquezes del Nuevo Reino de Granada. In *Venezuela en los*

Cronistas Generales de Indias, vol. 2. Biblioteca de la Academia Nacional de la Historia. Serie: Fuentes para la Historia Colonial de Venezuela, vol. 59. Caracas: Italgráfica.

Denevan, William
1971   Campa subsistence in the Gran Pajonal of eastern Peru. *Geographical Review* 61(4): 496–518.

Denevan, William, J. M. Treacy, Janis Alcorn, Christine Padoch, Julia Denslow, and S. F. Paitain
1984   Indigenous agroforestry in the Peruvian Amazon: Bora Indian management of swidden fallows. *Interciencia* 9: 336–357.

Descola, Philippe
1994   *In the Society of Nature: A Native Ecology in Amazonia*. Cambridge: Cambridge University Press.

Divale, William T., and Marvin Harris
1976   Population, warfare, and the male supremacist complex. *American Anthropologist* 78(3): 521–538.

Dueñas-C., Ariel, Julio Betancur, and Robinson Galindo-T.
2007   Estructura y composición florística de un bosque húmedo tropical del Parque Nacional Natural Catatumbo Barí, Colombia. *Revista Colombia Forestal* 10(20): unpaginated.

Early, John D., and John F. Peters
2000   *The Xilixana Yanomamo of the Amazon: History, Social Structure, and Population Dynamics*. Gainesville: University Press of Florida.

Eisenberg, John F.
1980   The density and biomass of tropical mammals. In *Conservation Biology: An Evolutionary-Ecological Perspective*, ed. Michael E. Soulé and Bruce A. Wilcox, 35–55. Sunderland, MA: Sinauer Associates.
1989   *Mammals of the Neotropics: Panama, Colombia, Venezuela, Guayana, Suriname, French Guayana*. Chicago: University of Chicago Press.

Elias, Marianne, Gilda Santos Muhlen, Doyle McKey, Ana Carolina Roa, and Joe Tohme
2004   Genetic diversity of traditional South American landraces of cassava (*Manihot esculenta* Crantz): An analysis using microsatellites. *Economic Botany* 58(2): 242–256.

Ernst, Adolf
1887   Motilonen Schädel aus Venezuela. *Zeitschrift für Ethnologie* 19: 296–301.

Febres Cordero F., Luis
1975   *Del antiguo Cúcuta: Datos y apuntamientos para su historia*. Biblioteca Banco Popular, vol. 72. Bogotá: Talleres Gráficos del Banco Popular.

Flowers, Nancy, Danial Gross, Madeline Ritter, and Dennis Werner
1982   Variation in swidden practices in four central Brazilian Indian societies. *Human Ecology* 10(2): 203–217.

Foster, Robin B., and Nicholas V. L. Brokaw
1982   Structure and history of the vegetation of Barro Colorado Island. In *The Ecology of a Tropical Forest: Seasonal Rhythms and Long-Term Changes*, ed.

Egbert G. Leigh Jr., A. Stanley Rand, and Donald M. Windsor, 67–81. Washington, DC: Smithsonian Institution Press.

Gabaldón Márques, Joaquín, ed.
1962 *Descubrimiento y conquista de Venezuela*, vol. II. Biblioteca de la Academia Nacional de la Historia. Serie: Fuentes para la Historia Colonial de Venezuela, vol. 55. Caracas: Italgráfica.

Galvis, G., J. I. Mojica, and M. Camargo
1997 *Peces del Catatumbo.* Asociación Cravo Norte (ECOPETROL–OCCI-DENTAL–SHELL). Bogotá, Colombia: D'Vinni Editorial.

Gessner, Fritz
1953 Investigaciones hidrográficas en el Lago de Maracaibo. *Acta Científica Venezolana* 4: 173–177.
1956 Das Verlaufder der Venezuela-Expedition 1952. *Ergebnisse der Deutschen Limnologischen Venezuela Expedition* 1: 1–22.

Ginés, Hermano
1982 *Carta pesquera de Venezuela (2): Áreas central y occidental.* Monografía 27. Caracas: Fundación Salle de Ciencias Naturales.

Goldbrunner, A. W.
1963 *Las causes meteorológicas de las lluvias de extraordinaria magnitud en Venezuela.* 2nd ed. Caracas: Publicación Especial, Ministerio de la Defensa.

Goldman, Irving
1963 *The Cubeo: Indians of the Northwest Amazon.* Illinois Studies in Anthropology 2. Urbana: University of Illinois Press.

Graf, C. H.
1969 Estratigrafía cuaternaria del noroeste de Venezuela. *Boletín Informativo de la Asociación Venezolana de Geología del Ministerio del Petróleo* 12: 393–416.

Gragson, Theodore
1989 Time allocation of subsistence and settlement in a Chu Kho Nome Pumé village of the Llanos of Apure. PhD dissertation, Pennsylvania State University.

Gross, Daniel R.
1975 Protein capture and cultural development in the Amazon Basin. *American Anthropologist* 77(3) 526–549.

Gross, Daniel, George Eiten, Nancy Flowers, Francisca Leoi, Madeline Ritter, and Dennis Werner
1979 Ecology and acculturation among native peoples of central Brazil. *Science* 206: 1043–1050.

Hames, Raymond
1979 A comparison of the efficiencies of the shotgun and the bow in neotropical hunting. *Human Ecology* 7(3): 219–252.
1983 Monoculture, polyculture, and polyvariety in tropical forest swidden cultivations. *Human Ecology* 11(1): 13–34.

1989 Time, efficiency, and fitness in the Amazonian protein quest. *Research in Economic Anthropology* 11: 43–85.

Hames, Raymond, and Patricia Draper
2004 Women's work, child care, and helpers-at-the-nest in a hunter-gatherer society. *Human Nature* 15: 319–341.

Harner, Michael
1973 *The Jívaro: People of the Sacred Waterfall*. New York: Anchor/Doubleday.

Headland, Paul
1973 *The Grammar of Tunebo*. Language Data, Amerindian Series 2. Dallas: Summer Institute of Linguistics.

Headland, Edna, and Paul Headland
1976 Fonología del Tunebo. In *Sistemas fonológicos de idiomas colombianos* 3, 17–26. Lomalinda: Editorial Townsend.

Heckenberger, Michael, J. Petersen, and E. Neves
1999 Village size and permanence in Amazonia: Two archaeological examples from Brazil. *Latin American Antiquity* 10(4): 353–376.

Hernández, Francisco A.
1988 *Región natural 6: Piedemonte colinoso sur de Perijá*. Sistemas Ambientales Venezolanos, Proyecto Ven/79/001. Serie II, Los recursos naturales renovables y las regiones naturales. Sección 2, Las regiones naturales. Documento #6. Caracas: MARNR-DGSPOA.

Hill, Kim, and Kristen Hawkes
1983 Neotropical hunting among the Aché of eastern Paraguay. In *Adaptive Responses of Native Amazonians*, ed. Raymond Hames and William T. Vickers, 139–188. New York: Academic Press.

Hill, Kim, and Hillard Kaplan
1988 Tradeoffs in male and female reproductive strategies among the Aché. In *Human Reproductive Behavior: A Darwinian Perspective*, ed. Laura Betzig, Monique Borgerhoff Mulder, and Paul Turke, 277–307. Cambridge: Cambridge University Press.

Hilty, Steven
2003 *Birds of Venezuela*. 2nd ed. Princeton: Princeton University Press.

Holder, Preston
n.d. The Motilones: Report of field-work. Unpublished report on file at the American Museum of Natural History, New York.
1947 The Motilones: Some untouched tropical forest peoples in northwestern South America. *Journal of the Washington Academy of Sciences* 37: 417–427.

Holmes, Rebecca
1993 Demografía médica de los Barí. In *Estado de salud indígena: Los Barí*, ed. Rebecca Holmes and Juan Scorza, 26–44. Maracaibo: Fundación Zumaque.

Hoopes, J., and O. Fonseca
   2003   Goldwork and Chibchan identity: Endogenous change and diffuse unity in the Isthmo-Colombian area. In *Gold and Power in Ancient Costa Rica, Panama, and Colombia*, ed. J. Quilter and J. Hoopes, 49–89. Washington, DC: Dumbarton Oaks.

Huber, Otto, and Clara Alarcón
   1988   *Mapa de vegetación de Venezuela*. Caracas: MARNR.

Hurtado, Ana Magdalena, and Kim Hill
   1987   Early dry season subsistence ecology of the Cuiva foragers of Venezuela. *Human Ecology* 15: 163–187.

Ibrahim, A., Abdel Babiker, I. K. Amin, I. Omer, and H. Rushwan
   1994   Factors associated with high risk of perinatal and neonatal mortality: An interim report on a prospective community-based study in rural Sudan. *Paediatric and Perinatal Epidemiology* 8(2): 193–204.

ICLAM (Instituto para la Conservación del Lago de Maracaibo)
   1983   *Informe sobre los muestreos exploratorios realizados en la cuenca del río Catatumbo*. Document C-83-06-023-0. Maracaibo: ICLAM.
   1991   Estudio preliminar de la Laguna de Sinamaica. Informe Técnico. Convenio CORPOZULIA-ICLAM, Maracaibo, Venezuela.

IGAG (Instituto Geográfico "Agustín Codazzi")
   1968   *Boletín climatológico de Colombia: Precipitación, década 1951–1961*. Bogotá: IGAG.

Jahn, Alfredo
   1927   *Los aborígenes del occidente de Venezuela*. Caracas: Comercio.

Johnson, Allen
   1983   Machiguena gardens. In *Adaptive Responses of Native Amazonians*, ed. Ray Hames and William T. Vickers, 29–63. New York: Academic Press.

Jordan, Carl F., ed.
   1989   *An Amazonian Rain Forest: The Structure and Function of a Nutrient Stressed Ecosystem and the Impact of Slash-and-Burn Agriculture*. Man and the Biosphere 2. Paris: UNESCO.

Jordan, Carl F., and P. G. Murphy
   1978   A latitudinal gradient of wood and litter production and its implication regarding competition and species diversity in trees. *American Midland Naturalist* 99: 415–434.

Kaufmann, Christian, and Hans Briegel
   2004   Flight performance of the malaria vectors *Anopheles gambiae* and *Anopheles atropoarvus*. *Journal of Vector Ecology* 29(1): 140–153.

Keyeux, Genoveva, Clemencia Rodas, Nancy Gelvez, and Dee Carter
   2002   Possible migration routes into South America deduced from mitocondrial DNA studies into Colombian Amerindian populations. *Human Biology* 74(2): 211–233.

Kiszewski, Anthony, Andrew Mellinger, Andrew Spielman, Pia Malany, Sonia Erlich Sachs, and Jeffrey Sachs

2004 A global index representing the stability of malaria transmission. *American Journal of Tropical Medicine and Hygiene* 70(5): 486–498.

Klinge, Hans, and W. A. Rodrigues

1974 Phytomass estimation in a central Amazonian rain forest. In *IUFRO Biomass Studies*, ed. H. D. Young. Orono: University of Maine Press.

Koivula, Minna, Esa Koskela, Tapio Mappes, and Tuula Oksanen

2003 Cost of reproduction in the wild: Manipulation of reproductive effort in the bank vole. *Ecology* 84(2): 398–405.

Lathrap, Donald

1968 The "hunting" economies of the tropical forest zone of South America: An attempt at historical perspective. In *Man the Hunter*, ed. Richard Lee and Irven DeVore, 23–29. Chicago: Aldine.

1970 *The Upper Amazon.* London: Thames and Hudson.

Leigh, Egbert G., Jr., and Donald M. Windsor

1982 Forest production and regulation of primary consumers on Barro Colorado Island. In *The Ecology of a Tropical Forest: Seasonal Rhythms and Long-Term Changes*, ed. Egbert G. Leigh Jr., A. Stanley Rand, and Donald M. Windsor, 111–122. Washington, DC: Smithsonian Institution Press.

Lizarralde, Manuel

1997 Perception, knowledge and use of the rainforest: Ethnobotany of the Barí of Venezuela. PhD dissertation, University of California, Berkeley.

2008 A life for a life: Barí responses to murder in the Sierra de Perijá. In *Revenge in the Cultures of Lowland South America*, ed. Stephen Beckerman and Paul Valentine, 79–92. Gainesville: University Press of Florida.

Lizarralde, Manuel, and Roberto Lizarralde

1991 Barí exogamy among their territorial groups: Choice and/or necessity. *Human Ecology* 19: 453–467.

Lizarralde, Roberto

1968 Trabajos con los Barí. MS. on file with the Facultad de Humanidades y Educación, la Universidad de Zulia (LUZO), Maracaibo, Venezuela.

1992 Barí settlement patterns. *Human Ecology* 19(4): 437–452.

2004 Sobre la violencia entre los Barí y los criollos en Perijá, Zulia, 1600–1960. *Boletín Antropológico* 60: 7–35.

n.d. *Una breve historia de los contactos con los Barí de la Sierra de Perijá, Venezuela y Colombia.* Under review.

Lizarralde, Roberto, and Stephen Beckerman

1982 Historia contemporánea de los Barí. *Antropológica* 58: 3–52.

n.d. Epidemics among the Barí. Unpublished manuscript.

Lizot, Jacques

1977 Population resources and warfare among the Yanomami. *Man* 12(3–4): 497–517.

MAC (Ministerio de Agricultura y Cría, Dirección de Planificación Agropecuaria)
1960   *Atlas agrícola de Venezuela*. Caracas: Litografía Miangolarra.
1961   *Atlas forestal de Venezuela*. Caracas: Editorial Senda Ávila.

MARNR (Ministerio del Ambiente y de los Recursos Naturales Renovables)
1979   *Atlas de Venezuela*. 2nd ed. Caracas: MARNR.
1985   *Atlas de la vegetación de Venezuela*. MARNR, Dirección General de Información e Investigación del Ambiente, Dirección de Suelos Vegetación y Fauna, División de Vegetación. Caracas: MARNR.

Mayobre, F., J. J. San Jose, B. E. Orihuela, and J. Acosta
1982a   Características morfológicas, anatómicas y fisiológicas que influyen sobre el crecimiento de *Manihot esculenta* Crantz var. Cubana. *Alcance: Revista de la Facultad de Agronomía de la Universidad Central de Venezuela* 31: 197–206.
1982b   Influencia de nivel de fertilización y riego sobre el crecimiento de *Manihot esculenta* Crantz var. Cubana. *Alcance: Revista de la Facultad de Agronomía de la Universidad Central de Venezuela* 31: 171–196.

Meggers, Betty J.
1954   Environmental limitation on the development of culture. *American Anthropologist* 56(5), pt. 1: 801–824.
1971   *Amazonia: Man and Culture in a Counterfeit Paradise*. Chicago: Aldine Atherton.

Melton, Phillip
2004   Molecular perspectives on the origins of Chibchan populations from the Sierra Nevada de Santa Marta, Colombia. MA thesis, University of Kansas.

Melton, Phillip, I. Briceño, A. Gomez, E. J. Devor, J. E. Bernal, and M. H. Crawford
2007   Biological relationship between Central and South American Chibchan-speaking populations: Evidence from mtDNA. *American Journal of Physical Anthropology* 133: 753–770.

Mendez, J. G.
1975   La exploración para hidrocarburos en Venezuela. Primeras Jornadas Venezolanas de Geología, Minería y Petróleo. Compañía Shell de Venezuela, Maracaibo. Mimeographed.

Millard, Ann, and Elois Ann Berlin
1983   Sex ratio and natural selection at the human ABO locus. *Human Heredity* 33(2): 130–136.

Milton, Katherine
1984   Protein and carbohydrate resources of the Makú Indians of northwestern Amazonia. *American Anthropologist* 86(1): 7–27.

Montaldo, A.
1973   Importancia de la yuca en el mundo actual con especial referencia a Venezuela. *Alcance: Revista de la Facultad de Agronomía de la Universidad Central de Venezuela* 22: 17–40.

MOP (Ministerio de Obras Públicas)
1973   *Distrito hidrológico 1: Isoyetas 1973*. Caracas: República de Venezuela, Ministerio de Obras Públicas, División de Hidrología.

Murray, G. W.
1988 [1915]   Un informe sobre los Motilones. *Boletín del Archivo Histórico de Miraflores* 125: 143–148.

Nectario María, Hermano
1977   *Los orígenes de Maracaibo*. Publicación del Instituto Nacional de Cooperación Educativa. Madrid: Villena.

Nemoto, Takeshi
1971   La pesca en el Lago de Maracaibo. Proyecto de Investigación y Desarrollo Pesquero (MAC-PNUD-FAO) Ministerio de Agricultura y Cría, Oficina Nacional de Pesca. Informe Técnico #24. Caracas.

Notestein, Frank, Carl Hubman, and James Bowler
1944   Geology of the Barco Concession, Republic of Colombia, South America. *Bulletin of the Geological Society of America* 55: 1165–1216.

Novoa, Daniel, comp.
1982   *Los recursos pesqueros del río Orinoco y su explotación*. Caracas: Corporación Venezolana de Guayana, División de Desarrollo Agrícola.

OCEI (Oficina Central de Estadística e Informática)
1985   *Censo Barí: Censo indígena de Venezuela 1982*. Caracas: Oficina Central de Estadística e Informática.
1992   Censados en Venezuela 314,772 indígenas. *Tiempo de Resultados* 2(2).

Odum, Eugene P.
1971   *Fundamentals of Ecology*. 3rd ed. Philadelphia: W. B. Saunders.

Osborn, Ann
1982   Mythology and social structure among the U'wa of Colombia. DPhil dissertation, Oxford University (St. Anthony's College).
1985   *El vuelo de las tijeretas*. Bogotá: Fundación de Investigaciones Arqueológicas Nacionales, Banco de la República.
1995   *Las cuatro estaciones: Mitología y estructura social entre los U'wa*. Bogotá: Banco de la República.

Ouhoud-Renoux, François
1998   De l'outil à la prédation: Technologie culturelle et ethno-écologie chez les Wayapi du haut Oyapock (Guyane française). These de doctorat, l'Université de Paris X.

Parra Pardi, Gustavo, et al.
1979   *Estudio integral sobre la contaminación del Lago de Maracaibo y sus afluentes*, part II: *Evaluación del proceso de eutroficación*. Caracas: MARNR, Dirección General de Información e Investigación del Ambiente, Dirección de Investigación del Ambiente, División de Investigaciones sobre la Contaminación Ambiental (DISCA).

Patiño R., Aníbal
1973   Cultivo experimental de peces en estanques. *Cespedecia* 2(5): 75–127.

Peña Vargas, Ana Cecilia
1995 *Misiones capuchinas en Perijá*. Documentos para su historia 1682–1819, vols. 238 and 240. Caracas: Academia Nacional de la Historia.

Pérez Lozano, Alfredo
1990 Peces de agua dulce de la cuenca del Lago de Maracaibo, Venezuela: Una contribución al conocimiento de su distribución geográfica con algunas consideraciones zoogeográficas sobre su origen. Trabajo especial de grado para optar al título de Licenciado en Biología, Universidad de Zulia, Maracaibo, Venezuela.

Picchi, Deborah
1982 Energetics modeling in development evaluation: The case of the Barairi Indians of central Brazil. PhD dissertation, University of Florida at Gainesville.

Pires, J.
1978 The forest ecosystems of the Brazilian Amazon: Description, functioning, and research needs. In *Tropical Forest Ecosystems: A State of Knowledge Report*. Paris: UNESCO.

Pittier, Henri
1920 *Esbozo de las formaciones vegetales de Venezuela con una breve reseña de los productos naturales y agrícolas*. Caracas: Litografía del Comercio.
1971 *Manual de las plantas usuales de Venezuela y su suplemento*. Caracas: Fundación Eugenio Mendoza.

Plumacher, E. H.
1894 Dispatch sent to Edwin F. Uhl, Assistant Secretary of State, from Maracaibo, 9 February 1894. Dispatches of United States Consuls, Washington, DC.

Pons, Adolfo, Adolfo de Villamañan, Alonso Núñez, Benigno Pérez, Epifanio de Valdemorilla, Vicente de Gusendos, and Gerardo Vargas
1962 Los Motilones: Aspectos médicos-sociales. *Kasmera* 1(1): 11–67.

Ramos García-Serrano, Carlos, and Juan Pablo Del Monte
2004 The use of tropical forest (agroecosystems and wild plant harvesting) as a source of food in the Bribri and Cabecar cultures in the Caribbean coast of Costa Rica. *Economic Botany* 58(1): 58–71.

Ramos Henao, Alonso
1963 Investigación preliminar sobre la biología del "bocachico" de los ríos Uré y San Jorge y los sistemas de ciénagas de Ayapel y de San Marcos. In *El "bocachico": Contribución al estudio de su biología y de su ambiente*, by George Dahl, Federico Medem and Alonso Ramos Henao, 55–91. Departamento de Pesca de la Corporación Autónoma de los Valles del Magdalena y del Sinú—CVM. Bogotá: Talleres Gráficos del Banco de la República.

Redfield, A. C., B. H. Ketchum, and D. F. Bumpus
1955 Report to Creole Petroleum Corporation on the hydrography of Lake

Maracaibo, Venezuela. Unpublished MS., ref. no. 55–9, Woods Hole Oceanographic Institute.

Reichel-Dolmatoff, Gerardo
1946 Informe sobre las investigaciones preliminares de la Comisión Etnológica al Catatumbo. *Boletín de Arqueología* 2: 381–394.

Robinson, John G., and Kent H. Redford
1989 Body size, diet, and population variation in neotropical forest mammal species: Predictors of local extinction? In *Advances in Neotropical Mammalogy*, ed. John G. Robinson and Kent H. Redford, 567–594. Gainesville, FL: Sandhill Crane Press.

Rodrígues, Gilberto
1973 *El sistema de Maracaibo*. Caracas: Instituto Venezolano de Investigaciones Científicas.

Roosevelt, Anna C.
1980 *Parmana: Prehistoric Maize and Manioc Subsistence along the Amazon and Orinoco*. New York: Academic Press.
1991 *Moundbuilders of the Amazon: Geophysical Archaeology on Marajó Island, Brazil*. San Diego: Academic Press.
1999a The development of prehistoric complex societies: Amazonia, a tropical forest. In *Complex Polities in the Ancient Tropical World*, ed. E. Bacus and L. Lucero, 13–33. Arlington, VA: American Anthropological Association.
1999b The maritime, highland, forest dynamic and origins of complex culture. In *The Cambridge History of the Native Peoples of the Americas*, vol. 2: *South America*, ed. F. Salomon and S. Schwartz, 264–349. Cambridge: Cambridge University Press.

Rubio-Palis, Yasmin, and C. F. Curtis
1992 Biting and resting behavior of anophelines in western Venezuela and implications for control of malaria transmission. *Medical and Veterinary Entomology* 6(4): 325–334.

Rubio-Palis, Yasmin, and Robert H. Zimmerman
1997 Ecoregional classification of malaria vectors in the neotropics. *Journal of Medical Entomology* 34(5): 499–510.

Salati, E., and P. B. Vose
1984 Amazon Basin: A system in equilibrium. *Science* 225: 129–138.

Salick, Jan
1989 Ecological basis of Amuesha agriculture, Peruvian upper Amazon. In *Resource Management in Amazonia: Indigenous and Folk Strategies*, ed. Darrell Posey and William Balée, 189–212. Advances in Economic Botany 7. New York: New York Botanical Garden.

Santos-Granero, Fernando
2009 *Vital Enemies: Slavery, Predation, and the Amerindian Political Economy of Life*. Austin: University of Texas Press.

Schubert, Carlos
1975   Evidencias de una glaciación antigua en la Sierra de Perijá, Estado Zulia. *Boletín de la Sociedad Venezolana de Espeleología* 6(12): 71–75.

Schultz, Leonard P.
1947   The fishes of the family Characinidae from Venezuela, with descriptions of seventeen new forms. *Proceedings of the United States National Museum* 95(3181): 235–367.

Segura W. W., Maia, and Ramiro Barrantes
2009   Dermatoglyphic traits of six Chibcha-speaking Amerindians of Costa Rica, and an assessment of the genetic affinities among populations. *Revista de Biología Tropical* 57 (suppl. 1): 357–369.

Service, M. W.
1993   Mosquitoes (Culicidae). In *Medical Insects and Arachnids*, ed. R. P. Lane and R. W. Grosskey, 120–240. London: Chapman and Hall.

Servicio Geológico Nacional e Inventario Minero Nacional
1967   *Geología del cuadrángulo F-13: Tibú*. Bogotá: República de Colombia, Ministerio de Minas y Petróleos.

Sieff, Daniela
1990   Explaining biased sex ratios in human populations: A critique of recent studies. *Current Anthropology* 31(1): 25–48.

Simón, Fray Pedro
1963   *Noticias historiales de Venezuela*. 2 vols. Biblioteca de la Academia Nacional de la Historia, Serie: Fuentes para la Historia Colonial de Venezuela, vols. 66 and 67. Caracas: Italgráfica.

Smith, Eric Alden
2004   Why do good hunters have higher reproductive success? *Human Nature* 15(4): 343–364.

Snow, J. W.
1976   The climate of northern South America. In *Climates of Central and South America*, ed. Werner Schwerdtfeger, 295–403. World Survey of Climatology 12. Amsterdam: Elsevier.

Solano Benítez, Guillermo
1970–1971   *50 años de vida nortesantandereana*. 5 vols. Cúcuta, Colombia: Librería Stella.

Solano M., J. M.
1974   *Reproducción inducida del bocachico*, Prochilodus reticulatus *Valenciennes*. Bogotá: INDERENA (Instituto de Desarrollo de los Recursos Naturales Renovables).

Stocks, Anthony
1983a   Candoshi and Cocamilla swiddens in eastern Peru. *Human Ecology* 11(1): 69–84.
1983b   Cocamilla fishing: Patch modification and environmental buffering in the Amazon *várzea*. In *Adaptive Responses of Native Amazonians*, ed. Ray-

mond Hames and William T. Vickers, 239–267. New York: Academic Press.

Sutton, Emory, and Ronald Arnett
1973   Ecological characterization and domestic and industrial wastes. Vol. 1 of *Study of Effects of Oil Discharges and Domestic and Industrial Wastewaters on the Fisheries of Lake Maracaibo, Venezuela*, ed. William L. Templeton. (Contract 212B00899, Research Report to Creole Petroleum Corporation.) Richland, WA: Batelle Pacific Northwest Laboratories.

Taphorn, D. C., and C. G. Lilyestrom
1980   *Piabucina pleurotaenia* Regan, a synonym of *P. erythrinoides* Valenciennes (Pisces: Lebiasinidae); its distribution, diet, and habitat in Lake Maracaibo, Venezuela. *Copeia* 2: 335–340.

Tergas, Luis, and Hugh Popenoe
1971   Young secondary vegetation and soil interactions in Izabel, Guatemala. *Plant and Soil* 34: 675–690.

Torroni, Antonio, James Neel, Ramiro Barrantes, Theodore Schurr, and Douglas Wallace
1994   Mitochondrial DNA "clock" for the Amerinds and its implications for timing their entry into North America. *Proceedings of the National Academy of Science* 91: 1158–1192.

Turke, Paul
1988   Helpers-at-the-nest: Childcare networks in Ifaluk. In *Reproductive Behavior: A Darwinian Perspective*, ed. Laura Betzig, Monique Borgerhoff-Mulder, and Paul Turke, 173–188. Cambridge: Cambridge University Press.

Vickers, William
1983   Tropical forest mimicry in swiddens: A reassessment of Geertz's model with Amazonian data. *Human Ecology* 11(1): 35–46.
1988   The game depletion hypothesis of Amazonian adaptation. *Science* 239: 1521–1522.
1989   *Los Sionas y Secoyas: Su adaptación al ambiente amazónico.* Quito: Abya-Yala.

Viloria, Angel L., and Rosanna Calchi La C.
1993   Una lista de los vertebrados vivientes de la Sierra de Perijá, Colombia y Venezuela. *BioLlania* (Guanare) 9: 37–69.

Waldron, Ingrid
1983   Sex differences in human mortality: The role of genetic factors. *Social Science and Medicine* 17(6): 321–333.

Walker, Robert, Mark Flinn, and Kim Hill
2010   Evolutionary history of partible paternity in lowland South America. *Proceedings of the National Academy of Science* 107: 19195–19200.

Wauters, Luc, and Luc Lens
1995   Effects of food availability and density on red squirrel (*Sciurus vulgaris*) reproduction. *Ecology* 76(8): 2460–2469.

Werner, Dennis, Nancy Flowers, Madeline Ritter, and Daniel Gross
  1979 Subsistence productivity and hunting effort in native South America. *Human Ecology* 7(4): 303–316.

Winterhalder, Bruce
  1983 Opportunity cost foraging models for stationary and mobile predators. *American Naturalist* 122: 73–84.

Yost, James
  1981a People of the forest: The Waorani. In *Ecuador in the Shadow of the Volcanoes*, ed. G. Ligabue, 95–115. Venice: Ediciones Libri Mundi.
  1981b Twenty years of contact: The mechanisms of change in Wao ("Auca") culture. In *Cultural Transformations and Ethnicity in Modern Ecuador*, ed. Norm Whitten, 677–704. Urbana: University of Illinois Press.

Yost, James, and Patricia Kelley
  1983 Shotguns, blowguns, and spears: The analysis of technological efficiency. In *Adaptive Responses of Native Amazonians*, ed. Raymond Hames and William T. Vickers, 189–224. New York: Academic Press.

Zaldívar, María Eugenia, Roberto Lizarralde, and Stephen Beckerman
  1991 Unbalanced sex ratios among the Barí: An evolutionary interpretation. *Human Ecology* 19(4): 469–498.

Zaldívar, María Eugenia, Oscar Rocha, Emilio Castro, and Ramiro Barrantes
  2002 Species diversity of edible plants grown in homegardens of Chibchan Amerindians from Costa Rica. *Human Ecology* 30(3): 301–316.

Index

Note: Italic page numbers refer to figures, maps, and tables.

vidual versus group returns on fishing and hunting, 112, 113, 120; interhearth group gifts of fish, 120; and marriages, 5, 7, 10, 12, 15, 17, 21, 166, 167, 169, 170, 174, 175–176, 177, 178, 179; and nuclear families, 5, 7, 25; and remarriages, 23–24, *24*; union of two hearth groups, 10, *10*, 12, 15, 18, *19*, 24; and visiting, 19
Heckenberger, Michael, 232
Heliconia leaves: for births, 17; for fishing, 118; as garbage, 109; for serving manioc, 8, 120
hepatitis, 3, 20, 147
Hernandez, Cecilio, 152, 159n2
Hill, Kim, 228–229, 230
Hilty, Steven, 131
historical Motilonia: climate of, 29, 31–36, *35*, *36*; colonization of, 77; and elevation, 97; map of current vegetation, *45*; map of soil types, *40*; map of vegetation around 1950, *47*; residential territory compared with total territory, 70, 74–75, 76, 78, 79, 81; riverine system, 52–60, 106, 119; terrestrial system, 36–39, 41–44, 46, 48–52
Holder, Preston, 76, 77
Holmes, Rebecca, 183, 189
hospitality, 101
Huambisa people, 225
Huber, Otto, 43, 44, 48
Hueck, Karl, 43
human ecology: and Barí demographics, 180–181; culture as digestion writ large, 235; and disease ecology, 154, 233; issues of, 213, 235–236; and natural and social environment, 236; and predation, 233; and production, 82–83; and reproduction, 160, 180–182, 228, 229. *See also* ecological anthropology
hunting: and agriculture, 91, 102; and altitude, 133–136, *134*, *135*, *136*, 139; and attacks on Barí people, 155, 223; buffering reserves, 139; distribution of game, 113, 133; early

morning jaunt, 129–130, 138–139; ethnographic comparison of Barí people with lowland neotropical horticulturalist peoples, 221, *222*, 223; and fishing, 111–112, 136–140, 222–224; game taboos, 221; individual versus group returns, 112–115, 135; jackpot game kills, 111, 113, 130, 139, 223; overview of, 110–115; and partible paternity, 209–210; places hunted, 132–133; planned versus spontaneous hunts, 129–130; and productivity, 83; and rainy season, 8, 85, 136–138, 222; and reproduction, 181, 196–198, 202, 229; and sexual division of labor, 23, 85; species taken, 130–132; and spoilage, 110, 111; as subsistence activity, 84, 102, 111, 113, 129, 194–195; techniques used, 113, 114, 129, 132–133; types of, 129–130; variation in productivity, 130, 133–136, *134*, *135*, *136*, 137, 138–139, 221, 222, 231–232
Hurtado, Ana Magdalena, 228–229

ICLAM, 54
Ihchidayosá, 179
ihchingbarida (spirit), 146
influenza, 20, 75–76, 147, 151
intestinal parasites, 147, 150, 151–152
Ishkandakaira (settlement), 152, 159n2, 179
Isthmic Chibchan language, 214

jaguars, 145, 146
Jaramillo, Orlando, 183, 184, 227, 228
Johnson, Allen, 217

Kainkokbarí Creek, 241–242
Kaplan, Hillard, 229
Kelley, Patricia, 221, 233
Ketchum, B. H., 54
kinkajous, 51
knifefish, 116, 120
Kogi people, 225, 227
kokshibadyi (skin disease), 16

and partible paternity, 2, 17, 22, 25; and pregnancy, 170–171; and rape, 179; and sexual availability, 161; and visiting, 174

Shuar people, 225

shungbaraba (earth spirits), 12, 21, 151–152

Sierra de Perijá, 27, 30–32, 37, 44, 46, 55, 189

Sierra Nevada de Santa Marta, 214, 218

singing, and ceremonial activities, 14–15, 18–19, 96, 101, 167, 169, 177

Siona-Secoya people, 230, 231

skirts. See *dukdura* (woman's skirt)

smallpox, 65, 233

Smith, Eric Alden, 181, 229

snails, 51–52, 141

snakebite, 15, 51

spear fishing: and bocachico, 59; and dry season, 8, 10; experience of, 26; methods of, 115, 117, 118; and weirs, 10, 16, 116–117, 118, 119–120, 138, 143n1, 219

spitting, as curing or blessing, 16, 17, 168–169, 170, 207, 211n6

Stocks, Anthony, 220

subsistence activities: and Chibchan language family, 215; and ethnographic comparison with lowland neotropical horticulturalist peoples, 216; and food availability, 82–83, 142–143, 225; overview of, 84–85; and rate maximizers, 83–84, 125–126, 139, 194–195, 219–221, 223–224; and settlement patterns, 226; and sexual division of labor, 16, 26, 85. *See also* agriculture; fishing; gathering; hunting

Sutton, Emory, 52, 54

taibabioyi (water spirits), 145–146

Taphorn, D. C., 56

tapirs, 51, 130, 131, 223

tarikbá (man's loincloth), 19

Tephrosia (barbasco), 115, 118, 119

Tergas, Luis, 109

Tibú, Colombia, 29

tigerfish, 116

Tótubi: biography of, 4, 25, 158–159; childhood of, 8, 12–13; daily routine of, 16, 26; hearth group of, 5, 7, 8, 9–10, *10*, 12, 14, 15, 16, 17–18, *19*, 21–24, *22*, *24*, 25; marriage of, 15–17; and mortality risks, 144, 152; pregnancies of, 16–17, 19–20, 24, 25; puberty ritual, 13–14; remarriage of, 23–24; and sickness as embarrassment, 20–21, 151; singing of, 14–15, 18, 19

trade, between lacustrine and terrestrial peoples, 64, 68, 219

tuberculosis, 147, 150, 233

Tukano people, 232, 234–235

Tukuko (Capuchin mission compound), 20, 21–22, 23, 24, 25, 149

Tunebo (U'wa), 214, 215, 225, 227

Turibakaig, 152, 153

turtles, in Barí diet, 51, 118, 141

typhus, 77, 147, 151

Uré River, 57

U.S. Homestead Act, 69

U'wa (Tunebo), 214, 215, 225, 227

Valle de los Motilones, 37

Veillon, Jean-Pierre, 43

Venezuela: and Barí natural environment, 27, 29–36; Barí reservation in, 81, 189; Barí territorial groups in, 11–12, *11*

Venezuela Indian Commission, 79–80

Venezuelan Bureau of Indian Affairs, 20

Venezuelan Cordillera of the Andes, 31, 33

Venezuelan Ministry of the Environment, 183, 189

Venezuelan National Census of November 2001, 182

Venezuelan National Indian Census, 182, 183, 187, *188*, 189, *189*

Vespucci, Amerigo, 63